AF574941

365 DAYS OF *Gratitude*

There's always something to be grateful for!

CAROLYN GRAY

365 Days of Gratitude:
There's Always Something to be Grateful For!
Copyright © 2015 Carolyn Gray

RevMedia Publishing
PO Box 5172
Kingwood, TX 77325
www.revmediapublishing.com

All rights reserved. No part of this book may be reproduced or transmitted in any form or by any means without written permission of the author.

ISBN-13: 978-0-9968715-2-5
Printed in the United States of America

No part of this book may be reproduced or transmitted in any form or by any means, electronic or mechanical—including photocopying, recording, or by any information storage and retrieval system—without permission in writing from the publisher.
Inquiries to info@revmediapublishing.com.

1 2 3 4 5 6 7 8 9 10 11 21 20 19 18 17 16 15 14

Foreword

Before you start reading my journal, I have a disclaimer: this is my journal and you may find misspelled words, incorrect grammar, run on sentences, incomplete sentences and many other mistakes. I did that on purpose! I decided to publish my journal without editing it because it was written from my heart and in a journal you just don't go back and make corrections. Well, I don't go back and make corrections; however, I have to admit that I said "yikes" at some of my mistakes (Miss Orr, I know better!).

The question I was asked most often was "what order did you write your gratitude posts?" My response was: I wrote in no particular order – I wrote about events, people and things from years ago to the present.

My original idea was to express gratitude to people, places and things that have contributed to me being the person I am today; however, I abandoned that idea when I met people who touched my heart daily with their acts of kindness that warranted my expressions of gratitude. For example, the four year old who gave me two hugs one day because he missed giving me a hug the prior week because he was on spring break! I would be remiss for not mentioning being grateful for the butcher, the sacker, the attendant at the cleaners and of course for the shredder I received as a gift.

The beauty of this "project" for me was the Facebook friends who followed me on a regular basis. Actually, some followed me every day (well, to be exact, it was not day but late night). I am extremely grateful for the heartwarming comments from those same FB friends who stayed up to read my post. I also learned that there are a bunch of people who are awake late at night just like I am.

Truthfully, it was not my intention to publishing my journal; however, after encouragement from a number of people who followed me, I changed my mind. They helped me to realize that publishing my journal might help others to see that small things can make a big difference in our lives and we all have so much to be grateful for.

If you were not able to follow me for the entire 365 days, here they are right here: 365 days of gratitude …There is always something to be grateful for! This project was reflective and gratifying. I encourage everyone to show expressions of gratitude even if you only write expressions for a short period of time…a week, a month, three months or for 365 days!

Thank you to everyone who stayed up well after midnight each night to read by post and to those who encouraged me to take the step to publish.

Love y'all,

Carolyn

Day 1
Jerri Evans

I have been blessed to have hundreds, maybe thousands of people in my life, to contribute to the person I am today. My goal this year is to thank 365 of those individuals - one each day starting NOW!

I met Jerri Evans in 1973, in San Antonio, Texas and for many many years she was my mentor, role model, sounding board and anything else I needed her to be. She saw more in me than I saw in myself and recommended me for a job in Washington, DC. I was selected for the job and that was the beginning of a wonderful career. My goal of becoming an HR Manager was realized.

I observed her, listened to her, didn't always like some of the things she suggested I do (but I did them anyway), I had -- have-- great respect and admiration for her. Jerri knew the way and showed me the way. I love her and CAN'T thank her enough for what she did to help me be the person I am today. Jerri Evans you are number 1 in my book.

Day 2
Toni Shirley

Toni, "Just so you know" there will be no specific order to thanking people who have impacted my life. When I set this goal, I just started listing names.

Today, I am offering a good gumbo cooking thank you to my friend... Toni Trahan Shirley!

Toni and I worked together in Shreveport, LA for five years. We complemented each other. Her goal everyday was to make me look good and she did that very well.

This lady could out-work five people. (Don't ask me how - I just know she did!). While we complemented each other, that does not mean we did not have a discussion or two more than once. But as the saying goes - at the end of the day, we were a united front.

We both worked hard and played just as hard. Toni showed great respect for me and always had my back. Actually, I got a two-fer because her husband Bill was there for both of us. (We affectionally referred to him as "Mr. Bill". (Tiffany Shirley Timms, Toni's daughter, started that Mr. Bill - promise). Mr Bill would bring us lunch and often patiently waited for Toni after work because "she was almost finished with whatever she was working on."

For several years, Tiffany and I were walking partners during the Susan G. Komen race for the cure. Tiffany has a special place in my heart because she is a devoted and committed educator. Thanks Tiff, for all you do.

Matthew Shirley, Toni's son, and I spent time chatting and he too checked in on us. I was so happy to be invited to Matt's wedding to Jennifer. Matt treated me like family.

Toni, thank you for being so supportive and making my time in Shreveport feel like being at home. I almost forgot -- the best gumbo I have eaten was made by T. Shirley. I am still trying.

Aurelia Evers Weems - *My mom taught elementary school for many many years in Shreveport while I was growing up.*

Carolyn Gray - *Aurelia Evers Weems Shreveport is a wonderful place. I could move back right now except I would have to go it alone! What school did you attend?*

Cheryl Adams - *What a heartfelt story! She is an amazing woman.*

Aurelia Evers Weems - *My mother taught at Caddo Elementary. We lived in Bossier City by the Air Force Base.*

Beverly Wallace - *What do you mean you would have to go it alone! You left family here in Shreveport!!! :) I am glad to know that you agree it is a wonderful place! Have a great day!*

Toni Trahan Shirley - *Carolyn, how proud you make me feel. Yes, we had a wonderful working relationship and a great personal connection. We managed to work together at two different times and were each glad to have that second opportunity. I realize this does not make me #1 or #2 in your memory book, but I'm at least sticking with the story that I am in the top group (even if it's #365!) You already know how I feel about you. It would take a book to express all the laughter, the things done together, the red shoes, yes...the gumbo!...the tearful trip to the Social Security office when I learned that at 55 I had to go on Medicare....I was barely holding together when you saw me going down the hall to the exit and got your purse and drove me there...you are, at heart, such a good and loving woman...you cared about the people we served...you knew that getting their paychecks on time was IMPORTANT to them...not"just an error; they'll get it in two weeks",.....the Susan Komen walks....serving hot dogs to every employee in the hospital...bringing food to the after hours crew...taking an interest in all of our families, that 5-second smile which lasted so long..see, I COULD write a book.... like you actually managed to do. With such affection and respect.....*

Pat Albarado - *WOW THAT IS SO SO AWESOME*

Tiffany Shirley Timms - *Thank you, Carolyn Gray, for the wonderful tribute to my mother. We all remember you just as fondly. Also, I still use the big coffee cup with the snowmen that you gave to me. It's my favorite!!!*

Leslie Turner - *These post made me Cry with genuine emotion. She is a vey classy lady and I can relate to how u all feel. Her present in the room...is like a* *glow in the air, that can sooth ur heart instantly. Her nurturing clasp of ur hand and the 5 second stare is simply peaceful. I like how ur friends are deeply moved by those things as well. U really do make a Huge difference.*

Carolyn Gray - *Toni Trahan Shirley and Leslie Turner, this made me cry. Toni, I remember everything you mentioned. I have not thought about it for some time but I remember the trip to the Social Security office. I am grateful we were there for each other.*

Carolyn Gray - *Tiffany Shirley Timms, OMGosh, you still have the snowman coffee cup. It's about time for a new one!*

Day 3

Alice Brown Bryant

I am grateful to have been blessed with good friends in my life. My very dear friend, Alice Brown Bryant in Hampton, Virginia shared "halfs" with me when we didn't (together) have money to each buy lunch. We put our "change" together to get a sandwich, french fries and a medium coke than split it.

We lived about 15 miles from each other and several days she would leave home early to pick me up (and get both of us to work on time) because my oil drinking VM would not start.

Alice got a new car, with a stick shift, that she could not drive! I would get up early, drove to her house, parked my car and we would take her car to work. We did that so that on our lunch hour I could teach her how to drive the stick shift. We would laughed so hard as she jerked us through the parking lot! After a few days, she got it.

Oh, the memories...real girlfriends are truly a blessing and Alice was a true friend.

Day 4

Lori Hughes, Max Taylor and Jack Balko

This is a special day for my gratitude check in on FB, because I'm grateful to three very special people. Lori Hughes, Max Taylor and Jack Balko. The connection - Toastmasters International.

Lori tried for a couple of years to get me to attend a Toastmasters meeting. All I had to do was walk up one flight of stairs to the conference room; however, I never had time. At least that what I told her....

She would invite me to the Toastmaster conferences -- no luck, I still was busy. The conferences were held on Saturday and I was not about to give up MY Saturday for a Toastmasters meeting.

One day Lori invited me to participate in a Toastmasters Division Contest by working the registration table. Actually, she all but begged me. I went BUT I was kicking and screaming all the way. She tried to tell me how much fun I was going to have and how interesting the conference was going to be. As I look back, she should have told me to go home because at that point, I needed a serious attitude adjustment. I told myself I would NEVER let anyone talk me into doing anything like "this" again.

Well, I stayed at the conference and met so many wonderful people. Ben Stephenson, the District Governor, Jack Balko, Max Taylor all made time to thank me for registering the conference participants. They did not have to invite me to the next meeting or conference, because I had fun and it was interesting. Oh my goodness, I was hooked!

I joined the local Toastmasters club - I now had time to walk up the flight of stairs to attend the meetings. Lori nominated me as President.

A few months later, Jack Balko was elected as District Governor, Max Taylor was elected Division Governor and I was elected as Area Governor. I started traveling to conferences and meetings in Dallas some 200 miles from my home in Shreveport. I received so much support from Jack and Max. They were always available when I had questions and Max traveled from Texarkana to Shreveport to help me start two new club. After Max completed his term as Division Governor, he recommended me and I was elected as Division Governor. Tough shoes to fill behind Max; however, I knew he was still there if I needed him.

Lori was my mentor in Toastmasters and she encouraged me from my first speech to me earning the highest award in Toastmasters -Distinguished Toastmaster (DTM).

I am grateful that Lori Hughes not give up on me and for Jack Balko and Max Taylor believing in me. It was a wonderful journey and I did not have to go it alone.

Thanks Lori, Jack and Max once I got hooked, I was hooked.

Jack Balko - *Carolyn, You are so kind with your compliments. Your outstanding success in Toastmasters is due to your very dedicated endeavor in serving at all levels of Toastmasters within District 50. Eastern Division and District 50 became great due to outstanding members like you. It was a real privilege working with you and your friendship is wonderful.. I trust all is well with you and that your business enterprise, book tour, and all the rest are diubg great.*

Day 5
Sherrie Wingate

Growing up with five sisters was wonderful. I am grateful for and appreciate ALL of them. Today I salute my sister Sherrie Wingate.

Sherrie is a United States Air Force Veteran and I say thanks to her for serving. This is not just about her serving our country, it is about the lessons we have learned and the fun we have had.

Sherrie LOVES to shop more than I do. We have spent many many days and evenings shopping in Houston, Tucson, Dayton, Hampton, Shreveport and Seattle. Sherrie can find the best bargains. She loves loves shoes and boots. When I am out shopping, I will take pictures of cute boots and send them to her. (That's not nice!)

She is loads of fun -- one year she came to visit me in Dayton and we decided to make our own Christmas ornaments. We got the idea from a craft show we attended. We purchased bags of curly hair, eyelashes, eyes, and beautiful wall paper. We used white styrofoam ball that I decided to spray paint brown - you know, have a little diversity. Well, that was not a great idea because the spray paint melted the styrofoam! We had the angel ornaments - hair, eyes, eyelashes and all. I took one to work and everyone thought they were cute and wanted to know where I got them. No one believed that I made them.

A few years later, my sweet little sister had to go on dialysis. (She was diagnosed with Lupus) I was sadden but her faith grew stronger! I admire her for not letting anything--not Lupus or needing a kidney -- weaken her faith or stop her from doing what she wanted to do. We believe there is a donor and she will have the kidney transplant.

In the meantime, she lives her life to the fullest. She has claimed her complete healing and knows everything is on God's time schedule. I am grateful to be connected to someone with such great faith. Love you my Sweet Sister.

Judy Mitchell - *Oh how true that is. I'm so thankful for every day the Lord gives me! Also thankful for the wonderful people He has placed in my life. I'm so blessed and it is all because of Him!!!*

Toni Trahan Shirley - *Oh, yes, I remember you as the night-owl and me up as early as 1:00 am sometime when I was on a roll and did office work the rest of the night before getting dressed to go to work. What a passion I had for it! I am still the early riser on a typical day!*

Carolyn Gray - *Toni Trahan Shirley I am better at getting up earlier now because some of my meeting start at 8 a.m. BUT on the days I don't have meetings, I* *sleep late.*

Kendra Wilson-Hudson - *Wonderful!*

Toni Trahan Shirley- What can I tell you Carolyn! You wrote this as a "night owl" and I comment on it as a super early riser!. Yes, I admire Sherrie, too, because of she years and years of dialysis God has graced her with. It means she is alive and sharing life with the rest of you. I remember meeting her having a dialysis treatment in Shreveport and saw how terrifically cold she was, shivering and shivering even though she was fully under covers. If you can imagine, so very cold that she just could not take even fingers out from under the covers we dialysis patients wear to maintain some warmth if we can. Some days that works, but some times it just doesn't. Friday I had on long Johns, two pair of socks, a down blanket, a blanket over that, and then a jacket over the foot-to-knee area and yet finally had to ask that the heat in the entire clinic be lowered so I might have a sot at getting remotely comfortable before they return it to warp cold!! I admire Sherrie for what she endures with the faith we are fortunate to have. I salute her for serving for the defense of our nation and for the part-time job she has as an on-going dialysis patient who has a good attitude about her duty to serve her health by being there day in, day out, by handling it when she has periods of running-out-of-steam as well as the times she is allowed the energy to roam those shopping areas with a sister like you. Yes, God has left us ESRD patients her for a reason and we need to be out there joyfully trying to accomplish that purpose, whatever it is and whether or not we know what it is. Have a great life, Sherrie. The human part of us says living life with dialysis 3 x weekly surely beats the alternative even thought we know our faith assures us of eternal life! God bless you Sherrie and God bless you Carolyn.

Deborah Higdon - *You know Shirley, Carolyn does not do mornings! (sorry Cal)*

Carolyn Gray - *Deborah Higdon, just so you know, I do some mornings!! Like today. Thank you very much Missy.*

Aurelia Evers Weems - *Inspirational!*

Sally Stubbs - *Please thank Sherrie for her service to our country! I'm grateful to her.*

Alicia R Badger - *I remember those ornaments! That was the same time we stopped on the side of the road and picked cattails and Uncle JB sprayed them with something to preserve them! And thats where I learned Mahjong that I still play (I played last night :)). Wonderful post Diva Aunt...now I know my shopping addiction is inherited!!!!*

Carolyn Gray - *OMGosh Diva Niece! I forgot about the cattails. I still play Mahjong too. Your addiction is deeper than you realize...your grand and great* *grandmothers had real b-a-d addictions!*

Judy Mitchell Carolyn--*what an awesome story!! Thanks for sharing! This really touched my heart and soul.*

Carolyn Gray - *Toni Trahan Shirley you know I am a "night owl" !!! Remember I did the late inservice meetings - 12 a.m. and 2 a.m. and you did the 6 a.m. We were a great team!*

Carolyn Gray -*Thanks Judy Mitchell. I have so many memories. I guess most people do when they get our age!!!*

Judy Mitchell - *Oh how true that is. I'm so thankful for every day the Lord gives me!!!*

Judy Mitchell - *Also thankful for the wonderful people He has placed in my life. I'm so blessed and it is all because of Him!!!*

Toni Trahan Shirley - *Oh, yes, I remember you as the night-owl and me up as early as 1:00 am sometime when I was on a roll and did office work the rest of the night before getting dressed to go to work. What a passion I had for it! I am still the early riser on a typical day!*

Carolyn Gray - *Toni Trahan Shirley I am better at getting up earlier now because some of my meetings start at 8 a.m. BUT on the days I don't have meetings, I sleep late.*

Day 6
Ed Thorsland

When the Medical Center Director (Dayton, OH) received approval of my appointment as HR Manager he called me to his office to notify me. I wasn't nervous but I did wonder why Mr. Thorsland wanted to see me.

I am grateful to have had the opportunity to work for and with Ed Thorsland. He was straight forward, no nonsense, sincere and very respectful.

One thing I appreciated about Mr. Thorsland was the way he treated everyone. He had great respect and admiration for our labor partners, in fact, the President of our local union, Art Jordan, was always kept "in the know." When new changes happened, he would make sure we notified Art, managers and employees. He did not want anyone hearing things through the grapevine.

I remember well, the year he made the decision to give every employee who received at least a satisfactory annual performance rating a monetary award. I was impressed. Of course, my rating was much higher (-:

He gave me lots of authority to manage HR. We were the first facility to implement a Partnership Agreement in our region and that was because he believed in doing the right thing. We had a huge celebration...our Regional Director, Mr. David Whatley, attended the signing ceremony.

Mr Thorsland recommended me for and I was appointed to committees outside of the facility to represent the medical center.

When I think of Quality, TQM, TQI, I always think of Ed Thorsland. I knew very little about TQM/TQI before going to Dayton; however, I had to put myself on the fast track because he was big on Total Quality.

He trusted me to do the right thing and I was ever mindful not to betray that trust.

Mr Thorsland, thank you. I am grateful for our paths having crossed.

Day 7
Harriet McCall

In the workplace, we have formal and on-the-job training. I received OJT from a high school student – Harriet McCall (Shreveport, LA). Harriet needed to "work" 80 hours in order to complete the requirements for graduation.

Harriet made an appointment to see me to ask if I would give her an opportunity to work 80 hours (volunteer) in Human Resources in order to complete requirements for... graduation. Of course I said yes.

The week after she started working, we had a huge projectó we had to prepare labels for approximately 1200 employee file folders. Because she was so computer savvy, that was a breeze for her and a relief for me and the staff.

In addition to completing the label project, Harriet taught me to prepare killer PowerPoint presentations and how to mail merge. She taught me how to add sound and different types of transitions to the slides. My instructor (Harriet) came to me and did not cost the agency any training dollars.

Harriet completed her work assignment in HR, graduated from high school, enrolled in college and started working for the agency as a compensated part-time employee.

You never know where your help comes from. Thank you Harriet McCall for being extremely patient with me and for helping me remove the "technopeasant" title after my name.

Dwan Milam-Reed - *She sounds like a very sharp young lady.*

Carolyn Gray - *She was-- she was in high school!*

Patricia Kim I *remember Harriet! She was great!*

Day 8
Madge Fletcher

Madge Fletcher In 1985, I met my very dear friend Madge Fletcher. We shared an office for over a year. She was my pillar during that time because I had plenty of occasions to cry on her shoulder.

That year, my son went to junior high school. He was always in the principal's office because he was in trouble for fighting. He was short and when the older kids picked on him and call him shorty, shrimp, ...squirt, etc. he decided to prove that he was tough.

When Ms Franklin, the Principal, called me at work to tell me she had Chris in the office. She would say "I have Chris in the office and I'll let him tell you what happened." I would get off the phone with her and cry and Madge would console me. The story was always the same; Chris was in a fight because someone called him pee-wee, squirt or some other name referencing his height.

I was concerned that the child would not make it out of junior high let along graduate from high school.

Madge was a former teacher and assure me that he would make it through that stage. I wasn't so sure.

Well, she was right; he made it through that stage and through high school on to college. I was thankful for her support and friendship as well as my son's behavior improving. Actually, he had some help from me with that -- if you know what I mean!

Madge is a warm compassionate person and was always there to encourage me personally and professionally.

Thank you Madge for your support, compassion and friendship. Love ya girl.

Carolyn Gray - *Yes, Judy Wootton McKee this is our Madge. She was wonderful to work with and as a friend, she was even better. We had some awesome times in that office. I have very fond memories of my time spent with her. Also, I have to credit Madge for my love of pimento cheese sandwiches.*

Carolyn Gray - *Frances Johnson we had the best carpool.*

Judy Wootton McKee - *The year I spent in Houston was special because of you and Madge. Your friendship meant so much!!*

Carolyn Gray - *Aww thanks Judy.*

Day 9
Bobby Morris

When I transferred to Washington, D.C. I was surrounded by a number of wonderful people. One in particular was my boss – (yes, boss) Bobby Morris.

Bobby Morris hired me based on the recommendation of Jerri Evans. (Jerri had clout!)

Bobby Morris was supportive and very generous to those who performed well. When I applied for the agency's Upward Mobility Training Program, Bobby gave me a... glowing reference and when I was selected, he gave me an award.

I learned to pay attention to details from Bobby Morris because he was VERY detailed oriented. I didn't want to disappoint him, Jerri or me!

He encouraged me, allowed me to take training classes to enhance my skills and always told me that I had lots of potential. I believed him!

I lost contact with him when I moved from Washington D.C. to San Antonio. I tried, unsuccessfully, to locate him. When I finally found a number to contact him, I learned that he retired and moved to Florida. I asked the person I spoke with to give him a message for me and I pray he got my message. I wanted him to know that I achieved my goal and he was instrumental in helping me. I am grateful for Bobby Morris helping me be the person I am today.

Margaret A. Volk - *There's a name that I haven't heard in a very long time....*

Caryn Ayers - *Nine down and how many more to go, I admire your tenacity and willingness to acknowledge others.*

Day 10
Former Supervisor

As I think about the people who have contributed to me being who I am, I reflect today on someone I learned from by observing him.

By observing my immediate supervisor, I learned that I did not want be anything like him. I wanted to be fair, treat others with dignity and respect, and display a high level of integrity and compassion for those who worked for and with me.

Although I found few positive attributes about him, I learned what I did not want to become. I am extremely grateful that my professional path crossed very few like him.

Casey Conner - *Well said :) lol*

Angelica ItsGodinmekowgurl Byrd - *I like that!*

Day 11
Alice Vaughn

This day has been a day of reflection about a lady who gives, gives and gives even more. I have not found anyone more giving than Alice Vaughn.

I met Sis Vaughn over 30 years ago. She gives of herself without thinking about getting anything in return. She has fed, clothed, transported, called, visited, given gifts, prayed and sent more "I missed you today at church" cards than 100 other people.

Sis Vaughn is very nurturing and does not mince words. She is a woman of her word and will give you words of sage advice just like you were one of her own children. I know--I have been the recipient of her advice on many occasions.

I am grateful for having Sis Vaughn in my life. She has consoled me, fed me, called me and prayed for and with me. In case you were wondering, yes, I have been the recipient of an "I missed you today at church" card! I love Sis Vaughn dearly and pray that God continues to bless her.

Thank you Sis Vaughn. I am grateful for you being instrumental in me being the person I am; there is some of Alice in me and that's a very good thing!

Sally Davis - *It's a very good thing! Thank you for always being there to encourage and HELP me with this calling from God! I wouldn't want to be on this journey with anyone other than you!! Love you!!*

Carolyn Gray - *Love you more Psal!*

Sis Vaughn passed away in October 2013 – she fought a GOOD fight. I think of her often.

Day 12
Beverly Vann

When I head outside, I have on sunglasses – sun or no! My friend, Bev Vann teased me every time she saw me leaving my office with my sunglasses on and there was "not a drop of sunlight to be found." (Her words!)

It was one of those things that affectionately stuck and some of my co-workers started asking why I had my sun glasses on and there was no sun.

I transferred from Houston and when I returned ten years later, the first thing Bev asked me was "are you still wearing your sunglasses when there is no sun." I had to respond in the affirmative because I was and still do wear my sun glasses during the day if I am outside, sun or no.

When I retired, Bev was not able to attend my retirement luncheon; however, she made sure she sent me a gift– a pair of sunglasses all wrapped up in a beautiful gift bag.

Bev taught me to embrace humor and not let anyone stop me from wearing my sun glasses regardless of how much I was teased. Bev, I hear you laughing at me or is it with me?

Sylvia Lacey - *Don't ever stop being you! Pearls, sunglasses and the ever famous double clutch. lol But seriously always protect your eyes from damaging UV rays sun or not.*

Donald Reel - *Ms. Gray that is you!*

Day 13
Emma Yerby

Today is set aside for my friend that I gained weight with after going on a diet! My girlfriend, Emma Yerby and I went on a diet because we wanted to lose five pounds. We recorded our weight (127 and 130 pounds) (this was a few years agoówell, maybe 30!) and at the end of the time designated, we both had gained weight! I should have learned my lesson but I didn't. I have been on numerous diets and the results have been the same–I gained weight! So, I have stopped dieting – given up while I was somewhat ahead.

Emma and I have laughed over the years about our unsuccessful attempt at wanting to lose "only five pounds." You gotta be able to laugh at yourself and we have.

On Day 9, I spoke about my boss Bobby Morris. I lost contact with him so I could not send him a handwritten thank you note. Well, guess what, my buddy, investigator Emma Yerby, called me after reading the post and said "I think I found Bobby Morris!" She went on to say she thought she had located a number for his son and was waiting for a return call from him.

About an hour after we spoke, sure enough, Emma had a number for Bobby Morris. She shared it with me and I contacted him. Bobby and I chatted for about ten minutes. Although he didn't remember me right away (I worked for him 30 years ago), he thanked me for the kind words and shared his address with me. I will get his thank you card in the mail tomorrow. I was excited to share with him how grateful I am that our paths crossed and for his support.

If I am trying to locate anyone else, I will be calling Emma Yerby.

Margaret A. Volk - *Gotta love that Emma! Thanks for sharing this funny story...*

Judy Otts Paine - *Marshall I am on a diet now. Heaven help me if I gain 5 more lbs!*

Carolyn Gray - *Judy Otts Paine-Marshall, don't do it! (-:*

Day 14
Chi-Chi Barrentez

While working at Fort Sam Houston, I met Chi-Chi Barrentez. Chi-Chi's hands were always busy. On her break, she would crochet. She made lovely scarfs, sweaters, shawls and Afghans.

On day I mentioned how much I loved her work and she asked me if I wanted to learn. I was "in" – of course I wanted to learn. She told me what supplies I needed to get started. Immediately after work, I went to Woolco to purchase the yarn, a crochet hook and a cute little bag.

Chi-Chi was very very patient with me. It took several days for me to get the hang of it. I made the l-o-n-g-e-s-t chain stitch you have ever seen. It didn't matter, I was happy because I was crocheting! After the chain stitch drill, I got down to some real crocheting; I started making single and double crochet stitches. Chi-Chi taught me to use a pattern and it was on! I made a shawl, in fact, I made many many many shawls. Everyone in my family and all of the neighbors received handmade shawls for every occasion.

I continued crocheting until I advanced to making Afghans. Yep, everyone got Afghans too.

Thanks Chichi for teaching me to crochet.

Melody Seale - *Love it, brings back my time of the learning process, the longest chain stich ever, lol!*

Carolyn Gray - *Melody Seale, you should have seen it. I probably could have stretched it from one end of the state of Texas to the other. I think she was trying to keep me busy will she crocheted! It worked. I concentrated on that chain!*

Phyllis Jenkins Isiminger - *My granny taught me to knit before I started first grade, but I could never get the hang of crocheting. Your story has inspired me to try again......thx*

Melody Seale - *You are so funny, i love it.*

Carolyn Gray - *Phyllis, they could not teach me to knit! I love crocheting -- I find it so relaxing. Knitting made me nervous!!*

Madge Fletcher - *Do you remember teaching me to crochet as we carpooled to work!!*

Carolyn Gray - *OMGosh, Madge I forgot that we crocheted our way to work.*

Chi- Chi's project grew --Love it! We had the best carpool.

Frances Johnson Can *you teach me?*

Carolyn Gray - *Of course. I am wondering why you were not in the "carpool crocheting class" - you must have been driving (-:*

Day 15
R.N. Marsall, Sr.

My pastor for many many years was Pastor R.N. Marshall. Pastor Marshall was a great teacher and I was truly blessed by his Bible teaching. He explained what he taught in such a way that my son (who was 6 years) could remember the content of his sermons.

In 1981, he introduced the church to Praise and Worship music. It took me several Sundays to appreciate the "new" music. I think the main reason was that I didn't know the words to "new" music. Once I learned the words, I enjoyed Praise and Worship and even tried to sing (which I cannot do) out loud.

Pastor Marshall, thank you for teaching me how to study the Bible, memorize scripture and for introducing Praise and Worship music to our church.

Pastor R.N. Marshall passed away January 2015.

Day 16
My Grandson David

I am a grandmother, my grandmother name is GiGi and my grandson is David. He use to tell me his name is David and his name is in the Bible a lot of times!

We have shared so many fun occasions that I am having a hard time deciding which one(s) I am most grateful for.

David and I have a few things in common but the one thread that connects us is that we are both serious night owls! On his weekend visits, we would frequently stay up until 2 a.m. building airplanes, playing radio station (he was the DJ and I was the caller and we recorded our interviews), write stories, make up songs and dance.

Then the little dude would go upstairs, get ready for bed then call me to bring him a grilled ham and cheese sandwich, potato chips and a diet DP and cut the sandwich in trangles (aka triangles). Coming right up! That's right, at 2 a.m., I was up making a grilled cheese sandwich, to order!

Now, the truth of the matter, had his Dad, my favorite son tried to stay up past 10 p.m. at that age – let's just say he wouldn't have asked.

At night, when we went out, I would let him drive in the subdivision once we are on our street. Did I mention I live less than a mile from Precinct 4? shhh!) Sitting on my lap driving was fun for him and I love seeing him happy.

He loves to shop (especially if we were shopping for him), swim, visit the library to check out books with his library card, visit the art museum, take in a play at The Texas Rep Theater and afterwards, stop by Sonic's for a foot long chili dog (he missed his GiGi on that one!).

When I decided to write me book, All About ME* (*Manners and Etiquette for TWEENS and TEENS), he was my "subject." I figured if he would read and apply what I had written, other TWEENS and TEENS would be able to as well. He also helped me present when I had Manners and Etiquette Workshops.

I have been loved, unconditionally, by my grandson and I am extremely grateful for every moment I have spent with him. He is my sweetie! Since he is in high school now, I might have to stop calling him my sweetie– maybe not!

Toni Trahan Shirley - I remember David since almost when he was born so that his GIGI could adore him. How many fast trips from Shreveport to Houston so you could bring David back to Shreveport to have such a good time with GIGI (never mind grandfathers here...GIGI was the rock!) How many fast trips to Houston and back to get him home. What a bond you too have. I am told that I overstep boundaries and, in essence, spoil a couple of my grandchildren; if not that, then it is that I am not seeing them enough. I'll tell you what! There is just about no level of "spoiling those children" that I really come close to. It is a miraculous privilege we grandmothers happen to have. It is character building that they each have someone in life that can be their fortress of warmth and safe haven, friendship, and the kind of love that comes from a loving grandmother. You modeled some of that for me Carolyn. David was and is such an important part of your life. If I can compare myself to you in any sort of way, it is in the depth of love I have for these 4 grandchildren of mine. As I have said many times before, "they are my heart". So very glad Day 16 belongs to David (and his GIGI).

Toni Trahan Shirley - *Oh, and I happen to have dear Leah spending the night here tonight. Of course, she falls asleep snuggling with Gramma in bed!*

Stacey DeMarco Jata - *This is a beautiful story. Thank you for sharing!*

Jane Warner - *I just came back from North Carolina and was introduced to such things as "Duck Dynasty", football, bowling and "grown up" talk. Wow where have these last 14 years gone!*

Rebecca Montgomery-Nelson - *Ms. Gray, this is so sweet....remind me of Betty when it comes to her grands....Ya'll spoil them rotten and then bring them back to the moms to get they minds right. Something Im looking forward too....but most definetly not no time soon....*

Melody Seale - *Such a sweet story Carolyn, you are a wonderful woman!*

Juliana Lucci Ashley - *Carolyn, he is so lucky to have you--everyone should have a GiGi like you. In fact, I want one--will you be my Gigi?*

Sylvia Lacey - *2:00am really? Grandmothers are a special breed, I'm not sure what happens to the strict no nonsense mother gene when you become Gigi. Maybe when it happens to me I'll understand. Until then I remain amazed.*

Judy Mitchell - *Love this story!! Yes -- GiGi does rock!!! Fantastic grandmother.*

Judy Otts Paine-Marshall - *You are truly an awesome grandmother!*

Carolyn Gray - *Toni Trahan Shirley Shirley, probably my most memorable trip was the one I drove from Jackson to Shreveport on a Friday afternoon, up at 5 am on Sat, drive to Houston to see David play basketball for about 30 minutes then back to Shreveport the same day because I was flying out Sunday for travel to somewhere. Now, that's love!!*

Toni Trahan Shirley - *Yes, Carolyn, it is love, great love!*

Freddie Garnett Jr. - *GiGi This is one of the greatest Loves that we my ever have in our lifetime. Hold on to this for life....Paw Paw*

Day 17
Nancy Campbell

If you have never work for your friend and had an awesome experience, I truly wish you could have worked for Nancy Campbell.

I had the privilege of working with and for Nancy Campbell. She was a great teacher, boss and friend. If you worked for her, you would give 110% because you wanted to make her look good all the time. Nancy earned the admiration and respect of her employees, peers and superiors because of her integrity, compassion and work ethic.

She was firm but fair with everyone. She laughed as hard as she worked and would stand up to a two ton gorilla!

Nancy made sure we were properly trained, held us accountable and supported her entire staff. She was our greatest cheerleader–she kept us pumped up! Nancy was concerned about work/life balance before it was cool. I never had a problem taking off to attend school functions for my children or if I wanted to take a day or two off to stay home and do nothing! Honestly, you could tell her you just wanted to be off–period.

You don't often find someone you can work for, be mentored by and maintain a friendship unless you worked for Nancy Campbell. Thanks Nancy for all the support and encouragement. You are one awesome lady.

Nancy Campbell - *You are too kind my dear friend! I think back so fondly of our shared time in Houston. We worked hard but we had so much fun!!*

Carolyn Gray - *Yes we did have fun A blessing for our paths to have crossed. You were a great leader.*

Day 18
Sandy Lawrence

When I started my business, I had NO idea what networking was all about; however, there was an angel on assignment–Sandy Lawrence. Sandy shared her knowledge, contacts and network with me.

Sandy invited me to events so that I could see just how things worked. She had holiday gatherings, book signings, meetings and I was invited to all of them. She knows everybody and her goal was to ma...ke sure I knew as many of her contacts as possible.

Sandy is passionate about what she does and has a heart the size of Texas. She taught me that "there is enough to go around for everyone so share." Sandy believes in making referrals – she holds nothing back from anyone.

She gives her time at her Marketing Bistro where everyone is invited and welcome to stop by to get and share ideas on marketing concerns. She gives, gives, and gives. I have never heard her complain about anything. Sandy finds the good in everything.

I love being in her company and appreciate her so very much. I am blessed to have her teach me the ropes!

Day 19
Evelyn Nabritt

When we lived in Augusta GA, my neighbor, Evelyn Nabritt, had two precious little girls, Stephanie and Bonita who though I was a little girl!

Evelyn and I became friends through the girls. This was wonderful for me because I did not know anyone. Evelyn would check on me to make sure I was doing ok and let the girls "play" with me. We moved, and moved again. We lost contact with each other for over 30 years.

I was working in North Carolina and mentioned I had a girlfriend in South Carolina that I would love to locate. Paula, a lady in the office happened to live in the same town my friend was from. She offered to help me find her. I drove to Paula's that weekend and we tried to locate Evelyn at her last known address. The street name had been changed! BUT we found someone who knew her daughter Stephanie and told us where they lived. We drive there -- no luck -- that was the wrong address.

Later the following week, Paula came to work excited and had good news, she located Evelyn. Evelyn and I spoke over the phone. I could hardly wait for the weekend to visit her.

I drove to South Carolina, saw the girls who had adult children and of course did not remember me. Evelyn and I had to catch up on the lost time. We told the girls about them thinking I was a little girl and wanting me to play with them. We had hours of laughs that day.

Evelyn and I stay in touch with each other regularly and promised to not lose contact with each other. Thanks Evelyn for being my friend when I didn't know anyone.

Paula McKnight - *I LOVE GEORGIA...I LIVED IN ATLANTA SHORTLY AND HAVE FAMILY THERE!*

Dedra Murchison - *What a wonderful memory and testament to friendship! Am enjoying your posts and find myself sharing my gratitude more easily this year!*

Tanya Ann Furtado - *What a fantastic story!! Thank you*

Donald Reel - *Carolyn, you are a truly blessed woman!!!!!*

Day 20

Deborah "Cookie" McCulloch

Is there a nurse in the house! Yes, there is and it is my little sister, Deborah or Cookie as she is affectionately referred to by family and friends.

Cookie is a Registered Nurse and a darn good one. She is compassionate and passionate about being a nurse.

Having a nurse in the family is GREAT. We call her for every scratch, scrape and bump. When her boys, my grandson and nephew were younger, they took advantage of the in home nurse and she had a treatment plan for their hurts–an ice bag! That bag of ice cured everything in a minute. That's just about how long they kept the ice bag on their injury.

Now, some of the adult members were not a whole lot better. The request from my husband every time the doctor gives him a prescription is: "call Cookie to see what this is that doctor has given me." Once she explains to him what the doctor told him, he has the prescription filled.

Deborah is the most patient nurse you will every meet! Whether at work or home, she is awesome in emergency situations - grace under fire! I have seen her in action and she is the nurse you want to be there by your bedside. She is truly one who has been "called" to this profession.

This little sister, Number 7 of 8 in our family has brought me years of joy and laughter. She is a wonderful wife, mother, sister and friend. I am blessed to have her as my sister and friend. I love this nurse.

Marco Cruz - *I love me some cookie! Sweet as a cookie.*

Rosemary Slade - *I love nurses too!*

Judy Mitchell - *It's nice having nurses in the family. Love this inspirational and heartfelt story. Look forward every day to your post. Keep them coming.*

Day 21
Don Reel

Have you read The Greatest Salesman in the World or A Better Way to Live by Og Mandino was a question posed to me in 1992 by Donald Reel. My response of course was "no, I have not." I had to admit that I had never heard of Og Mandino.

Sir Don's next question was what about The Richest Man in Babylon by George S. Clason. I had to give the same response.

That was my response that day; however, the next day, I was excited to tell him I purchased The Greatest Salesman in the World by Og Mandino as well as The Richest Man in Babylon. I read both books and had my son, Chris, who was a senior in high school read The Richest Man in Babylon.

Don introduced me to other great authors and books as well as shared wisdom and business ideas with me. The following year, I read The Return of the Ragpicker by Og Mandino–thought I had one up on my teacher. Not so! He had already read it.

My life has been enriched by reading these and other books. Don, I am grateful to you for introducing me to some of the best books I have every read.

Frances Johnson - *I think Sir Don introduced all of us to these books.*

Donald Reel - *Thanks Francis!!!!*

Carolyn Gray - *Frances Johnson, he helped all if us to grow. He's that kinda guy!*

Day 22
Roslyn Evans

It is no secret that I cannot keep a plant alive for more than a couple of weeks. For this reason, I love receiving fresh flowers rather than plants.

Roslyn Evans knows this – she has for years sent me flowers for Christmas/

my birthday and sometimes on Mother's Day. She is so very thoughtful and caring.

We worked together for a number of years and when I transferred from Ohio, she wro...te me regularly to check on me to see how my new home and office environment were coming along.

Roslyn and other staff members gave me what I liked on Boss's Day, Valentine's Day, and just because day -- fresh flowers and chocolate-- not plants! I was blessed to have worked with the staff in Dayton. They treated me like family (that they liked!).

Roslyn, thank you for remembering me on holidays and for making me feel so extremely special.

Crissy Butts - *Ditto! I got two plants at Christmas, a poinsettia and a little herb garden and both lived about as long as a bouquet of flowers I bought for the table. Maybe my plants don't like florescent lights, and chlorinated tap water. I guess my environment is not ideal, my intentions are always hopeful though. :)*

Judy Otts Paine-*Marshall I grow pansies in the winter! They are surviving outside.*

Day 23
Judy Mitchell

"*The Joy of My Heart*" is a wonderful devotional I use every day. Judy Mitchell gave me this little book for Christmas years ago. There is a scripture reference and a wonderful story (two or three paragraphs) related to the scripture. I have made notes in the book, recorded important dates and have given copies of the book to several other people.

Judy Mitchell and I worked together in Shreveport. Within the first month of working with her I learned that she was detailed oriented and oh so thorough. Judy was knowledgeable, organized, punctual, fun to work with and low maintenance. She was one of the absolute best people to have on your team. She was like a little duck in the pond–quietly and gracefully moving along.

I loved that all I had to do was give her a project, leave her alone and the next thing I knew the project was completed and she was ready to move on to another project.

If Judy Mitchell said something, it could be taken to the bank! Thanks Judy for my book, your loyalty, your high level of integrity and your friendship.

Carolyn Gray - *Judy Mitchell, I love that devotional! The first thing I do each morning is read The Joy of My Heart and pray. I have others that I read but this* *one I use every morning!*

Cheryl Adams - *Judy is one great friend to have on your side. She told me many times not to get married until the right one came along. Oh how right she was. She spent many times praying with and for me when my mom was dying from cancer. I so missed her when she left Shreveport*

Toni Trahan Shirley - *Well, since you two recommend it, I have ordered it.*

Judy Mitchell - *Toni and Cheryl -- I sincerely appreciate your kind and thoughtful words. You will never know just how much they mean to me. Make God continue to bless both of you!!!*

Day 24
Eva Smith

Fore! My friend Eva Smith had two tickets to the Masters Golf Tournament in Augusta, GA and she invited me to go along with her. I had watch golf on TV a time or two which was the extent of my involvement with or knowledge of golf.

When we got to Augusta National, I found out she knew less than I did about golf! I at least knew you had to have golf clubs, balls and a caddy. I also k...new the terms "tee" and "par." Never mind that I didn't really know the real meaning of par.

Not being known for my shyness, I decided to ask! Yep, I walked right up to a man who looked like he knew about golf and fired off several questions. I got the answers and along with our programs, we walked around Augusta National like we were pros. It was a fascinating experience and made me want to learn to play, especially since I knew golf terminology. After all, I had been to the Masters!

We had so much fun, met some "stars" and saw so many important looking people. I say important looking because I am so sure Eva and I looked important to them too.

That one trip to the Masters made me an expert of the game (at least in our circle) as well as appreciate the beauty of the golf course. Thanks Eva for exposing me to the sport of golf up close and personal.

Melody Seale - *You are an amazing woman Carolyn!*

Judy Mitchell - *Wow. Attending the Masters--what an honor. You have had some fantastic life experiences.*

Frances Johnson - *Way to go Ms. Gray!*

Day 25
Bonnie Burt

Being able to play a game of golf was realized when I met Bonnie Burt. Bonnie mentioned to me one day that she and her husband John played golf. I was excited – I told her I have always wanted to learn to play golf since my Masters experience.

I told Bonnie I had never played golf, and didn't own a single club. That was not a problem. Bonnie said I could use John's clubs. The next after... noon we were headed to the golf course at Barksdale AFB. I had my sneakers and John Burt's golf clubs.

Bonnie gave me a thirty minute crash course and I was ready. I was swinging like I was playing softball. All Bonnie could say was "you have the most amazing swing I have ever seen!" We played 18 holes which took us A-L-L afternoon because we had to let the real golfers through. I was exhausted and decided trying to play 18 holes was a bit much for me. I went home, took a shower, did not eat dinner, went to bed and slept until the next morning!

I could not wait to get my own clubs. My husband cautioned me not to go overboard because I might night like playing golf. I purchased a pair of golf shoes, a glove and some real cute golf clothes. I took his advice about the clubs. I hit the thrift stores and found a set of clubs. They needed new grips and since my husband did not want me to go overboard, I figured he would not mind replacing the grips.

Bonnie and I found a really nice 9-hole course and we frequently took off work in the morning (because we had a 7:30 a.m. tee time), played 9 holes, got ready and went to work in the afternoon.

Guess what I got for Christmas that year? A new set of golf clubs! By that time, my swing was much better and we even played in a couple of charity scrambles.

I am grateful for John loaning me his clubs and for Bonnie Burt being patient while I learned to play a game I love.

Carolyn Gray - *you betcha! Fair warning, I love the game...not that good!*

Roxie Tabor - *I remember that you are a good golfer, Carolyn.*

Carolyn Gray - *Roxie, you are too kind.*

Melody Seale - *Woman of many talents!!*

Day 26
Norma King-Joiner

Norma King-Joiner took me under her golf wing after Bonnie moved to Arizona. Norma and I worked one awesome schedule. On Sunday, I attended 8am service, 9:30 am Sunday school then home by 10:40 for a nice breakfast and nap. I had to nap to be ready for our 1 p.m. tee time.

Norma could play 18 holes but not me. Well, I could play 18 holes; it just took me two days! Front 9 one day, back ...9 the second day. During the week, we played the twilight round to take advantage of the lower green fees.

Norma helped me improve my swing and much needed help on my short game. She was patient and fun. One of my most memorable outings was when Norma hit a ball which soared then landed in the pond but not before hitting a duck in the head! We ran to the pond to see if the duck was ok 'n the duck was out of sight!

Norma taught me to tee off with my 5 iron on par 3 holes that were 100-125 yards. I could actually get the ball on the green off the tee and par the hole. She was a great golfer and didn't mind sharing her knowledge. If she had not moved, I just know she could have gotten me ready for the senior circuit!

Toni Trahan Shirley - *And such a nice, nice person!*

Toni Trahan Shirley - *You were up very late, Ms. Gray!*

Carolyn Gray - *Always Toni Trahan Shirley! I am working on not staying up so late.*

Day 27
Sandra Byrd

Most people know I don't like to cook; however, like most people, I have a dish I am known for. I have to thank my friend of 30+ years, Sandra Byrd, for my specialty dish.

Almost every Thanksgiving, we had dinner at work. Those who could cook would prepare a dish and the rest of us (I was in the rest of us group) would bring paper items, drinks or donate money for the meat dish.

Sandra would prepare a HUGE dish of string beans and potatoes seasoned to perfection. Talking about delicious – yum! One year, I brought a dish–twice baked potatoes. Everyone raved about the twice baked potatoes. They were good but the truth of the matter was that I only put the cheese on the potatoes. I had to admit that my husband prepared them--but I helped!

One year, I asked Sandra if she would tell me (not just give me the recipe) how to make her string beans and potatoes. She did and for years, I have been serving up Sandra Byrd string beans, new potatoes! That is what we call my dish. When my family asks me to prepare something, it is my "Sandra Byrd string beans and new potatoes dish." They are delicious; however, they don't compare to Ms Byrd's.

I have a specialty dish thanks to Sandra Byrd.

Carolyn Gray - *Judy Mitchell, you know I don't either. I'll send you the recipe.*

Frances Johnson - *Sandra was a great cook...........we had many great cooks in HR. And the Thanksgiving dinner was a feast.*

Toni Trahan Shirley - *Send me the recipe, too. They let me eat green beans, so I cook them often & a variation would be welcome. Bill can eat the potatoes since I am not allowed.*

Judy Mitchell - *Thanks Carolyn. Does the recipe make a large portion? If so, I'll c if I can make a smaller portion.*

Day 28
Margaret Volk

MGT is the abbreviation for Margaret as in Margaret Volk. Margaret and I worked in the same section. She was an expert (as far as I was concerned) on the WANG. I had no idea where to start on the WANG. I mean I did not know how to turn it on. Margaret taught me everything I needed to know.

Margaret was quiet, industrious, generous and a great friend. My children loved MGT. She found ...the coolest gifts for them. Like a mug with Mary Jane shoes as a base for my daughter and one with sneakers for my son.

We did lots of things together - like crying when her dog Skippy got sick, shopping for her a new car, going to plays with my children, taking pictures of the Purple Phantom and planning parties for our section.

When I applied for the Upward Mobility Program, MGT, Emma and I were always on mail patrol waiting to see if I got selected. Everyone said I would receive a short letter if I "made it." Well, the letter finally came–it was a long letter. The three of us were reading it with sad faces until we got to the last paragraph which read that I had been selected to participate in the program. We were jumping up and down like three little girls. We were all so very happy.

Of course, I was given a huge send off and MGT gave me a 5X7 yellow "junior executive pad" with a verbal reminder not to forget where I came from. Well MGT, I did not forget. Without your help and friendship, I may have "made it" but it would not have been as enjoyable. Thanks MGT for your support and friendship.

Margaret A. Volk - You have such an incredible memory for details! The Purple Phantom - I haven't thought about that in many years. Thanks for the wonderful write-up and for the friendship we shared. Working with you and Emma all those years ago gave me a wonderful start to my career. You made me see that work could also be fun! Thanks for acknowledging me on "Day 28" :-)

Carolyn Gray - *We worked hard and played just as hard. We were truly a great work family.*

Mgt, I have *wonderful memories of my years spent in Washington DC.*

Do you and *Emma Yerby remember Miss 4:25?*

Sylvia Lacey - *You have been blessed to have some very wonderful, supportive and interesting people in your life and career. So many are equally blessed because you choose to "pay it forward."*

Margaret A. Volk - *I'm sure that I should remember Miss 4:25, but my memory is not as great as yours! Emma Yerby - Do you remember?*

Day 29
Deborah Higdon

I love traveling by automobile. It is so much fun especially when you have a great travel partner.

Deborah Higdon and I have taken many road trips and I tell you, she is one of the best travel partners I have ever known. We have turned five hour trips into eight hour trips. How? Glad you asked! We stopped at every interesting looking place on the side of the road. We ate, shopped, antiqued and I talked to every stranger in sight.

Deborah knows Louisiana history so traveling with her through the state of Louisiana was a true history lesson. We took tours of antebellum homes in Louisiana, shopped at the best antique shops from Louisiana to Florida, laughed out loud and silently and of course we ate lots and lots of good Cajun food.

Debbie is a nurse, a darn good one. She is all about providing excellent care to each and every patient she has contact with. Along with her clinical skills, she also has exceptional administrative knowledge. She taught me to write competencies and prepare for Joint Commission surveys. By observing her, I learned to be focused.

On a completely different note, I grew to love LSU football because of her. Debbie is the best football player LSU has ever had. When LSU is playing,

I will call her and her response is always "do you know the game is on?!" When the game is a close one, she is WORN OUT from playing so hard. There are LSU fans and then there is Debbie, THE LSU fan.

Deborah Higdon -Thanks Carolyn, Those were special times. I have yet to meet anyone who can "silently" laugh as well as you! Those were the best laughs. And, YES - you learned the life history and aspirations of everyone we encountered while I tried to pretend I didn't see them. You are a genuine "blue" - through and through!

Day 30

Ricky and Monica Hall

When you think of church school for adults, you don't generally think of a class with 40+ adults in attendance on any given Sunday morning. Well, that is exactly what Monica and Ricky Hall's class looked like.

When I decided to attend Lake Bethlehem, I wanted to attend church school to get a feel for the church. I loved the class, the people and the teachers. They made studying the Bib...le very interesting and encouraged class participation. After about a year, they introduced a new book for the class which helped us to study and apply the Word to our everyday lives.

We had a class Christmas party where we played games, ate delicious food and fellowshipped which allowed us to get to know each other better. I found out that Ricky had a funny side! I was heartbroken about leaving my church, church school family and friends when we decided to relocate to Houston.

I am grateful for the experience of being taught by one of the nicest couples I have had the pleasure of knowing. Their light shines before men and not for their glory!

Day 31

Anita Hall

Transferring to a new job can be stressful. You don't know anyone, don't know phone numbers or the layout of the building.

When I got to Dayton, I only experience this for a very short period of time. Anita Hall had worked for the agency for a number of years and she knew everything about the building and the phone numbers to every department. Anita showed me around. When someone came into our office and she knew I did know them, she would speak to them and use their whole name.

If I reached for the telephone directory to look up a number she would ask "who are you calling?" and then give me that person's number.

Anita made life easy for me – she was the historian. Regardless of what I need to know or get done, she was my resource. I had a wonderful work experience while there and I owe much gratitude to Anita. Thanks Anita Hall for showing me the ropes!

Day 32

Hattie Higgins-Greene

Having mentors was the one thing that helped me to achieve my career goal of becoming a Human Resources Manager.

My first HR mentor was Hattie Higgins-Greene. She was a walking FPM (you gotta be old school to know that one!) and she had lots of tough love for me. Hattie trained me and trained me r-e-a-l good. When she was explaining something or going over a process/ procedure, I alway...s had my steno pad and pen ready to take notes.

When she spoke, I listened. If she held up her index finger while she was explaining a process/procedure, I underlined those insturctions in red because I knew that was something very important. If she said Carolyn, "you must" do so and so, I put asterisks around those statements.

Hattie had me research EVERYTHING--I had to read the regulations first. She always told me to know the answer for myself and not rely on others – including her – for answers to my questions. It was like being in a classroom. She ensured I understood what I read and that I knew how to apply the guidelines to real life situations.

Talking about appreciating my "schooling" -- I was well trained and prepared to go it on my own. I still had my steno pad with all those notes for a just in case moment. If I didn't have an answer to a particular question, I knew where to find the answer. I was able to share my knowledge with others which means there is a little piece of Hattie Higgins-Greene in everyone I trained.

Hattie and I became very good friends and remain friends to this day. We had some good laughs about my steno pad notebook with the red markings. I MUST say that I am grateful to my friend for preparing me and helping me achieve my career goal of becoming a Human Resources Manager. Thank you Hattie.

Sylvia Lacey - *Having a great mentor is a wonderful experience, makes all the difference in the world.*

Donald Reel - *Carolyn, being of the "Ole School" I can appreciate the post.*

MaryAnn Ederhoff was a walking FPM. I used to always call her when I was in South Dakota to get answers to Personnel Issues. The first P.O. that I had with Forest Service, made me read and re-read the FPM everyday for 8 hours for many months. BORING!

Day 33
Buzz Bellmont

I love going to the theater and my recent trip to the theater is one to remember.

I had the honor of attending opening night of "*Knock Me a Kiss*" at the Ensemble Theater with Buzz Bellmont, The Critic's Critic. "Knock Me a Kiss" was written by Charles Smith and directed by Chuck Smith, and they were both in attendance. They were standing close enough to me that I could have touched them but I didn't!

Buzz introduced me to so many people I can't remember any names. We took pictures and I saw two ladies I worked with years ago.

The play was wonderful with great humor and superb acting. I recognized one of the performers and finally remembered I saw her on stage years ago. She was good back then, too.

At the conclusion of the play, I shared my thoughts with Buzz and told him how much I enjoyed the play. I am so blessed to have friends who don't mind sharing with me.

Thanks Buzz Bellmont for the invitation. It was a night I will remember for a long time.

Day 34
Alicia Stamps

My youngest sister, Alicia, is a teacher. She taught first and second grade for about 15 years. She taught in a school where the parents were not as supportive as they could have been. When her class went on field trips, she had to have adults accompany her and I raised my hand!

I took trips with her class to the zoo, picnics and participated in their holiday celebrations. I enjoyed s...haring with the "little people" as I referred to them. They said the funniest, most truthful things and gave THE best hugs.

My sister had a second grade class one year that I fell in love with. I would take off from work to spend time with those little people. I was so attached to them that the next year when they were in third grade, I still went to the school to see them.

A professor from Prairie View A&M University addressed a conference I attended years ago and he said "preachers and teachers are called!" My sister was called and she loves her calling. I am grateful that she answered her calling and for all of the teachers who answered their calling.

Alicia, thank you for accepting the call and I appreciate you allowing me to enjoy the ride with you.

Jane Warner - *Alicia is blessed to have you as a sister.*

Melody Seale - *You are a wonderful woman Carolyn, you are so full of love and it shows always!*

Day 35
Mrs. Gerri Foster

One year, a family friend, Mrs. Foster, told me she had one more Christmas gift to wrap; however, she was out of wrapping paper. She pulled out a used and very very wrinkled piece of wrapping paper and asked me what would I think if someone gave me a gift wrapped in that paper.

My flippant teenage response was – "the person receiving it should be glad you thought enough of them to purchase a gift for them!" When I went to visit her on Christmas morning to deliver my gift to her she said "Carolyn, this is for you." It was the very very wrinkled wrapping paper. I smiled and she laughed. I thought to myself I had no idea she would wrap MY gift in that used paper.

I unwrapped the gift to find a beautiful blue and white cashmere cap to match the cashmere sweater I received from my parents.

That experience taught me to never ever give anyone anything I would not want for myself. I received a beautiful gift and learned a valuable lesson.

Judy Wootton McKee - *I love your stories too, especially this one. You are a special friend!!*

Donald Reel - *Carolyn, a great lesson for all of us. Have a great weekend!*

Day 36
Pastor S. Riley

I learned many things from my former pastor. I am grateful he encouraged me to read Proverbs daily. Since 2008, I have read Proverbs every day. I must admit that there have been times I have gone to bed and remembered that I did not read Proverbs for the day. When this happens, I get up and read the Proverbs that corresponds with that particular day.

I have read Proverbs for four years and every time I read it I find something that I didn't notice the month before or the year before. Reading Proverbs does not replace my daily Bible reading and studying, it enhances and strengthens what I study. I am grateful and wiser for this lesson. I have shared this with a number of people who want to have more wisdom. It works.

Day 37
Annette DeFazio

We spend so much time at work that it is important to have at least one person you can relate to and cut up with. Annette DeFazio was my all day long cut up buddy.

I met DeFazio in San Antonio. We both transferred there from Washington DC so we had a few things in common which made us "different" according to the locals. Our primary mode of communication with each other was with our eyes.... Mostly rolling our eyes at some of the things we heard and saw happen.

Annette was my life preserver and I was hers. It seemed that we just didn't fit in. They seemed to always want to "get" people. Both of us came from organizations where people worked as a team. A favorite expression in that office was "get your licks in on 'em first." We got our licks in on them - we left!

I so appreciated my coworkers at my new job and I am grateful that I never worked in an environment like that again.

Annette and I lost contact with each other for years; however, through Facebook we reconnected. We had a nice long chat about getting our licks in on ëem. DeFazio, thank you for helping me through that period of my career. Grateful it was only eight months and not years.

Carolyn Gray - *Annette we ate our way through that ordeal-- Church's Chicken and Carl Jr's hamburgers!*

Annette DeFazio - *We sure did...I have got the cholesterol #'s to prove it...thank goodness we didn't drink...although at times a shot of Cuervo would have deadened the pain ;)*

Carolyn Gray - *well, you are as funny as ever!)*

Annette DeFazio - *Have a beautiful rest of the day & thank you again for the "shout out." I wish we had reconnected while I was still living in Tx...we would still be chowing down on some "cluck." My daughter plans on moving back when she finishes school...I hope we get to meet up again one of these days :)*

Annette DeFazio - *Car-O-lyyyn, this is one of the best posts to ever appear on my crazy FB wall...I am truly humbled. I look at my life as a big patchwork quilt...a bag full of remnants that I am constantly piecing together, then every* *now & then God sends me this wonderful, unique piece of material that stands out among the rest & reminds me of the blessings he sends to us when life is kicking is down. You are one of those beautiful, unique pieces in my "life quilt" & he blessed me again by reuniting with you after all those years. God bless you & thank you for being my lifeline at a time when I most needed it:)*

Carolyn Gray - *Ann-NETTE, we would have both perished. I am so thankful we held each other up. God was watching over us for sure!!!!*

Annette DeFazio - *Oh, we definitely took a bunch of "sour grapes" & made some vintage wine!! I was telling a friend about our experiences a while back... lol... How you would walk by my desk, finger scratching the back of your ear (ala Mary E.) & say in your best syrupy Southern drawl..."Ann-ettte how ya' feeeeelin? What can I do to YOU today???" LOL... I looked forward to lunch time like a first grader...when you picked up your purse & headed my way, I heard recess bells in my head...then your famous words as we departed for Churchs fried chicken...."Come on DeFazio...lets blow this place & go get some "cluck." Haaahaaa... chuckling as I type this...good memories:)*

Toni Trahan Shirley - *I can just see Carolyn's mischevious, rolling eyes!! Yes, it is hard to live or work in an environment where people are looking for something to "get" you with! Thank God for the blessing of peaceful hearts.*

Day 38
Darla Powell Phillips

Darla Powell Phillips and I are members of Houston Coaches. Darla shared the history of Houston Coaches with me when I joined and always made sure I felt welcome.

Darla invited me to attend the annual conference of another organization she is a member of. We have also worked together on a couple of Houston Coaches initiatives. Darla knows people in and around Houston which makes her an excellent resource for me. A big plus is that she does not mind sharing her knowledge.

Darla sponsored a conference and wanted to give the participants a gift so she purchased copies of my book: Hot Chicks and Attentive Dudes for them. There were 1001 other books she could have purchased as gifts; however, she chose my book. I was honored and grateful for her support. Darla, thank you.

Cecilia Strahle Engquist - *Darla Powell Phillips rocks! She is always supportive, a wonderful friend, and great coach. I love our breakfasts. Thank you Darla!*

Cecilia Strahle Engquist - *You rock too Carolyn :-)!*

Madge Fletcher - *Carolyn, your picture was on the front page of the Cy-Fair Newspaper yesterday. What a surprise when I open the section of the Chronicle and saw your beautiful face! Way to go Girl!!!*

Carolyn Gray - *Madge Fletcher, I saw it on FB but was unable to get a copy of the paper. How are you?*

Madge Fletcher - *I will mail you a copy!*

Carolyn Gray - *Thanks Madge Fletcher.*

Day 39
Ida Jo Officer-Davis

One of my favorite fragrances to wear is Chloe. I have worn Chloe for years–like 35+ years. I have my friend and mentor Ida Jo Officer-Davis to thank for introducing me to Chloe.

I visited Jo at her apartment and that fragrance was ALL over the apartment. Because of my inquisitive nature, I immediately asked: "what is that I smell?" Jo laughed and said "I don't know what you smell!" She... handed me a bottle to sniff and that was it. That is what I smelled--Chloe. I had never heard of and of course never smelled anything that smelled so darn good.

Jo had a small purse size bottle of Chloe and she said "you can have this since you like it so much." I took it, said thank you and quickly put it into my purse. I didn't want to take a chance on forgetting it.

When I got home, I went to Joske's and purchased a BIG bottle of Chloe. I wear other fragrances; however, Chloe is still one of my favorite fragrances. Jo was also instrumental in helping me jumpstart my career and I am very grateful for her guidance and of course for the bottle of Chloe.

Lori Cernosek Velez - *aww, I love Chloe. only scent I wear...*

Frances Johnson - *You really dated yourself on this post..........haven't heard anyone mention Joske's in a long, long time........loved their EOM sales every month.*

Day 40
Paul Loudermilk

I have been blessed to work with some very supportive colleagues. Paul Loudermilk and I worked together for about five years. While we did not always agree on how to get to the destination, we always got there and still remained friends.

What I like most about our friendship is that we are able to talk through things. I know under that steel vest of his is a warm, compassionate and kind ...man. I remember wanting to see Stomp live. No one wanted to see it because it was toooooo loud and it was. Paul agreed to go so I would not have to go alone. It was absolutely wonderful.

He didn't mind having me on his golf team if we were playing a scramble. That might have had something to do with me being able to slam the ball off the tee -- of course, that's my take on it! (- ;

As serious as Paul is, he has a sense of humor --- like the time he decorated a broom with a Tiara and a scarf and left it in my chair as a Halloween gag. My staff tried to warn him that it might not be a good idea but he did it anyway. Fortunately for him, I thought it was funny! If someone else had done that, it might not have been so humorous. I knew he wasn't trying to call me Broom Hilda!

Paul is a good friend and I am very happy that our paths crossed

Toni Trahan Shirley - You know, I feel that about Paul, too! I always called him a passionate friend to those he chose to befriend. His gruff was so much bigger than his bite. Yes, he actually has a marsh mello heart. We share a birthday and I will always remember that and think of him especially on my birthday. Look forward to running into him one of these days. I think he is a good man with some little boy left in him and it's appealing!! Hey Paul!

Day 41
Donna Carter

My friend Donna Carter and I have a favorite scripture--Psalms 116:12 "What shall I render unto the Lord for all his benefits toward me?" For years we recited Psalms 116:12 to each other as we passed in the hall at work, before the start of meetings and on e-mail messages.

I transferred from Houston but when I returned for a visit, we still greeted each other with Psalms 116:12. That's... how we said hello.

I was attending a conference and someone walked up to me and said I have a note for you. I opened the note and read it: Psalms 116:12. I smiled and said this is from Donna Carter! The person said Donna said you would know who the note was from. Of course I would!

Donna Carter and I shared many many special scriptures but this one was our favorite. Every time I read Psalms 116, when I get to verse 12, I think of Donna. Donna, this is still on my list of favorites. "What shall I render unto the Lord for all his benefits toward me?"

Rhonda Holst Redmon - *One of my favorite stories so far...can't sleep now till I read these! Nite and thank you.*

Carolyn Gray - *I was just about to make you go nite nite!*

Stacey DeMarco Jata - *I absolutely loved this story! Thank you, Carolyn!!*

Judy McCurdy Mitchell - *Very inspirational story. Enjoy reading these every day. Thanks for sharing.*

Day 42
Kiki Aristidou Koymarianos

Many thanks to Kiki Aristidou Koymarianos for introducing me to WOAMTEC (Women on a Mission to Earn Commission).

I attended WOAMTEC, The Woodlands Chapter luncheon the day after being told about it. I was excited--the room was full of women business owners who were serious about growing their business and mine! After the luncheon, I came home and got on the WOAMTEC website because I needed to know more. After checking the organization out, I clicked on the join tab and joined. That was about ten months ago.

Since that time, KiKi has encouraged the "birthing" of five other chapters in the Houston area (Houston (Northwest), Galleria, Magnolia, Cypress and Conroe). I have attended the launch of each of these chapters and they are all awesome with phenomenal dedicated directors. What is so amazing about WOAMTEC in this area is that the oldest chapter (The Woodlands) will celebrate its first anniversary in March.

Two weeks after joining WOAMTEC, KiKi appointed me as an Ambassador and encouraged me to take advantage of the one hour coaching session offered to all members. I took her advice. The coaching session alone was worth more than the membership fee. Seriously!

Being a member of WOAMTEC, The Woodlands Chapter has given me so much exposure in the area. I have held Personality Assessment and Manners and Etiquette workshops and sold many many of my books.

I am grateful to KiKi Aristidou Koymarianos and the support I received from the members of WOAMTEC.

Kiki Aristidou Koymarianos - *Thank you Carolyn Gray. You are a great person and I am blessed to have you in my life.*

Day 43
Kathleen Hawkins

Shortly after joint WOAMTEC, The Woodlands, I made an appointment for my one hour free business coaching. To my surprise, my appointment was with Kathleen Hawkins, Founder and President of WOAMTEC.

While the free business coaching call is a benefit, there is no "fluff" at all. As requested, I forwarded my marketing and workshop material and other information to Kathleen prior to the call.

For one solid hour, she went through everything I had forwarded, asked lots and lots of questions, made comments, suggestions and recommendations and told me I would be receiving a written summary of our meeting. I received a report so thorough that it took me a week to digest the information. I shifted into action and was extremely busy for two months accomplishing those things Kathleen suggested and I knew need to be done.

Never in a hundred years did I expect to receive a follow-up call but I did. It was quick and to the point – "how are you coming along?" "Is there anything else I can do to assist you?" We spoke for about 10 minutes and I was on my way.

I am grateful to be a part of an organization that delivers on what it says it will do. I could not have purchased that level of coaching for what I invested in my WOAMTEC membership. I know that I have resources not just in my local chapter but from the corporate level. Kathleen Hawkins, thank you for all you do to help others be successful. Membership does have its privileges!

Day 44

Lillian Barnett

Living in Dayton, OH was a special time in my life. I made new friends; everyone was so accepting of me, the lady from Texas.

Lillian Barnett made homemade bread better than any bakery in the country. When she baked bread, she would bring me my own stash along with soft butter. I couldn't eat them all in one sitting (believe me I tried); however, I had the microwave in our break room working overtime warming my bread. Oh my goodness, that Lillian could bake some bread.

One Christmas Lil gave me a box of pencils with my name on them. I was like a second grader when I opened that box and saw my name on those pencils; I said "they have my name on them." (I am chuckling as I write this) Lil and the entire staff knew I loved any and everything with my name on it. I guarded those pencils like they were gold. I actually kept them under lock and key.

Years later when I was down to my last pencil, I call her and asked her if she remembered where she got them – she didn't remember. Instead of getting more pencils, Lillian sent me four dozen homemade rolls! I had the microwave in my kitchen working overtime.

I called to thank her for thinking of me. I enjoyed the rolls more than I would have pesonalized pencils. I am so grateful for wonderful friends.

Day 45
Pastor Harold Marshall

I had the privilege of being taught some Bible truths by Pastor Harold Marshall. Rev Harold (as he was affectionately called) was our Christian Education Director. He taught us to read and study the Word, always, always bring you Bible to church anytime you were going to church and to pray the Word back to God.

I learned several things from him like satan goes around like a roaring lion.... He explained to us that satan roars but he has no teeth! I have never forgotten that and that is how I look at satan–toothless!

Rev. Harold also taught us the importance of forgiving others and not to harbor unforgiveness because it will EAT YOU UP.

He often referred us to Psalm 119 (verses 1 – 176) where I have three scriptures highlighted in my Bible and for years have used them as my foundation. Psalm 119:11, 105 and 133 have kept me from doing some things and not saying soooo many things that would not have been the right thing(s) to say. Psalm 119: 11 - Thy word have I hid in my heart, that I might not sin against thee.

Those scriptures along with him teaching us to ask ourselves three questions before saying something: 1. Is it true? 2. Is it kind? and 3. Is it necessary? I am blessed to have had Rev Harold help me have a solid foundation and grateful that he is a man of humility, patience and love who always has time for everyone. Thank you Pastor Harold Marshall.

Day 46
Lois Tonsall

Lois Tonsall was the beauty queen of our office. She was always, always "well put together"– from head to toe. Her makeup was flawless and she tried to teach me to apply makeup without any real success. I just could not get it.

Her tip for me since I could not get the hang of applying makeup was to keep my lips polished. I have followed her advice and rarely will I leave home without "polishing my lips."

In the office, Lois taught me how to make corrections to typed documents. Her secret weapon was a piece of chalk. Yes, chalk! After erasing the mistake, she instructed me to gently touch the space with the chalk before typing the correct letter. It took practice but I was able to master that little trick.

Before word processors when a document had to be correction free, that was one neat little trick and it kept me from starting over on many occasions. Make up no, correcting typos yes! Thanks

Toni Trahan Shirley - *Both life-time helpful hints! Thank you Lois! She did keep those lips in place and glossy when I worked with her!*

Carolyn Gray - *Toni Trahan Shirley, I may not grasp some things but those that I do...I really do!*

Day 47

Rhonda Holst Redmon

I was looking for a venue to hold a book signing for my book Hot Chicks and Attentive Dudes when I was introduced to Rhonda Holst Redmon, GenuWine Tasting Room in Magnolia.

I walked into GenuWine and thought it was the absolute coolest place and perfect for a book signing. All I had to do was convince Rhonda that it would be a good idea. Things sorta took a different turn. When I told Rhonda I had written a book and I wanted to have some book signings, she said "you can have one here." That was easy!

Rhonda suggested the date because Duane Vincent would be there playing and some of her high school classmates would also be there. I can't tell you how excited I was. Rhonda set up a table for me, served me lots of goodies and told me to feel free to walk around and chat. Well, that wasn't a problem.

GenuWine had not been opened very long but Rhonda was willing to help me promote my books and coaching practice with no strings attached.

When I think of women helping women grow their business, I think of Rhonda opening the doors of her new business to help me build mine. Rhonda and I have a wonderful relationship – the only challenge we sometimes encounter is deciding on who gets to talk first!

Thank you Rhonda -- Love ya girl.

Day 48

Anita Long

Conjuring up visions of chocolate and blues is what aroused my interest and made me attend a Chocolate Blues event a couple of years ago. That is where I met Anita Long, Director, WOAMTEC Galleria (and lots of other titles). The event was wonderful.

A year later, Anita and I met again at WOAMTEC, The Woodlands luncheon where we chatted and agreed to meet for a one-on-one. She told me about her famous dad, Huey Long and the Ink Spot Museum.

That day, Anita was wearing an elegant white blouse with a black pants suit. She looked so sharp. I had to tell her how good she looked and I confessed to her that I have a "fetish" for white blouses!

We shared stories about white blouses which made me determine that we share the same "fetish" – we both love white blouses. Actually, we decided we especially like white cotton blouses although neither of us particularly likes ironing them so we look for white blouses that are made of fabric that requires little or no ironing.

When you have a one-on-one and decide to be transparent, you discover the strangest commonalities.

Day 49
Twyla Davis

It is such a pleasure working with people who go above and beyond what is required or expected. I have been blessed to have worked with more people in that category than those in the "just do enough to get by" category. Maybe I should refer to that category as the "not in my job description" category!

Twyla Davis was in the above and beyond category. Twyla was always at work EARLY and... did not mind staying late to finish projects she was working on. She would drop what she was working on to complete any project I needed done. I loved the fact that Twyla was as accurate as she was punctual.

Twyla would take off – like use her leave – to bake goodies for the office at Christmas. I mean real homemade, everything from scratch goodies! Goodies loaded with pecans, peanuts, butter (Paula Deen would love Twyla) and Ghirardelli chocolate. I'm talking about seriously delicious mouthwatering goodies. She prepared so much that it took us several days to eat all that she made.

She shared her Italian Cream Cake recipe with me and I baked it for my family. They loved that cake and it was good but not as good as Twyla's.

On a personal level, I adore her husband (George), daughter (Kim), son (Chris) and grandkids. It was not just about work with us, we supported each other after work. I am grateful to have people like Twyla and her family in my life.

Day 50
Freddie Garnett, Jr.

My brother Freddie has been my sounding board for years. When I want an honest "straight, no chaser", no fluff answer, I consult with him. He is very serious and a shrewd business man.

Before I release my books, I asked for his input because I feel that he knows what works. When I published my first book: All About ME* (*Manners and Etiquette for TWEENS and Teens) I asked him to let me... know what he thought – and he did. He said "Sis, the book is good, very good but it is not just for TWEENS and Teens." He went on to say "some adults could use the information in your book."

I did not remove TWEENS and Teens from the title of the book; I should have because I have had the same response from other adults. As I prepare to publish another book, I will again ask for his input. This time, I will listen to my brother's sage advice.

Freddie and I are friends; we can discuss any subject, confide in each other, disagree from time to time, as well as respect each other's privacy. I am grateful for my siblings. Freddie, thanks for being my friend.

Beverly Wallace - *How can I get a copy?*

Day 51
Pastor Gerald Jones

I met Pastor Gerald Jones at a networking meeting. I introduced myself to him because I was interested in a program he spoke about for the youth. Pastor Jones introduced me to his wife Gwyn; she and I became friends.

I attended their Bible study for a while which Gwyn taught. She is a phenomenal teacher and speaker. For my birthday, she treated me to lunch at Grand Lux. We had a wonderful time and I of course ate too much.

When Gwyn retired, she invited me to her retirement ceremony. It was fabulous! They had a live jazz band, a delicious spread and so many wonderful well-wishers.

We had a women's conference at my church and I invited Gwyn. It was a launch party for my pastor's lipstick line. We had a great time. Gwyn and I don't speak with each other on a daily basis but when we do, we pick up where we left off. I love friendships like that. Gwyn is an awesome woman of God and I am grateful that Pastor Jones introduced me to his lovely wife.

Day 52
Pat Durham

I met Pat Durham at a networking meeting. Later that week, I had a session with my coach and I told her I had met one of the most elegant, poised and professional woman that I have had the pleasure of meeting in a long time.

The second time I attended that particular networking meeting, Pat offered a "free," (seriously) one hour etiquette class for anyone who wanted to attend. Well..., I showed up. She held the class in her beautifully decorated office. We chatted for a while waiting to see if anyone else would show up.

I teach manners and etiquette so for me this was going to be a great refresher and I had Pat Durham all to myself. She taught just like there was a room full of participants. We shared family stories and visited for about an hour and a half.

Pat could have told me she was not going to have the class or that she would reschedule since I was the only one there but she didn't. I am extremely grateful for Pat sharing her knowledge about etiquette with me. That was such a generous act of kindness on her part. I left her office excited.

Florence C. Hagnere - *I <3 it! Thanks! The way you felt special and she handled the situation is very interesting!*

Day 53
Rebecca Montgomery-Nelson

Living in New Orleans was interesting, fun and rewarding. One of the rewards of living in New Orleans was meeting and mentoring Rebecca Montgomery-Nelson.

Becky was instrumental in orienting me to good eating places, second line, where to get me hair done and helping me "run" the office.

I had the pleasure of watching Becky develop professionally and personally. Becky was eager to learn anything new and I always had something new for her to learn. She shared with me that she liked my "whole ambiance!" That phrase became our inside joke.

She accepted feedback from me with respect and appreciation. Believe me; I gave her lots of feedback. I know she knew I loved, respected and wanted her to be prepared for her next level.

Becky had two children that she adored – she was a wonderful mother. She became a home owner only to be displaced by Hurricane Katrina.

That didn't deter her in any way – she relocated her family to Houston and purchased another home.

Her daughter graduates from high school this year and will be heading to college in the fall. Her son is excelling academically as well as being a star football player. Becky has reason to be proud of them and herself–she had overcome so much and she is still standing.

Mentoring someone who wants to be mentored is sooo easy and rewarding. I am grateful for Becky for being extremely respectful and appreciative of those things I recommended and suggested she consider doing. I am also grateful that she liked my "whole ambiance!"

Becky, I am proud of you and happy for your successes. You are a great mother and have done an AWESOME job with the children.

Courtney Coats Topini - *What...ya went to the Home Land and didn't tell me....I born and raised there....and Living In New Orleans is a challenge....we eat too much good food. I miss that living here now :(*

Courtney Coats Topini - *H2O or John Jay for the Hair?*

Carolyn Gray - *Courtney Coats Topini, I ate myself crazy. Even the food at the food court in the mall was good.*

Rebecca Montgomery Nelson - *Carolyn Gray aka "Fox"....I am "clutching my pearls" while reading this. Next year, will be 15 years working at the VA, and one of the best part of it all is when I met you! You have always been a cheerleader for me and Elizabeth and I greatly appreciate it. One thing for sure that I am really grateful that you never judge me and accepted me from day one for who i am. I will always honor and love you for being who YOU are and that is a "Great Woman" and you have truly been an awesome role model. There are many "Jewels" in my life, and Carolyn Gray, you are one of them...Love you much Foxy Lady...*

Day 54
Jane Boyd Moughon

Jane Boyd Moughon called me one day to ask if she could treat me to a cup of coffee. I agreed; however, I must admit my first thought was: what is she trying to sell.

Well, to my surprise, she was not selling anything. She wanted to get to know me better and find out what it is that I do. True to her word, she treated me to a cup of tea and we asked each other real serious questions--some personal and some about each other's business.

We learned we are both passionate about helping teens excel personally and academically.

During our meeting, Jane asked me if I was familiar with Success magazine. I replied that I was familiar but had not read the magazine. She told me the magazine had excellent articles and each magazine comes with a CD.

I left the meeting and went straight to Barnes and Nobles to see if I could find a copy of Success Magazine. I purchased a copy, removed the CD and put it into the CD player before leaving the parking lot. The CD had interviews of authors, entrepreneurs, educators, social media tips and John Maxwell on leadership. The interviews were spectacular.

When I got home, I read the magazine and noticed an article written by Mel Robbins– one of my new best friends! I met Mel, a dynamic conference speaker, at the Texas Conference for Women a couple of years ago.

Jane, I am grateful you wanted to get to know me better and for introducing me to Success Magazine. Thanks for sharing

Day 55
Angie Key

Some older adults have a problem accepting and learning new information from young people. Not me! I have learned so much from young people it is not funny. One of those young people is Angie Key. As Lieutenant Governor for Education for Toastmasters, District 50 Angie held numerous training classes. The one that had the most impact on how I conduct training and workshops was her Train... the Trainer class. I drove two hundred miles to attend the class and didn't regret the drive nor the time spent in the class.

I still use the Time Grid she shared with us. In fact, I have shared it with a number of others who were having difficulty staying within specific time limits for their workshops. I am sure there is new material out there; however, I still use Angie's material. It ain't broke so I ain't trying to fix it!

Angie is an excellent instructor who is patient, extremely knowledgeable and does not mind sharing with others what she knows. She presented fresh new ideas and loved and encouraged feedback.

I haven't see Angie in a few years; however, I follow her on FB as she posts some of her photographs of Audrey and Chris Reeds' children, The Reedlets (that is how they affectionately refer to Tegan and Logan) and Veronica Key.

Her photographic work is as exceptional as her training presentations. She has a spirit of excellence that shows in whatever she does. I am grateful to Angie for being patient, sharing her knowledge and tips on how to effectively present to groups. Thanks Angie.

Day 56
Olaide Banks

Olaide Banks and I service on an advisory board together. He is a gentleman and extremely concerned about the wellbeing of others. He goes way out of his way to help others. Olaide is also an exceptional speaker who keeps an audience engaged throughout his presentation. Let me not forget to mention he is also an outstanding attorney.

Olaide helped me out with the use of his conference room several evenings. I needed a conference room near downtown to meet with a client. I was almost in panic mode when I contacted Olaide to ask if he would allow me to use his conference room for a couple of hours and he said sure.

He is a great listener and an awesome sounding board. He is direct, concise and to the point; however, always very very diplomatic and compassionate.

I am grateful to have Olaide in my circle. Thank you Olaide for helping me out and keeping me from going into a full blown panic mode!

Day 57
Joyce Adams

"Hey baby!" is how Joyce Adams addresses everyone. I met her the first day I reported for work in Houston. She had a warm smile and made me feel welcome and the rest is history.

We have enjoyed a thirty plus year friendship supporting each other during some fun times and some not so good times in our lives

Joyce invited me to her church to see a play she was "staring" in. I told my children we were going to a play that NaNa (that's what family and close friends call her) was "staring" in. My son informed me that she was not a movie star because he knew where she lived and she did not live in Hollywood! Trying to get across to my seven year old son that all movie stars don't live in Hollywood was just not happening.

When he saw NaNa perform, he declared that she is a movie star and needs to move to Hollywood. Joyce and I had a good laugh for years about that one.

Every Mother's Day since meeting Joyce, she gets up EARLY and heads to Fannin to purchase flowers for the mothers of her church. This is one of the few charitable things she does that gives her so much pleasure. She just loves to give and share. Joyce is very low maintenance – you can give her a box of rock and she will be excited.

I am blessed to have a friend like Joyce for all these years and have never had a disagreement, never had her say no when I ask her to do something -- she make a way.

Day 58

Jackie Hopkins Craver

In the movies when ladies go shopping, the consultant brings out racks and racks of dresses, slacks, blouses, suits, or jackets for them to try on. All they do is try on clothes; the consultant is there to put them back on the hanger. The consultants offers them snacks, brings in accessories and more clothes for them to try on.

Well, I wasn't in the movies but I was treated like a star ...when I was introduced to the Don Caster private selection line of clothing by Jackie Hopkins Craver.

After answer questions about what colors I like, what styles, dresses or pants, dressy or casual I made an appointment with Jackie to try on a few items. When I arrived at her show room, based on my responses, Jackie had two racks of clothes ready for me to try on. All I did was try on clothes; she put them back on the hangers, provided refreshments, brought in accessories and offered her honest assessment of each and every item I tried on.

Jackie gave me a compact from her Mary Kay line to go along with my new gorgeous wardrobe. I didn't have the heart to tell her I couldn't apply the eye shadow; however, I did apply the blush and of course the lipstick.

I left Jackie's show room feeling very special and couldn't wait to return to see the fashions for the following season.

I have done a little bit of shopping in my days, however, I have never received the personal attention I was given by Jackie. Those ladies in the movies were acting; my shopping experiences with Jackie were very real.

Kendra Wilson-Hudson - *Sounds like a really nice experience. That would be wonderful!*

Florence C. Hagnere - *Awesome! I like this one :-) The personnalized service does really it all!*

Carolyn Gray - *Kendra Wilson-Hudson, it was awesome. I have shopped in stores...really nice stores...but that was truly one I will never forget. Check out the Doncaster line. Hope you get a consultant like Jackie!*

Judy McCurdy Mitchell - *Wow!! That is awesome!! I think I could adapt to that type of treatment*

Day 59
Barbara Orr

When I was in junior high school, I had a really hip/cool English teacher, Miss Barbara Orr. She was from Hawaii and was the heart throb of every boy in the class and all of the girls tried to dress "like" Miss Orr.

Miss Orr did not (she would be proud of me for that one) like contractions. In fact, she would "bleed" all over your paper with that red pencil of hers when she found a contraction. Second on her list were abbreviations – you better not abbreviate a single word in your composition. She wasn't particularly fond of the usage of "slang" in our writing.

I don't recall the entire content of my composition but I remembering writing the phrase "and all that jazz" in one of my papers. Talking about bleeding!! Her comment on my paper read: "Miss Garnett, we have discussed this on more than one occasion!" My Dad was disappointed with me when he read her comment. I got the message!! Miss Orr stressed that our bad casual writing habits would not help us become better writers. She made us practice, practice and all that practice made us better writers that year.

I am grateful that Miss Orr give us regular reading and weekly writing assignments. Bleeding on my compositions did not kill me – but it made me sad just seeing all that red on my paper! Having to prepare a weekly composition helped me with my creativity although it didn't stop me from using contractions and abbreviations in my casual writing. (Not your fault Miss Orr, I like contractions and abbreviations!) Thanks Miss Orr, you were my favorite teacher that year.

Day 60
Ovit Pursley

Sometimes I think of things that I would like to do and have no earthly idea how to make "it" happen.

When my book Hot Chicks and Attentive Dudes was published, I wanted to have a book signing in a nice setting. I contacted several hotels to check on rental rates only to learn that they were a bit pricy. So much for that bright idea!

One day, I decided to call a hotel in the Galleria area. I spoke with the nicest young man, Ovit Pursley, who invited me to stop by to take a look at what they had to offer. Ovit showed me around the hotel. It was beautiful and way out of my price range so I thought. After showing me around, Ovit sat down with me and asked me what I wanted to accomplish. I told him and he made me an offer I couldn't refuse.

Since this was my very first time attempting something like this, I needed all the help I could get and that is what Ovit did. He held my hand every step of the way and worked within my budget. He made suggestions and recommendations and basically bent over backwards to help me.

I had the event, it was very nice and I was supported by my friends. One of my girlfriends sent me a beautiful floral arrangement for my table. I met new people through this experience and by my definition; the event was a success. I learned what worked and what didn't work. My next event was very successful because I had some experience–Ovit taught me well.

It is wonderful when we share our knowledge with others and look for nothing in return. That is what Ovit did for me and I am grateful for his patience, compassion and integrity.

Day 61
Juliana Lucci Ashley

As a coach, I know the value of having a coach. I have accomplished so many of my goals thanks to my Coach, Juliana Lucci Ashley.

Juliana is a wonderful caring, giving, kind, DRIVING and compassionate person. Juliana helps me stay on track with accomplishing my stated goals and I have a lot! She is one of my BIGGEST and loudest cheerleaders.

Juliana coached me through a lot of my "first"... in business. She helped me locate a venue for my first WOO to WOW: 5 Stages of a Relationship (WOO, WHAM, WHOA, WHEE, WOW) workshop and attended the workshop.

When I decided to write my book: Hot Chicks and Attentive Dudes, she was there, coaching me through getting that finalized. If I stated a goal, Juliana held me to it (good coach!). There were times when I had to report that I had not completed a goal-- Juliana encouraged me for what I accomplished and helped me to move on.

There is a very serious side to Juliana and there is an extremely funny side of her also. I love her humor. She is poised, articulate and professional as well as an excellent presenter who I enjoy working with. I am grateful that Juliana is not just my coach; she is my friend who does not judge or criticize. Thanks Jules, you are the bestest!!

Judy McCurdy Mitchell - *I think we all need folks in our lives who are there to coach and encourage us. Sounds like you have really been blessed in this area--so have I*

Juliana Lucci Ashley - *Thanks for your kind words Carolyn. I have learned so much from you and have so enjoyed our fun times together as well as our col-*

laborations. You are one of my FAVORITE people to be around--always welcoming, encouraging and laughing with me! Everyone needs a Carolyn in their life! XOXO-J

Day 62
Willie Hunt

My friend Willie Hunt and I shared some of the best laughs at work. Although we worked on different floors of the building we ran into each other during the day at the Xerox machine.

We usually had an inside joke about something. We would have a quick release of laughter about something crazy one of us would say and get back to work.

Willie's daughter was involved in a number of activities and my daughter and I supported heró her ballet recitals were my favorite. His wife was extremely talented. She made beautiful dolls and their clothes which were to die for.

We ran into each other a while back and it was just like old times right there in Randall's. We spotted each other about the same time. He said "Hey Gray" and I yelled "Willie P." We chatted a long time because we had lots of catching up to do.

When I left Randall's, I was smiling as I reflected on all the good times we had and how grateful I am to have him as a friend. He is such a gentleman and one of the funniest guys I have had the pleasure of knowing.

Alane Bertrand Roberts - *I'm enjoying your stories, Carolyn!*

Nancy Campbell I *remember Willie; super nice guy!*

Donald Reel - *Carolyn, what ever happened to Willie Hunt?*

Day 63
Stacey DeMarco Jata

My Mom has eyes in the back of her head! We have probably all said that about our Mom. Well, my friend Stacey DeMarco Jata wrote and illustrated a book with that title. The story was inspired by her seven year old son. The art work is amazing.

Stacey and I met at a local networking meeting in Conroe. We were new BFFs right off. She shared her book with me and I shared my book: All About ME* (*Manners and Etiquette for TWEENS and Teens) with her.

A few days later, Stacey called me to see if I would be interested in participating in a vendor show. Of course, I said yes. We had a fun time setting up and selling our books. Before that show was over, she had another ëgig" for us the following month.

Stacey invited me to her home for her book signing. I drove way up there (smiles) the first thing I saw in her front yard was a moose. Yep, a moose! Granted, it was not a real live moose but a moose none the less. The connection, Stacey's blog handle is Texas Moose House. I was hooked on the moose.

I purchased one of Stacey's books for my sister because she always said that our Mom had eyes in the back of her head. My sister would ask my Mom if she could brush her hair because she wanted to get a look at those eyes! My sister's teen age son thinks she has eyes in back of her head.

As I was leaving the book signing, Stacey told me she wanted to introduce me to the Director of the Woodlands Children's Museum. Stacey made the call and I showed up at the museum with my book in hand. The director, liked the book and my ME* modules. I started teaching manners and etiquette at the museum a few weeks later.

Stacey and I work well together. We have participated in several vendor shows along with her beautiful daughter, The Butterfly Princess. I am grateful for Stacey getting me involved in local vendor shows and for introducing me to the Director of the Woodlands Children's Museum. Thanks Stacey you are tops in my book.

Judy McCurdy Mitchell - *Love reading your stories. They are so inspiring.*

Melody Seale - *same here, love reading them every day!*

Day 64
Lynette Mims

I worked for Southern Bell as a long distance operator back in the day. I'm talking, back in the day when there were toll boards with plugs and cords –we have come a long way baby! If you remember seeing pictures of an operator sitting in front of a toll board with cords going everywhere, well that is what my board looked like.

We worked in a large room with an "L" shaped toll board along ...two walls (about 50 yards each). There were -- I don't know how many women working at any given time. They were all very professionally dressed (that would include me!), I mean super sharp -- but there was more drama in that room than on General Hospital, The Guiding Light and All My Children combined!

Lynette Mims stood out because she was not just sharp, she was classy. I am talking classy on steroids! She was very friendly but didn't get involved in the drama that was stirred up of the "floor." I admired her and and said to myself "I gotta get to know this lady–I want to be like her when I grow up!"

I got my chance–I had a shift she wanted and I was HAPPY to switch with her. (I hated working 1:30 to 10:00 pm and she had a split shift) Lynette introduced herself to me and we became friends. She was from Chicago and in her 30s. She gave me some sage advice on how to be successful on any job. Lynette told me to stay out of "other folks business," dress appropriately, come to work when scheduled, be on time and do what I was paid to do!. That wasn't hard for me to follow because my parents drilled that same advice into us.

When I read the second chapter of Titus I think fondly about Lynette. She was the aged woman whose behavior was to be emulated. I have no idea where she is today but I am grateful that our paths crossed.

Rhonda Kuykendall Flowers - Wow! Inspiring story. It would be nice if we could get this behavior instilled in today's young people. You should try to find Lynette or at least her family and share your story.

Toni Trahan Shirley CAROLYN: great recollection, Lilly Tomlin! I don't remember you having that.skill, but I do surely remember you settling into warm professionalism as you entered what you knew might be sensitive or touchy or conflicting phone calls.

Frances Johnson - *Brings back a few memories...my first job at D&B, included releaving the switchboard operator for her lunch and breaks and during vacation. But ours was only about a 50 person office which was plenty.*

Carolyn Gray - *Ah, the old switchboard! I enjoyed my time working as an operator. I left to go work for the government.*

Day 65
Iantha Scott

I love to sing; however, there is a small problem with that: I cannot sing. At all! Mrs. I. Scott could sing and play the piano--she had a beautiful voice. One day she told the class whoever learned the words to a particular song could lead the song.

I went home, had my grandfather help me and I learned the words to the song. Much to Mrs. Scott's chagrin, I was the only one who knew al...l of the words to the song. I remember being excited thinking I was going to be able to lead the song.

Mrs. Scott had to do me like they did Barney Fife on the Andy Griffith Show–find a way to shut me down! She called me to her side, told me she had a "special job" for me. She handed me two red sticks and told me I was going to keep rhythm. She said she would let me know when to hit the sticks together. I was really excited with the sticks because I was the only one in the class given that assignment. I am sure that had something to do with everyone else being able to hold a note!

As a child, Mrs. Scott could have shattered my self-esteem by telling me my voice was bad (which it was– it is); however, she instead boosted my self-esteem. She made me believe I was the only one in the class able to keep rhythm. I don't remember how many times I got to "keep rhythm" but once was enough to make me feel special. I didn't care about singing that old song, I had my sticks.

Teachers are extremely crucial in the development of students and I am grateful that Mrs. Scott found a way to build my self-esteem and not destroy it.

> **Judy McCurdy Mitchell** - *What an inspiring story!! This one really touched my heart. You are a very blessed and gifted person!!!!*
>
> **Melody Seale -** *I love it , you are such an inspiring woman, you can bring a smile to my face always.*
>
> **Deborah Higdon** - *OK, I laughed til I cried!*
>
> **Carolyn Gray** - *Why! Why! Why are you laughing...just 'cause it's true.*

Day 66
Cathy Bracey

We say we want people to "tell us the truth" or we sometimes say "all they had to do was tell me." I don't know if we are ready to accept the truth when it is handed to us especially if it is not delivered in a "softer gentler manner.

The agency I worked for had a tuition support program which would pay for employees to earn a college degree. I was very interested in the program because at the time I had not graduated from college.

I gathered the necessary information on the admissions requirements from the University of Maryland and headed to the Training Section to apply for the tuition support program. Cathy Bracey, the Training Specialist, was outspoken and direct, very direct!

Cathy asked me how I planned to manage going to school and work full time. I made the mistake of not having a concise response. I started telling her how I had to find a sitter for my children and that I thought I wanted to take one easy class. I went on to try to tell her why I only wanted to take one easy class. She stopped me right there, looked me square in my eyes and said "you come back and to see me when you don't have so many problems."

I was speechless. What did she mean I had so many problems? I asked her – what do you mean? She responded that I needed to resolve my sitter problems and decide what classes I wanted to take. She told me she was there to help me with tuition support when I was ready.

Well, Cathy told me the truth, she was not there to listen to me talk about my sitter issues or why I wanted to take one easy class. I learned from that point on in my career that if I wanted or needed help, I had to have my stuff together.

If Cathy had entertained my conversation that day, I probably would not have "figured" it out. I am glad she was her usual direct self because it made me do what I needed to do to earn my degree.

Day 67
Claudia Parker

The day I arrived in Shreveport, LA, I met Claudia Parker. Claudia was my stylist for several years. She had very nice salon where she pampered me (and others), served me hot tea and cookies and did not have me waiting all day before servicing me.

Claudia loves hair and is passionate about her patrons having healthy hair. She used the best products, took her time and would not let me out of her salon until she was satisfied that my hair was a masterpiece. Claudia was committed to perfection which showed in her styling and cutting of hair. I recall asking her one day to stop working on my hair because I thought it looked great (I was in a hurry) and she said "not to me!"

I have had people stop me while walking through the mall to ask "who does your hair" after leaving Claudia's salon. When I relocated from Shreveport to New Orleans, I would drive back to Shreveport to have Claudia cut and style my hair.

Claudia would ask me from time to time to try different styles -- I gave in a time or two only to go back to my bob because it is easy–wrap, brush and go! She would probably not be real happy to learn that I am still wearing my hair in the bob she introduced me to years ago.

I am grateful for Claudia impressing upon me the importance of taking good care of my hair and that using good hair products make a difference.

Day 68
MaryAnne Kaylor

Deciding to have a mentor to help make climbing the career ladder is a very wise decision. I have had a number of mentors in my time – oh the joy and excitement of being asked to be a mentor.

MaryAnne was a Supervisory Dietitian who applied for a leadership program within our agency and was accepted. She honored me by asking me to be her mentor. I said what happened – did you run out of people to ask? She very seriously said "no, you were the first person I asked." I was ashamed for saying that to her and immediately asked how I could help her.

MaryAnne told me she had observed me and felt she could learn from me. She said she had the clinical skills but not the administrative skill to become a better leader/manger. The agency sent us to Cleveland, OH for training and MaryAnne and I got to know each other better. I encouraged her to purchase and use a planner to stay organized which she did. We also had fun visiting the Rock and Roll Hall of Fame while there (we were off duty!)

The program ran for a year. We discovered our personality traits; me the extrovert and her the introvert -- a perfect match! We completed the program and continued our mentor/mentee relationship on our own. MaryAnne applied for and was selected for an Administrative Officer position of a service line. She also served as the coordinator for a mentoring program the agency sponsored for administrative and clerical employees.

MaryAnne gave me a special handmade gift for Christmas that year – an angel made of tin. I love handmade presents.

When I left the agency, I told myself there is a little piece of me still there. MaryAnne Kaylor is there helping others.

Day 69
Pastor Sally Davis

It is awesome being in a church where the pastor teaches (and preaches) the Word. My pastor, Pastor Sally Davis or PSal as we affectionately call her is one dynamic teacher. She makes it plain and backs up everything with a scripture. She is the co-pastor of Embassy Church in Kingwood along with her husband, Pastor Jerry Davis.

She is effective and fervent about praying for people and situations. When someone asks her to pray, she stops in her tracks regardless of what she is doing and prays. Also, let me not forget to mention that she is VERY transparent, direct and compassionate. Her love for people is phenomenal.

PSal loves to teach but she CAN preach. She has been invited to churches across the country to preach at conferences. (I have been blessed to accompany her on some of her trips.) Don't let her looks fool ya, she is a dynamic preacher/teacher. She has been invited to speak at the Women Who Win conference at New Light this year. Dr. Fred Price prophesied over her several years ago that people would come from all over to sit at her feet to hear her preach the Word of God–well, what he prophesied is about to come true in a few weeks.

She has stood on the Word, sowed, prayed, preached, taught, loved and given her time and I am overjoyed to be able to witness this come true. Watching her go through some traumatic life changing events and remain standing has strengthened me. I am grateful and blessed to witness this for myself.

PSal has preached/taught hundreds of sermons. My personal favorite is The Father Factor. The Father Factor is my favorite because she teaches about how she loved and forgave her physically abusive father. PSal tell us in that sermon how grateful she was that her Poppa accepted Christ before he passed away and that she will see him in heaven.

In addition to being an awesome teacher and preacher, she is a creative decorator. She can dress up a cardboard box and make it look like a mansion! PSal also has a very humorous side and she shares her humor in her sermons. I am blessed to have her in my life.

Day 70
Dick Cullen

Dick Cullen interviewed me for the Personnel Intern position in his department. I was excited when I received the selection notification–really excited. I sent him a handwritten thank you note and made an appointment with his secretary to see him. I wanted to thank him for selecting me before I went to work for him.

Dick was laid back and very easy going. I entered his office and felt right at home. He said he appreciated the thank you note which made me even more relaxed. I told him I wanted to personally thank him for selecting me. He asked me if I had any idea why he selected me and I said no. He responded: because you didn't tell me you wanted to work in Personnel because you like people!

That sorta took me by surprise because at that time, I thought you needed to like people to work in Personnel. He went on to explain that Personnel is about rules and regulations and being able to interpret and apply them.

He said "you may not have much experience in that area; however, you are very inquisitive." I thought to myself: did he just call me nosey?! I thanked him because that is all I could do. I did not know him well enough nor was I secure enough to ask what he meant by his comment.

When I reported to work, Dick introduced me to the staff and one lady said "so this is our new nosey little intern!" I chuckled and Dick said you weren't supposed to repeat that. I knew I was right, he did call me nosey to my face with that euphemistic "very inquisitive" comment.

That phrase became the office joke for some time. It is a good thing that I didn't wear me feeling on my sleeve. Dick, said I asked so many questions during the interview that he was sure I would be able to interpret the regulations and if I had a question, I would ask. He was right, I would ask.

Dick had an open door policy and allowed the staff (including the intern) to ask questions and question anything that seemed to be out of line with the regulations. He always told us we could come into his office anytime we wanted to "chew the fat." (I had to learn the meaning of that one!) Dick was a hard act to follow as a supervisor. He was awesome to work for as well as the most fun person to have lunch with on The Mall.

He treated everyone with the utmost respect regardless of the person's position. His managerial skills were to be emulated -- I certainly tried.

Day 71
Dwayne Redman

There are some gentlemen and then there is Dwayne Redman in a class all by himself. Dwayne is THE most precious young man. He always has a kind word, a warm friendly smile, will literally give you his last and will pray for you on the spot.

Working with Dwayne was a pleasure. He always "helped" everyone. When someone was in need, he was the go to person. He was an excellent mentor to young men at work, in the church, and in the community.

He is a wonderful wonderful husband and the best father anyone would ask for. He loves his little ladies.

Dwayne invited his work family to hear him preach his first sermon. The scripture for his message was II Corinthians 5:17. Therefore, if any man be in Christ, he is a new creature: old things are passed away; behold all things are become new. The church was packed and I am so happy that I was able to share in that chapter of his life. Truly, everybody loves Dewayne!

When my Mom passed away two years ago, Dwayne called me, prayed with me and of course in very Dwayne Redman style wanted to know what he could do to help me. I assured him and others that I was ok and for them to continue praying.

I am grateful to have Dwayne Redman – Pastor Redman as my friend.

Day 72
Dick Koprowski

Classification was my least favorite discipline as a HR specialist. Actually, I could say I hated it. I shared an office with Dick Koprowski who was an excellent Classifier. Dick could look at a set of duties, read the classification standards, set them aside, take a smoke break and return to his desk and write his report.

He was amazing to watch, it was like a ritual. The only time he deviated from his ritual was when he had to conduct a desk audit. I accompanied him several times trying to learn from him. I never really "got it" and I believe that was because I didn't smoke!

Dick was a fun office mate. He was from New York and told some of the funniest stories ever. My favorite story was the one he told about not going to church. Dick said his parents sent him and his brothers to church; however they would go play pool. They would swing by the church to get a program before going home (proof they were at church). He said when they got home (I am cracking up writing this) his Mom would ask what they learned and his reply was: they talked about Jesus.

I loved to listen to him talk on the phone as he gave the person on the other end his name because he would say his name and then spell his last name – Koprowski, Kop (as in Peter)rowski. That's how I learned to spell Koprowski.

Dick was a patient and practical teacher. While I did not get to the point I liked classification, Dick help me to "just do it!"

Day 73
Lawrence Ackles

Lawrence Ackles was an intern in our Research Department. He was ALWAYS reading something. What made him stand out to me was he read rather large books while walking. One day I saw him and he was reading a small paperback book. I was curious so I asked him what he was reading. He replied with a question: are you familiar with Dr. Viktor Frankl? I said no. He told me I needed to read Dr. Frankl's book, Man's Search for Meaning. He said I would be intrigued.

I love to read but in the early eighties, I was into Ludlum and the likes so I didn't race to the book store to get Dr. Frankl's book. Honestly, I thought it was probably a book on finding a cure for something because that is what they did in Research.

Sometime later, I looked for Man's Search for Meaning. I found it, read the back cover and decided I needed to read the book. Man's Search for Meaning changed the type of books I read, changed how I react to situations and people. I encouraged my son to read Man's Search for Meaning– he did. I purchased copies of the book for friends and family because I felt it was information that would them learn to cope with everyday life situations.

My gratitude to Lawrence for introducing and exposing me to different types of books– a "whole nother world." Dr. Frankl's logotherapy and the basis for his development of logotherapy is fascinating.

Day 74
Sue Gold

I am a member of the Diplomat Team of MCABW (Montgomery County Association of Business Women). As a Diplomat, I get to do what I love which is greet members and visitors. I want them to feel welcome and have a great networking experience starting the moment they enter the room.

That is where I met Sue Gold, Creek Mortgage Company. I realized Sue was new and might not know anyone at the meeting so I asked her to sit at my table. She was my new BFF! Just for the record, Sue is an established professional and would have been fine without my help – I just wasn't taking any chances.

We had an opportunity to learn more about each other during the speed networking portion of the meeting. After the meeting, I invited Sue to come back and told her it was a great group to be a part of.

A week or so after the meeting, I checked my mail and found a note from Sue Gold. I ripped it open right there in the Post Office because I was curious. I was so surprised; it was a handwritten thank you note! First of all, most people don't take the time to send thank you notes and they certainly don't stop to hand write one.

I had to call her--I really did. Why? Well, to thank her for the handwritten thank you note of course!

I am extremely grateful for Sue Gold for taking time out of her day to send a handwritten note. That act of kindness reminded me that I needed to get back to doing the same thing. I went out and purchased four boxes of thank you notes (they were really cute and I couldn't decide on just one so I got them all!). I have been sending handwritten thank you notes to some of the people on my gratitude list.

Thank you Sue Gold for reminding me how wonderful it is to receive a handwritten note.

Day 75
Dock Voorhies

When I received the call that they wanted me to fly to Shreveport for a face-to-face interview, I was excited. When I saw the itinerary I freaked out. What was I going to do for two hours before the interview? An even better question was what I would do for two hours after the interview before my flight back to Ohio.

I called a friend of mine in New Orleans to see if she knew anyone in Shreveport who would not mind me hanging out in their office for an hour or so. Well, she had a friend who had a friend. That friend of a friend was Dock Voorhies.

When I arrive at his office, Dock gave me the warmest smile, introduced himself and seconds later he walked out and told me to make myself at home. He said he had meetings to attend and would not return for two hours.

I got the job and a whole host of great friends–Dock Voorhies being one of them. Dock was one awesome resource person. From my perspective, Dock was the go to person who knew everything and could get anything done.

Dock could decorate, cook and coordinate events. He supported the local schools, was active in his church, sang in the choir, like I said you name it and he could do it or get it done. Dock believed in sharing and helping others. When I met his wife, I found out they are two peas in a pod.

One year, he prepared homemade Shrimp Alfredo for an event he sponsored... I am talking from scratch, real butter (a lot of butter), whipping cream, fresh parmesan cheese with a large shrimp in every bite! I ate so much I was dizzy. Not to dizzy to ask for the recipe. I made Dock's Shrimp Alfredo for Christmas that year and everyone ate until they were dizzy.

Normally, I don't get very many compliments about anything I cook but thanks to Dock I did that year and I now have two specialties and the best friends anyone could ever have.

Day 76
Gwen Gistarb

We are often asked "what are you passionate about" or told to "pursue our passion." Gwen Gistarb is an educator who is passionate about helping mothers and daughters have better relationships. She is the author of The Lesson Plan ~ A Workbook for Mothers and Teenage Daughters. In The Lesson Plan, Gwen shares practical steps to help mothers learn how to keep open lines of communication with their daughters.

The Lesson Plan includes educational, inspirational, motivational lessons and activities taught through metaphors, poems, and short stories.

She conducts workshops she has titled: Cupcakes and Conversation. Her workshops are informative exchanges of valuable information for young ladies. As an educator, Gwen presents the information in a manner that promotes easy to understand dialogue for mothers and daughters.

Another way she gets her message distributed is through her radio show: Making Life Easy with Gwen Gistarb. It's real easy to be a guest on her show – how do I know? Well, I was a guest on her show that's how! All I had to do was go to www.makinglifeeasywithgwengistarb.com and complete the registration form and her producer took care of everything -- all I had to do was talk!

I am grateful for Gwen's commitment to helping mothers and daughters having open lines of communication. She has her moving, I mean a powerful transparent story that she shares which is titled: "My Story–Healing from My Secret" on her website.

Thanks Gwen for your passion and commitment to making a difference in the lives of mothers and daughters. I appreciate what you do.

Day 77
Neil Falkner

During my career, I had some wonderful co-workers, supervisors, and subordinates. Neil Falkner and I were co-workers, we were subordinates and we supervised each other.

When I first met Neil, we were co-workers – we were section chiefs. Then, I worked for Neil. Talking about being put on the fast track. Neil had me hit the ground running. He taught me the ropes in the Employee Labor Relations discipline; he was the best at researching case law and framing charges. Neil freely shared his knowledge, impressed the importance of having an air tight case, corrected and commented on my documents with a green ink pen. He felt red ink was too in your face.

Neil always asked: what would a third party (judge, EEO examiner or arbitrator) say? Neil trained me to look at every case as though I was the third party reviewer. He prepared me for my role as Assistant HR Manager. When I accepted the Assistant position, I was confident that I would be ok because I had soaked up everything Neil taught me.

As an Assistant HR Manager, I was rocking and rolling, making things happen and less than a year later, I was promoted to the position of HR Manager. That meant I needed an Assistant HR Manager. I selected Neil as the Assistant HR Manager and we were back together. We were a great team– I had adapted the Falkner traits – green ink pen and all.

A year or so after selecting him, Neil went on to become an HR Manager and beyond. I am grateful that my relationship with Neil at all levels was so rewarding. He taught me how to "examine" a case and make sound decisions based on the documentation. I attribute "his way" of approaching a case as the reason the agency prevailed in EEO, disciplinary and adverse action cases. Neil taught me to love this discipline in HR.

Day 78
Lilli R.

When we encounter people who are not like us, we tend to not want to associate with them and that can be a mistake. Lilli R. was a masters prepared educator whose degree was in English. She was well read, enjoyed traveling and being doted over by everyone. Her family was wealthy so she was used to having what she wanted and how she wanted it. We became good friends but initially, Lilli thought I was bum!

Lilli and my sister were good friends. They lunched together, visited new neighborhoods and model homes, shopped and anything else they wanted to do. My sister took Lilli to her medical and hair appointments.

One day, I was dressed for work – I mean dressed (yes, I had on my pearls!) when my sister called and told me she was not feeling well and asked if I would take Lilli to her doctor's appointment. I agreed. When Lilli saw me, she was furious. She wanted to know where my sister was and why did she have to go with me "looking like that!"

Of course, I wanted to drive off but I knew I couldn't so I explained that my sister was not feeling well and asked if I would fill in for her. Lilli told me I was not cute and I looked awful because I didn't have on make-up. She went on to tell me how beautiful my sister was (and she was) and that my sister always wore make-up and that she was decent woman. Now, I really wanted to drive off! I didn't– I took her to her appointment and got her back home.

I called my sister and told her about the insults which didn't seem to bother her. Now I am angry with her. I got over it and went on about my business. Nothing like taking off from work to do something for someone and they insult you.

My sister told Lilli that I was a supervisor, that I like to read, travel and I loved the theater. Well, that changed everything. I was no longer a bum, I was a professional who wore suits to work and Lilli liked me. She had my sister invite me to join them on one of their outings where she quizzed me like I was going to be in charge of her life savings.

On that outing, I learned that Lilli had a mental illness. Things started to make sense. She didn't like change; however, she changed her mind about me. We had long discussions about some of the books we had both read and our love for the theater.

Lilli brought so much joy to my life after we became friends. When I relocated, she wrote me regularly to keep me involved in her life. I am grateful we learned to love each other.

Day 79
Andrew

My gratitude today is to a wonderful 4 year old who is in my Manners and Etiquette Class.

He is adorable and a real jokester. Today when I knocked on the door, I could hear his sweet little voice announcing to the class "it's Miss Carolyn." Then he correctly asked: Who is it. (I see he was listening to that part of the class!) I said "Miss Carolyn" and he opened the door. He gave me a BIG hug and a kiss, then another hug and another. He said I got a triple hug today because he had not seen me in a long time because of spring break.

Talking about melting my heart – oh yea. This little guy loves to sit on my lap; actually, I am not sure how he stays on my lap since he sits right on the edge because he does not want anyone else to sit on my lap. He will tell them "there is no more room if they ask."

He has shared with me that his brother is mean to him and gets him in trouble ALL the time. He actually said his brother lies on him and he gets sent to his room. Not sure which one of them might not be telling the truth. The brother is 6 and my little guy is 4. Mom has her work cut out for her.

Teaching this class is like being on the Art Linkletter Show. You never know what will be said or done until it happens. I love them and their innocence. I didn't realize how much I would enjoy and look forward to teaching Manners and Etiquette to ten 4 and 5 year old boys. They are so much fun and I am grateful that I have the opportunity to share with them. They will have stories for their grandkids–

Day 80
Paula Thames

Paula Thames, an intern from Washington, DC, trained in our office. She was perky, very intelligent, and friendly with enough humility for ten people. We bonded because I had lived in Washington so we were able to chat about DC.

Paula shared a very very valuable tip with me: never ever be seen in the hall without paper and a pen. She said her grandfather (a high ranking official in another agency) gave her that tip. I immediately added it to my tool box and shared it with others because it made sense.

Paula said her grandfather told her when you are at work, you should at least look busy and being in the hall empty handed gave the wrong impression to everyone.

I was grateful to Paula and her grandfather for that sage advice. I never left my office without a steno pad and pen. I later graduated to my fancy Day Timer.

Day 81
Jeffery McCulloch

Sometime when people think of "in laws," they have visions of not so nice members married into the family. Not so with my brothers-in-law.

I am grateful to have wonderful brothers-in-law. Actually, I refer to them as brothers-in-love because they are truly a part of my family. My brother-in-love, Jeffrey is a wonderful husband, father and friend. He always has time to help others although he has a VERY busy schedule. He works full time in law enforcement and is actively and totally involved in everything my nephews participate in and they participate in lots.

Jeffrey had what I referred to as the curse of the pickup truck. A curse because when I needed something picked up I called Jeffrey and he always came to my rescue. My husband instructed me to STOP bothering Jeffrey and rent a truck when I needed to have something picked up. I did do that a couple of times and them my husband decided to get an SUV.

I have great respect, love and admiration for Jeffrey because he walks the talk. He is appreciative of any and everything done for him. I gave him a pen once and you would have thought he "hit" the lottery.

Jeffrey is one of the most optimistic, sincere, loving and compassionate individuals I have ever met. I am extremely glad he is one of my brothers-in-love.

Day 82
Mia King

My youngest niece is now in college, in fact, this is her third year in college. My how time flies.

I lived in Ohio for several years so when I came home, my niece, Mia, enjoyed having "coffee" with me. She was adorable sipping her "coffee" because it was too hot to drink. We would talk about cartoons and for several years, she would recite –word for wordóthe entire movie The Lion King. She had everyone saying "is gat a challenge." (the line was "is that a challenge" she was 3 or 4 years old). My husband purchased the VHS because he loved the sound track and listening to Whoopi Goldberg saying "Mufasa!" " Mufasa!"

Mia loved going shopping, dancing (ballet), eating out and coloring. When we ate out, she placed her own order – soup and a salad.

Before publishing my first book: All About ME*(*Manners and Etiquette), I "consulted" with Mia for her input on the title of the book. We had several discussions before making a decision. She was sooooo serious.

When Mia graduated from high school, we were chatting about things she enjoyed when she was little. She mentioned how much she enjoyed having coffee with me when I visited. I laughed and told her she wasn't drinking coffee! She said in a real soft voice "I wasn't drinking coffee?" I said "no, you had a cup of milk with about "that" much coffee." She said "GiGi, all these years I thought I was drinking coffee!" We both had a good laugh. I felt like I had just told her there was no Santa!

Those were fun times for me too Mia. I remember them well – I was drinking coffee and you were also drinking coffee with lots of milk! Love you baby niece.

Day 83

Rhea Davis

I met Rhea at an awards luncheon several years ago. During our conversation, she mentioned her degree was in Journalism and that she loves to edit. I tucked that information away because I was in the process of writing my second book: WOO to WOW: 5 Stages of a Relationship (WOO, WHAM, WHOA, WHEE, WOW).

When I finished writing WOO to WOW, I contacted Rhea, asked if she remember me and she did. I asked her to edit my book and she agreed. She edited the book, gave me some very positive feedback and off to the printer I went.

I thank God for having FAVOR with Rhea. She worked on my schedule and timeline although she worked a full time job. Rhea allowed me to contact her with any questions and make changes.

Rhea was great to work with so when I wrote Hot Chicks and Attentive Dudes, I called her to see if she would be able to help me out a-g-a-i-n. Rhea gave me feedback and candid comments about the addition of the Song of Solomon in the book. She said some people might not understand the addition of the Song of Solomon and suggested I write a little something in the intro to prepare them. I took her advice.

Rhea was correct, I have had a number of people suggest that I write a version without the Song of Solomon which I have not decided to do. However, as I prepare for the third printing of the book, I am mindful of the fact that some might not understand.

Thanks Rhea for your kindness and advice and I extremely grateful for your help with my projects.

Day 84

David Christian

Customer service is extremely important to me and so is a good product. I want it all and that is exactly what I got from David Christian at the FedEx Office Print & Ship Center on 1960.

I had a workshop scheduled and the printer did not have my books ready... no where near ready. I must admit that I panicked a bit. That was before I put myself in "time out" to think. I told myself that I HAD to figure something out and I did.

With jumpdrive (flash drive) in hand, I walked into the FedEx Office and asked if they could print my book. There was one small problem, the book had odd measurements. Dave (we are now friends so I can call him Dave) was so calm that he settled me down. He looked at the document, wrote some dimensions down and explained what I needed to do in order for him to print the book. I flew home, made the changes and back to the FedEx office.

Dave gave me a quote and told me he would have a proof for me to review the next day by 5 p.m. Well, he exceeded my expectations – the proof was ready before noon! I reviewed the proof and gave it the ok. I asked him if he was sure he could have the job completed by the following day. He assured me the books would be ready. Again, he exceeded my expectations by calling me before the promised delivery time to say the books for ready for pick up.

Talking about being grateful, I was beyond grateful for Dave helping me out. Not only did he get my product to me ahead of schedule but it was a good looking book.

I wrote a nice thank you letter to Dave's store manager because I wanted him to know how much I appreciated the way Dave treated me and that the books looked great. I let him know that I was extremely satisfied.

When I need something printed, FedEx Office is where I go – excellent customer service and a great product.

Day 85
Col D. O. Reddy

Find the indispensable man and fire him! That was on a sign in Col D. O. Reddy's office. It was the first thing you saw when you walked it – it was huge. I hated going into his office because of that sign.

I think my fear was based on the fact that I really did not understand the sign. I overheard Col Reddy asking another officer if understood the meaning of the sign. My ears perked up because I wanted to know myself. I couldn't hear the why.

Col Reddy loved coffee and was always asking someone to get him a cup of coffee. I told myself the next time he yells for coffee, be first to jump up and get him a cup. I heard him and I got him a cup of coffee. That was my excuse for going into his office to ask about the sign.

I don't remember everything he said about the indispensable man but I do recall he had no use for that man (or woman). He said when someone becomes indispensable they are harmful to the organization and a weak link because they only think about themselves.

I learned to do a good job, be a team player, be helpful and share ideas and information with my coworkers and certainly not ever think of myself as indispensable. I can close my eyes and still see that big embossed sign on the wall. Col Reddy thanks for the lesson-- never will I set myself up to become indispensable.

Dawn Kirke Kendrick - Love this! I see this all the time in the Fortune 500 company I work for......I have chosen the route you have Carolyn Gray. Team players rock!

Carolyn Gray - Dawn Kirke Kendrick, I have not seen the quote since but have never forgotten it. Team players totally rock.

Rosemary Behrens - Your days of gratitude reminds me of writing referrals at SCA. People don't think they have a referral for anyone in the room because they aren't thinking that way. Most of us when confronted with 365 days of gratitude would knee jerk with 'I don't have that much!' and many with that knee jerk (not all) would quickly retreat and reframe. Thank you for helping us all to see the corners of our own lives where small good things are hiding!

Day 86
Barbara Calloway

Friends are so precious – I have been blessed to have some very precious friends in my life and Barbara Calloway is one of those very precious friends.

Barbara and I worked together at Fort Sam Houston for several years. She had a daughter who was the same age as one of my younger sisters. During the summer, Barbara and I took the girls and her son on field trips.

My favorite was our trip to Austin to the state capitol. The trip was for the girls; however, I think I enjoyed the trip more than they did. That was my first trip to the capitol and it was an educational one. Touring the capitol building was also fascinating because I was actually there seeing with my own two eyes what I had seen on TV. As a Texan, it was indeed a pleasure to be able to say that I had visited the capitol and the city of Austin.

After our tour, we had the best picnic ever. The weather was perfect and I took pictures and more pictures with my Kodak camera with the cube flash.

Barbara was always ready for a road trip and I was always ready to drive. She was calm and very humorous. Another quality I remember about her was that she loved to share – she was extremely kind to everyone. I am grateful for Barbara's friendship, guidance and wisdom during a time when I really needed someone with her temperament in my life.

Day 87
Courtney Coats Topini

About a week ago, I attempted to save my gratitude entries to a disc because a number of people have asked me what I intend to do with them. My answer has been: I am not sure. Everyone has recommended that I save them somewhere other than on FB because if my account gets closed, I will not have access to any of the entries.

Well, my FB account did not get closed; however, I lost about 10 of my entries. Gone, no where to be found or so I thought. I messaged my friend Judy Mitchell and asked her to see if any of the missing entries were on her FB page. She looked and she was missing the same ones. OMGosh, thank you Judy!

Courtney Coats Topini and I attended an event yesterday and I mentioned my challenge to her and she flew into action. She pulled out her laptop, had me log in to my FB account and she went to work.

The miracle of the hour (actually, it only took her about three minutes) was that Courtney found the missing entries! She showed me how to search for them. When I got home, I got busy. It took me about an hour but I found nine of my lost entries. The one I could not find has been missing for some time. I was elated to find the nine.

I am grateful for Courtney stopping in your tracks to help me recover the lost entries. I saved the nine I found and will make it a practice to save them daily starting now. Courtney, you know you rock!

Sheila-Nate Blue - *There is truly power in numbers! What a fantastic story of what WOAMTEC is about. Co-mission.*

Dawn Kirke Kendrick - *That is one reason I have been friends with Courtney Coats Topini since 9th grade. I know I can always count on her in my time of need.*

Courtney Coats Topini - *Funny.....and look how you showed up in my "time of need". Thanks for helping me out this morning, they really appreciate it.*

Dawn Kirke Kendrick - *Anytime girl! I have said it so many times......I never felt completely at home in Texas until you showed up. I am glad you are around me.*

Day 88
Darlene Scallion

Darlene Scallion and I were best friends in fourth and fifth grade. She was tall and wore glasses. I wanted to wear glasses.

We ate lunch together and walked around the campus checking everything and everybody out. We did not jump rope, play dodge ball, four square or play jacks – guess we were too sophisticated for that. Sometimes we would sit on the steps and read the Weekly Reader....

My family moved away so in 6th grade, I had to make new friends. Darlene and I kept in touch regularly by way of the US Mail.

She wrote and told me she got her hair cut and I was jealous. It didn't matter if it was cute or not, it was cut. She sent me a picture and that made me want a short do even more because it was cute. My parents said "no" and that was the end of that discussion. I didn't get my hair cut but I had to have glasses and I chose a pair of sky blue cat-eye glasses.

We moved back to Texas and my friend and I were together again in 7th grade. We looked like teachers because we were so tall. I was 5'4" and she was probably two inches taller than that. The boys were all short! We both wore a size 7 shoe and I was afraid I would be wearing a size 12 when we graduated from high school if my feet didn't stop growing! (That prayer was answered)

At the end of that school year, my family moved again. Darlene and I kept in touch by way of the US Mail. We did not see each other until we were adults. We had an awesome time catching up–our friendship really did withstand the test of time.

Day 89
Phyllis Fluellen

J. California Cooper was an author I was not familiar with until I moved to Dayton. Phyllis Fluellen introduced me to J. California Cooper (Some Love Some Pain Sometime, In Search of Satisfaction, The Matter Is Life, Family, and so many many more).

Phyllis loved to read and was good about sharing what she read with me. In addition to introducing me to J. California Cooper, Phyllis also introduced me to BeBe Moore Campbell (Your Blues Ain't Like Mine). I could not put that book down. I would get out of bed to read the next chapter because I had to know what happened. Finally, I took a day off from work to finish the book!

One year Phyllis was my Secret Santa and I made out like a bandit. The entire week y she gave me something to read – an inspirational book, inspirational cards, a devotional and a novel. I am grateful for having worked with people who loved to read; we had subject other than work to discuss. It also helped us develop wonderful friendships.

Carolyn Gray - *Amber Slaughter, you are correct. Who are some of your favorites?*

Amber Slaughter - *Pearl Cleage, Kimberla Lawson Roby and my all time favorite is Langston Hughes.*

Carolyn Gray - *I have read What seems like crazy and Mad at Miles. I also like Hughes-- have not read Roby but I will.*

Carolyn Gray - *Amber Slaughter, that shd be what looks like crazy on an ordinary day. I also like Gaines and Taulbert*

Day 90
Mrs. Rose Small

Mrs. Small was my Mom's BFF. Their friendship was truly the definition of what a best friend should be. There was nothing they would not do for each other day or night. They would call each other in the middle of the night or early morning and it was ok.

If one was not feeling well, the other would drive ten miles to deliver homemade soup, magazines, juice or just to sit and chat.

Observing my Mom and Mrs. Small's devoted friendship was like reading a story book. Their friendship was authentic and sisterly. Mrs. Small helped my Mom become accumulated to rural life and that was a blessing because my Mom was a city girl and knew little about "living in the country."

My gratitude for Mrs. Small can't be measured or described in words (although I have tried) because she is such a phenomenal woman of God. She is someone who will find a way to share a penny with five people. She is wise and ever so resourceful, kind and giving. A stranger can knock on her door and she will invite them in and make them feel like a beloved family member.

She is a wonderful family friend and I love her dearly. Lord, I thank you for Mrs. Small.

Judy McCurdy Mitchell - *Beautiful story. True friendship is a very special and precious gift in life!*

Toni Trahan Shirley - *Great testimony about Mrs. Small (and your mother).*

Day 91
Naomi Pradia

Maya Angelou is one of my favorite authors. I have read a number of her books and poems. Naomi Pradia knew I was fond of Maya Angelou's writing and how excited I was that Maya Angelou read her poem "On the Pulse of Morning" at President Bill Clinton's first inauguration.

I tried to get a copy of the poem without any luck. Several months after the inauguration, Naomi gave me a copy of the ...poem "On the Pulse of Morning" and a VHS copy of Maya Angelou reciting it. It wasn't my birthday, Christmas or any other holiday; it was her gift to me "just because." I was elated to have that little book in my hands – Maya Angelou's "On the Pulse of Morning" a beautifully book with gold lettering.

Naomi passed away several years ago but I have never forgotten how much I appreciated her going the extra mile to get me a copy of the poem. She was always doing something nice for people she liked. Naomi was one classy lady. Her husband, L.B. was just as kind to us (her co-workers). We affectionately referred to him as meal-on-wheels because he would bring us lunch when we were too busy to leave the building for lunch. Two wonderful people!

Day 92
Janice Garnett

I was blessed with not one, not two but five sisters! We envied my sister Janice because she could dance better than everyone within a 100 mile radius. Even as a little girl, she could dance. We never know where or how she learned all of those moves. It was like she woke up and had mastered the latest dance.

Jan and I were great travel companions when we were younger. Of course I did... all of the driving "on account" of she drove faster than I did and that was frightening! She didn't really mind – she was content to kick back in the passenger's seat listening to music.

My sister has the greatest sense of humor. Most of the time she doesn't realize how funny she is until I start laughing and she will ask "what's funny?!" When I tell her, she laughs – uncontrollably! Now, on those few occasions she realizes she is funny; it will take her forever to tell the story because she can't stop laughing.

I have four prize voicemail messages I saved from her. When I play them back, I get the biggest laugh. In one message, she is chiding me for not calling to thank her for a watermelon (yellow meat) she sent me. She concludes by telling me "see if you get another yellow meat watermelon from me anytime soon." Of course she was laughing like crazy.

Having sisters (and brothers) is wonderful and in my case, it is awesome because we are all different and that represents a beautiful bouquet of personalities. Grateful for the diversity -

Marco Cruz - *Thank God for family? It is the first lesson we get from God on how to identify His characteristics in people. Also, that helps us appreciate how* *fearfully and wonderfully we are made in his image. Love you mom! Thank you for helping me see God's love for me trough all the individuals I've cross paths with and He has used to get me where I am today. And He will use to help me fulfill His purpose here on earth.*

Carolyn Gray - *MDC, thank you. I am grateful...so very grateful, ready and available to fulfill His purpose here on earth. Love you.*

Judy McCurdy Mitchell - *What an awesome story. You r so blessed to have so many siblings. Love this!*

Day 93
Elvira Riggo

Elvira Riggo could type faster than any word processor with great accuracy. We were cube mates and I learned lots of adminstrative stuff from her.

Elvira helped me to understand that it was ok to take things back if they were broken, torn or if I just didn't like or want them. I hesitated in the beginning because I thought I had the item too long. She told me to take it back and if they told l me "no" to ask to speak with the manager.

True confession, Elvira created a monster!! My worse offense was a pair of shoes I purchased from Fayva's. I had those shoe I know for three week and they hurt (ouch) my feet every time I thought about wearing them. Well, first of all, they were cheap but that was my level at the time (true confession) and secondly, they had a buckle that just did not want to work with me.

I still had the box so I put them in that box and back to the store they went. I was nervous but determined. I had my speech ready for him if he said "no." When he asked me why I was returning them, I said "they hurt me feet!!" and he said OK would you like to look for something else or do you want a refund. I found another pair, wore them to work the next day and they hurt too! Yep, I took them back, got my money and went to a better store– Bakers! (-:

Lord, I thank you for Elvira teaching me to be bold and I thank you even more for delivering me from cheap shoes

Day 94
Wayne and Phillipa Spencer

My second trip to New York was so much fun because we had our own personal tour guides – our dear friends Phillipa and Wayne.

Phillipa was from the Bronx and Wayne was from Georgia. They met in college and when they graduated they got married and move to "the city." They invited us to come up for a visit and we took them up on the invitation...spring in New York. WOW, what a wonderful f...our days!

Philippa's family was from one of the islands so we ate the best food the entire time we were there. It seemed like we at six full course meals every day. Her brother was a musician so we were treated to a grand evening of music at a very nice jazz bar. We toured "the city" and I was fascinated because I actually got to see touch and feel all of the the things I had read about and seen in the movies.

I was a teen the first time I visited New York and I just didn't get to experience "the city." My second trip was filled with shopping, New York style shopping, a show, partying and spending time with friends.

I have been back to New York since then but I did not enjoy myself like I did on that second trip. Our friends rolled out the red carpet for us and I will never forget that trip.

Toni Trahan Shirley - *How fortunate you have been in terms of travel and ENJOYING travel....especially with friends and loved ones. You made experiences such an adventure! You are among the best, my dear!!*

Toni Trahan Shirley - *And your own personal tour guides, Philipa and Wayne sound wonderful to know.*

Carolyn Gray - *Toni, I am so sure they had to rest after we left. Phillipa's family (esp her Mom) was wonderful. Her Mother cooked and served everyone the entire time we were there.*

You know I *love having fun.*

Judy McCurdy Mitchell - *What an awesome experience!*

Day 95
Kris and Vickie Allums

Some people are givers and some people are GIVERS! Kris and Vickie Allums are GIVERS.

We attend church together and I have observed them and admire how they love to GIVE of their time, talents and treasure One night, a man walked up to the church and give us three different versions of the same story within a span of three minutes. The man finally said he was trying to get to the bus station and wanted to know if there was public transportation. I forgot to mention our church is in the Kingwood/Porter area. There is no public transportation that I know of in that area. Kris volunteered to take him to Humble to the bus station.

The man had a need and Kris had the means. We prayed and waited for Kris' return and he came back with a mission accomplished smile on his face.

Vickie always has the coolest pens with colored ink. I think I might have been coveting one of her pens (maybe just a little) so she gave it to me. The very next week, Kris and Vickie gifted me with a small Bible and dedicated it to me. It is a small green NIV Bible. Kris gave Vickie one in her favorite color.

They are very thoughtful and helpful. I am grateful to know people who still GIVE to others those small things that make people happy because someone was thinking about them. Thank you Kris and Vicki for being cheerful GIVERS.

Day 96
Shelia McCulloch

Observing personal and professional growth in others is so awesome. It is especially rewarding if you feel you had a very small part in that person's development.

I must give Shelia McCulloch lots and lots of credit for her development; however, I like to feel I had a part in helping her get there. My small part in helping Shelia was that I made her feel comfortable during her interview for a job.

Shelia landed the job and from there, her creativity flowed. She was a very supportive member of our HR team, came up with a program to celebrate each and every employee's birthday by sending them a birthday card and started HR celebrating Customer Service Week.

Now, helping her feel comfortable during the interview paid off in a big way for me. Shelia and I were members of Toastmasters; she was VP, Education for our club. She was the best VP of Ed I have had the pleasure of serving with. The truth of the matter is that I would not have received my DTM when I did had she not held me accountable. She helped me set attainable goals and made sure I met those goals OR I had to answer to her – and I did not want to do that.

I am grateful for Shelia making me "report in" on a weekly basis and encouraging me to have those stretch goals. She was responsible for helping the members of our club develop goals to help us get to the next level in Toastmasters. Shelia was tough and it paid off as our club was President's Distinguished. When I share my accomplishments in Toastmasters with others, I always think of Shelia because she motived me and held me accountable until I finished my course.

Day 97
Derry McCurdy

I have had the pleasure of knowing some very creative people. Some people who can take the smallest items and make something beautiful. Derry McCurdy is that person; she is very creative. Derry makes jewelry, she can embroidery, make beautiful scarfs, floral arrangements, bake and quilt.

Derry is always making something cute. She made me some personalized dish cloths. Everyone know...s how I love "stuff" with my name on it and Derry went overboard with my name on the dish cloths. She even put my business name on a couple of them. I enjoy using the dish cloths with my business name when I conduct workshops where food is being served.

Derry's big project in my opinion is the patchwork quilt she made that tells the story of the Underground Railroad. She does presentations about the Underground Railroad at churches, civic organizations, schools and during Black History Month using the quilt she made.

Unfortunately, Derry's creativity has not rubbed off on me. I am grateful however that she was able to teach me how to wrap and tie scarfs and accent them with pretty pins. Derry is the scarf Queen. She has a scarf of every color, size and shape with a pin to compliment the scarf. She is one elegant lady.

> **Stacey DeMarco Jata** - *What an interesting individual! Thanks for sharing. I am intrigued with her Underground RR presentation, you'll have to let me come with you one day!! :)*
>
> **Judy McCurdy Mitchell** - *Wow. So many talents! Wish I had just one of these. Sounds like a very special lady.*

Day 98
Christopher (The Dude) Gray

It gives me great pleasure to write about the joy "The Dude" has brought into my life. The moment I laid eyes on his sweet little face I loved him.

I am extremely grateful for the many roles I have played in the life of "The Dude": Mother, disciplinarian, cheerleader, teacher, sports fan, warden (yes, warden) chef, housekeeper, chauffeur, banker, spiritual leader, counselor, coach and everything else in between.

"The Dude" is my favorite son Christopher. My sister Jan and I gave him that name along with "Mr. Christopher" when he was a toddler. He is also referred to a Chris Gray – yep by his whole name because there were at least three Chris' in every class he has been in since kindergarten. He was independent, resourceful, organized, respectful, loveable and intelligent.

As a toddler, he "could" dress himself. Not to mention the heel of his sock would be on top of his foot and the right and left shoes were always on wrong but he "could do it by himself" and I let him!

We both love to read, so we share books and articles. He and my son-in-love treated me to a game of golf a few years ago and I whipped up on them! I actually did it with the custom made club "The Dude" gave me for Christmas. He has not played with me since! He said it was no fun having to tell his co-workers his Momma beat him playing golf.

He has taught me how to maintain good records for my business and some really valuable tips on how to run my business. Looks like the roles have changed – he is now the teacher and cheerleader. When he wants to really get his point across, he calls me "Cal!" I pay close attention when I am called "Cal" because I know he is sharing some good stuff with me.

I thank God for my son and for him being a joy to his Mother.

Nick Sr Flores - *fight! fight! fight! LOL*

Susan Downs - *It is an amazing privilege to be a Mother. I loved reading you Mother Job Description--my favorite was" warden." I bet there are lots of stories behind that word. Been there.*

Carolyn Gray - *Susan Downs sure we could share stories! The end of the story is he turned out just fine!! I was a tough warden!*

Susan Downs - *Let's talk. I'm sure we could bring hope to the many parents struggling with wayward teens. Maybe another Debra Duncan show?*

Day 99
Deborah Duncan

Being a guest on Great Day Houston may not be what others would like to do; however, I wanted to be on stage with Deborah Duncan.

I got the bug after my Mom and I were part of the Great Day audience. When we got seated and my Mom saw Deborah, she was excited. She turned to me and said, you should "tell Deborah Duncan you want to be on her show." Being the obedient adult child, I followed my Mom's instructions–well, sorta. I mentioned to Deborah I had written a book: All About ME* (*Manners and Etiquette for TWEENS and Teens) and I am a Personality Assessment Trainer.

Deborah took pictures with us as well as any other guest who wanted a photo. Before we left, I gave my business card to the Associate Producer. About three weeks later, I received a message asking if I would like to be a guest on Great Day Houston. I was excited and my Mom was on cloud 9.

To my Mom, I was a celebrity. To Deborah, I was a guest who she treated like an old friend. I wasn't nervous because Deborah made me feel so comfortable. She is witty, friendly and treats her guest like VIPs.

I saw her a year later and she spoke like we were old buds. I am so grateful to have had the opportunity to be a guest on Great Day and to meet Deborah Duncan in person. She made me and my Mom very happy.

Claudia Suarez - Did you see The Price is right game show is coming to Houston we should go be a guest and maybe make it on stage and win fabulous gifts & prizes lol

Joy Clements Brasington - Two awesome women on stage. Great story.

Judy McCurdy Mitchell - Excellent story. Glad you appeared on her show and fulfilled dreams--your mom's and yours.

Susan Downs - Good for you being so obedient yet bold. Mothers sometimes do know what is best for us.

Rhonda Friend Welter Morgan - I have met her once myself,, she was such a nice person and I know someone who worked with her, she has never had anything but the nicest of things to say about deborah, as a friend, a woman and a coworker, it doesn't surprise me that you got along so well with her,,, after all you are very simular women,, and I adore the both of you.

Toni Trahan Shirley - *Ahhhh, my stage-struck friend. I love it!*

Day 100
Mrs. Carrie Davis

I am grateful for teachers. I am able to read because of teachers and that is reason enough for teachers to be very very special to me.

My third grade teacher, Mrs. Carrie Davis encouraged me to read everything I could get my hands on. As an adult she was my Sunday school teacher -- she taught us the Word. She told us if we study the word we would grow, grow, grow and if we don't study the Word, we will shrink, shrink, shrink! She demonstrated this every Sunday and recited II Timothy 2:15: *Study to shew thyself approved unto God, a workman that needeth not to be ashamed, rightly dividing the word of truth.* (I am smiling because I am remembering her standing in front of the class shrinking as she said this)

She also reminded us that every tub has to sit on its own bottom. I am so thankful that I heeded her advice. (Most of the time anyway!)

Day 101
Eddie Wingate

I am so blessed to have wonderful brothers-in-love. My brother-in-love, Eddie Wingate is phenomenal. He rolls out the red carpet every time I visit.

My Mom and I went to Arizona for my niece's graduation and Ed got us addicted to sun tea. Seriously, he made a gallon of sun tea every day – that would be sweet sun tea! They have a lemon tree in their back yard so the sun tea had fresh le...mon juice. We also had lemonade. Yum!

Ed barbequed the best ribs, chicken and sausage while we were there and I ate some of everything he cooked. Did I say I had glass after glass of sun tea and lemonade? I sat in the Arizona Room (that is their lovely glass enclosed patio) drinking sun tea and/or lemonade like I was at a resort. He is a great host.

When I returned home, I purchased three thank you cards because I could not decide on just one. I mailed all three cards and the really cool thing was he received thank you cards for three straight days. He called me to thank me for the thank you cards.

Ed is generous and I am grateful that he takes extremely good care of my sister. I will send him a thank you card to let him how grateful I am.

Robin Mize Calicchia- *Love sun tea and tea mixed with lemonade!!*

Kim Gebron - *I so enjoy seeing your daily posts! It's wonderful how you are expressing you gratitude and sharing your memories!*

Carolyn Gray - *Robin Mize Calicchia, the fresh lemons were so good. I have tried to make sun tea outfit does not taste like Ed's...must be the AZ Sun that's missing. (-:*

Carolyn Gray - *Kim Gebron, thank you. I have sooooo much to be grateful for. I am truly blessed.*

Patty Rottmann - *Love your posts!*

Judy McCurdy Mitchell - *Awesome story. Family is a gift from God. We should cherish every moment we have w our families.*

Susan Downs - *You must be a professional writer. You express yourself so eloquently.*

Carolyn Gray - *Thank you Patty Rottmann.*

Carolyn Gray - *Judy McCurdy Mitchell, you know I love my family and friends*

Carolyn Gray - *Susan Downs, I was told yesterday to say thank you when given a compliment...thank you. I don't even consider myself a good writer so Thanks again for the very very nice compliment.*

Carolyn Gray - *Robin Mize Calicchia, auto correct is great sometime...outfit should have been although. Sure you figured that out.*

Day 102
Lisa N. Alexander

Titles are important to some of us and some of us proudly introduce ourselves as so and so, the director of everything! I assigned myself a title that I am not particularly proud of; however, it was an accurate title so I had to claim it.

I was a somewhat of a technopeasant until I hear Lisa N. Alexander's presentation at Sandy Lawrence's Bistro. The truth of the matter is even after hearing her presentation, I was still a little lost. Lisa was so eager to make sure we understood how to get the most from FB and Google Analytics that I felt comfortable asking her for a one-on-one meeting and she graciously accepted.

Lisa came to the meeting armed with her computer, prepared to help me have a breakthrough and I did. She spent one solid hour of her time showing me a number of how to's. I took notes because there was no way I would remember how to check analytics, create an event in FB on anything else. I was so grateful for her spending time with me and for her patience. I had to immediately get home to put my new found knowledge to work. I practiced what I had been taught.

Last week, I walked into the Bistro networking meeting and there she was–The Lisa N. Alexander. It has been months since I have seen her and I was so excited to see her that I gave her at least three hugs before speaking to the rest of the group. After the meeting, I had to give her another hug – don't know when I will see her again.

I knew Lisa was on my gratitude list for this week so seeing her at the Bistro makes Day 102 even more special!

Day 103
Colonel Peter Withers

Colonel Peter Withers was one of the best supervisors anyone could ever have. There were four administrative civilians employees in the office and he recognized us as vital members of the team. He allowed those of us with the appropriate security clearance to have responsibilities that others thought we could not handle.

Colonel Withers was firm, fair, caring and helped everyone advance if they so desired. He offered training, included the cost of off station training in the budget so that we could stay current in our field.

He was a dedicated family man. Colonel Withers let us know that anytime we wanted to take off to participate in school functions, medical appointments, and sporting events for our children that it was ok. We were able to take leave as often as we needed/wanted to without feeling guilty. He would jokingly tell us we could take off "all day" as long as our work was completed at the end of the day.

We all loved and respected Colonel Withers and worked liked crazy to make him look good. That was so easy to do because he was one awesome boss.

Day 104
Patricia White

Beautiful, feminine, witty, intelligent, loving and a woman of God – I just described my sister Pat. She was generally quite; however, she had a comeback for anything that came her way.

Pat stayed make up and dressed up; I am talking every day. June Cleaver had nothing on my sister. Well, maybe she did. June wore an apron and Pat never covered her cute dresses, pants or whatever she chose to wear on any given day. When you saw her, you saw a sheerly feminine lady.

We were going somewhere one day and I was dressed and ready to go. Pat was still in the bathroom perfecting herself and I said: "come on girl, I have been dresses and ready and you are still not dresses." Her comment to me was "you get up and get dressed; I get up and get ready!" We didn"t leave until she "got ready."

Pat was constantly trying to get me to another level of girly girl. She did succeed to a degree and I am grateful for her efforts. I would rather keep my lips polished (my friend Lois encouraged me to do that) and call it a day. And as our friend Lilli reminded me, Pat was beautiful and she was. Love me some Pat.

Day 105
Ben Barley, Sr.

Clark Kent might have been Superman to most but my PaPa was Superman to me! PaPa was loving, kind, firm but gentle and wise. He could do ANYTHING. He was a handy man; he was smart, funny and could fix anything and everything.

PaPa taught me how to write in cursive, to add and subtract three digit math problems. He also taught me the words to a song that I thought I would have the opportunity to sing; however, that didn't quite work out as planned. My brother and I loved crawling into his lap and watching him make magic with a string and a button.

The real thrill was that PaPa would let us drive! My brother and I would alternate days driving. Papa would sit us his lap and let us drive from the gate to the house (about 150 yards). This gave us bragging rights at school.

My grandparents lived on a farm so we were able to feed the chickens, gather eggs, as well as do things like "help" make homemade sausage. We "helped" by turning the handle on the grinder. My brother and I would fill the feeders and see who could quickly turn them over without wasting the feed.

PaPa taught us to be respectful to everyone, not just adults. He told us it would take us a long way. He was a man whose word meant something–if he said it, that is what happened. He drove that point home: keep your word! I am grateful for everything he taught us and he was right, those things have opened many many doors for me.

PaPa was a pillar in the community – neighbors often checked with Mr. Ben before making major decisions. He knew the ropes whether it was banking, farming or raising cattle. The only thing I don't recall him getting involved in was trying to make automotive repairs.

As we got older, we stopped calling him PaPa and called him Pops and we all said that Pops was the man!See More

Prophetess Sharon Gillum - *I really love your story and I know this is so true.*

Amy Leigh Thomas *Koesters I knew what you meant!!*

Alane Bertrand Roberts - *I love this one!*

Frances Johnson - *Thanks for sharing your stories.*

Day 106
Louise Martin

Some people enter our lives and we don't really understand why; however, before too long, we figure it out. Louise Martin was much older (and wiser) than I was, she had three children and she was a minister. I had no idea why she entered my life but I was grateful she did.

I met Louise at work. She worked in the Supply warehouse and I worked in the Supply office where it was nice and co...ol (no heat for me!). Louise was quiet, hardworking, wise and did not get involved in the office drama. She never took breaks nor ate lunch with the other ladies in the office. I inquired and she inquired! I asked her why she didn't eat lunch with the other ladies and she asked me the same question.

As it turned out, we were both absent from the lunch bunch and breaks for the same reason: all they did was talk about the people who were not there. My solution to that was they could talk about me because I would not be joining them.

Louise had fallen on some very hard times and they took pleasure is discussing what they thought they knew about "her business."

Louise helped me understand how my job duties dovetailed with her position. It made my job so much more meaningful. It also helped me learn some of the duties of the other positions in the office. I was grateful for Louise teaching me how to research and cross-reference supply items. One of the first supply terms I learned was nomenclature. I had arrived!.

I transferred but I kept in touch with Louise. Her situation improved tremendously and she got a new job–an office job.

> **Jan PurposeFilled Cade** - *Thank you for sharing this story. Oftentimes, especially in the corporate work setting, you find yourself sitting "outside the crowd" wondering if there was something you did or said, but this is a reminder to me that God allows us to be separate for a*

> **Judy McCurdy Mitchell** - *Thanks for sharing. This is a great life lesson for all of us. Keep those messages coming. I love reading them!*

Day 107
Janet Carroll

Networking can be educational, fun and entertaining. I met Janet Carroll, RN at a networking meeting where she was the speaker. Janet talked about the brain, left brain-right brain.

The portion of her presentation that was very educational for me was the discussion about Cortisol and Oxytocin. Janet explained that Oxytocin is the happy hormone for women. The entertaining portion of h...er presentation was when she stood in a chair to make a point. I just knew she was going to fall–but she didn't. She knew exactly what she was doing.

When she finished speaking, I told her I thought she was going to fall. With that Janet Carroll confidence, she just smiled.

I ran into Janet months later at a different networking group and we were like old buds. I was grateful that she recognized me! We had a nice chat; she made me feel very comfortable. Janet's warm smile and big heart just does that to people.

Janet gave me a bit of advice: never leave home without my books and my boa. I left home once without them and there were people who wanted to purchase my book. I had to tell them I didn't have any with me. Since then,

I have left home without my boa, but never my books. Janet, I hear you!

Toni Trahan Shirley - *And you handle a boa so well...makes me envious. Makes me thing you are taller than my 5' 4-1/2" height!*

Carolyn Gray - *LOL....I am, I am 5'5"-- Thank you very much!*

Day 108
Monique Price

While living in New Orleans, I learned the slogan *Laissez les bons temps rouler*-- "Let the good times roll."

I worked with Monique Price and she gave me a pad of "things to do today" checklist printed on colored paper to help me stay organized. I liked the checklist so much that I have had it reprinted several times and still use it regularly. The big thing for me was not the checklist..., it was that she was part of the Krewe of Zulu and she would be in the Mardi Gras parade.

For the first time in my life, I had the opportunity to attend Mardi Gras. I was super excited and the fact that I personally knew someone in the parade was even more exciting. The day of the parade, the office look outs told me when the Krewe of Zulu float was near and I ran out of the office and stood on the corner waiting to see if I could catch a coconut.

There were people everywhere and I knew they had more experience than I did but I was more driven than they were. I was going to get a coconut-- not beads, not a cup but a coconut. I was running alongside the float when I spotted Monique and seconds later she saw me. She threw the coconut and I jumped up and caught it! Honestly, I have no idea how I managed to catch that coconut but I did.

I was happy! I went back to the office and showed off my coconut. I was grateful Monique saw me and that her throwing arm was so accurate. Now, what was I going to do with the coconut? I had no idea. All that mattered was that I had beads, cups and a coconut from Mardi Gras in New Orleans. Laissez les bons temps rouler!

Nancy Zimmer Evans - *I really want to know more about the "day" thing you are doing!*

Day 109
Pam Tilton

Carpooling was not something I ever wanted to do but living in Alief and working in the medical center I had to rethink that one. The carpool I joined was the best. We were all aggressive drivers and we didn't mind stopping after work if someone needed milk, bread or a soft drink.

Working in the same department was a big plus because we understood having to work a few minutes late sometime and we could bounce questions off of each other. We would tell stories and laugh all the way home. Pam Tilton told the funnies stories; she had some really good ones.

Pam was from California and most of her stories were about the beach. I loved the beach so I was always interested in what she had to say. The carpool broke up when I moved to Katy and Pam moved back to California. The other person decided she did not want to carpool with anyone else.

Pam and I stayed in touch over the years. One day, she called and told me she recommended me for a job as Assistant HR Manager. I was thrilled because the timing was right and I was ready to advance to the next level of management. I applied and was selected and off to Ohio we went.

I was grateful for the recommendation and elated the HR Manager selected me. It was an excellent opportunity. I loved my job, loved Ohio, love my home and loved the weather. The only negative thing about the move was that we were 1800 miles from Texas! That did not stop me from returning home five times to visit the first year we were there. I did better the second year; I only made three trips.

So glad I impressed Pam and happy for the carpool experience which changed my thoughts about carpooling. I just have to find the right one!

Carolyn Gray - Dayton--We were about 76 miles from Columbus and regularly traveled to Columbus. Cleveland was farther but only during the spring and summer, we loved spending time there. It was tooooo cold in the winter (sometimes in the fall) to think about Cleveland.

Ohio was a favorite for me.

Judy McCurdy Mitchell- *Another great story. Looking forward to tomorrow's.*

Tanya Ann Furtado *Burton - Ohio (35 miles ne Cleveland) geauga county*

Frances Johnson - *Oh those carpooling days...*

Day 110
Elizabeth Gay Pou

My Mom and Mrs. Pou, Army wives, kept in touch with each other for years. My Mom and I visited the Pou's in South Carolina and had a fabulous time. A few years later, Mrs. Pou passed away. My Mom kept in touch with Elizabeth Gay Pou, one of Mrs. Pou's daughters.

When my Mom passed away, I didn't think to notify Gay until I found a letter she had written to my Mom. I called to tell her; however, my sister-in-law had already informed her.

Gay and I chat regularly and have developed a relationship of our own. We have something in common: we are both entrepreneurs. Gay, the Highhill HomeMaker, creates some of the most interesting delicacies and presents them in the fanciest ways.

Because Gay has worked through the loss of her Mom, she has been very supportive in helping me through the loss of my Mom as well as sharing ideas with me about growing my business.

She is always thinking about how to improve whatever she is doing. I am grateful for her friendship and her vast knowledge and resources on how to help me grow my business. Gay is wise and an awesome strategic thinker. She is such an inspiration.

Amy Leigh Thomas *Koesters - I love this story, too! I can relate to a degree. It's always nice to have that person whom you can stay close to and share that common bond, especially when it's someone as special as your own Mom. Very sweet and endearing.*

Judy McCurdy Mitchell - *Very inspiring story. Isn't it wonderful how God places people in our lives????*

Carolyn Gray - *Judy McCurdy Mitchell, it is amazing. I was calling her to tell her about my Mom thinking that would be the end to that conversation. That was my thought. God had another plan and I am grateful he did.*

Frederick Blackwell - *HELLO MRS GRAY, JUST WANT TO SAY, IS YOU OK AND YOUR MOM.*

Day 111
Sonya Ware

Joining Toastmasters International has been one of the best gifts I have given myself. I have developed awesome relationships with Toastmasters all over the country. One cherished relationship I have developed is my relationship with Sonya Ware.

Several years after meeting Sonya, we ran into each other through another organization. We chatted and caught up on the years in between. We had both left our corporate jobs and were on our own.

What I love about Sonya is that she is so very very authentic and transparent. She shares and looks for nothing in return and is always looking for opportunities for others. Sonya is an exceptional motivational speaker. I can listen to her speak for hours because her speeches/presentations are chocked full of substantive information from her heart.

When I need to "kick" an idea around, Sonya is my go to girl. We don't talk often; however, when I need a sounding board, I call Sonya. I trust her and never wonder what she is thinking because what she says is what she means. I am also grateful that she is sooooo low maintenance –I love our friendship.

Toni Trahan Shirley - *That is a wonderful way to have a friendship, natural, low maintenance, helpful, just pick up from where you left it. So wash and west and wrinkle free! Way to be Sonya. Way to be Carolyn.*

Carolyn Gray - *Toni Trahan Shirley, that is exactly the way we do it ...pick up where we left off. She is such a sweetheart.*

Carolyn Gray - *Arnetta Yardbourgh, miss you. Talking about catching up...we need to chat. Love you back.*

Toni Trahan Shirley - *Yep. In Lafayette area; shd be home tomorrow night.*

Day 112
Barry Barley

Extended family members are so wonderful; I am extremely grateful for my Uncle Barry. He tolerated me at a child, loved me, spoiled me and let me attend his birthday party. I was elated to be in the room with all those teenagers. After they let me pin the tail on the donkey "one lousy" time, he made me leave. I begged and begged but it didn't work that time.

He would occasionally take me with him when he went to visit his girlfriend (my lovely Aunt Blanche). Well, I probably wore him down to the ground begging to go with him.

When he announced that he was going to see his girlfriend, I would cry, beg and anything else I could think of to get to make that trip. My uncle would tell me "no" and his reason was: I would not sit down and be quiet (and I wouldn't!). I would promise, seriously promise that I would sit down and be quiet (I meant it when I said it).

The minute we were out of the gate heading toward the little store, I would spring up, stand on the hump and asked if we could stop to get some root beer barrel candy and he would stop. That kept me quiet until we got to my Aunt's house. Once there, I had the best time–my aunt had three sisters about my age and I loved playing with them. On the way home, my uncle was probably very happy because I slept all the way home. He would carry me inside being very careful not to wake me because he knew if he did I would wake up talking!

As an adult, I had to call on him to help me with plumbing issues in my home and he was right there for me. I love my uncle and writing about him makes my smile and think of many other wonderful memories of him nurturing me as a child and helping me out as an adult.

Sylvia Lacey - *Love it. Thanks, that's an image of you that I probably would not have ever imagined. LOL*

Carolyn Gray - *LOL! What ya tryin' to say Sylvia Lacey.*

Day 113
Pastor Dennis Everett

Finding a church home every time I moved has caused some angst for me. When I moved to Shreveport, I visited several churches and could not find a church. The one church that I did not visit was Lake Bethlehem. Why? Because it was too large and I felt no one would know I was there.

I was SO wrong. The first Sunday I decided to visit the Lake, I arrived early to attend church school. I told myself that I could learn a lot about a church by attending church school and Bible Study. I was met at the door that Sunday by a beautiful lady with a very warm friendly smile. She welcomed me in, escorted me to the class and introduced me to the Bertha Odom because she did not want me to sit alone.

After church school, I attended the 11 a.m. service. The music was wonderful and the minister who spoke was good. He was not the pastor and I needed to hear the pastor before I made a decision about joining. I returned the next Sunday and the pastor, Pastor Dennis Everett was there and he delivered a powerful message and sang! I wanted to become a member. I prayed about joining and the following Sunday, I joined the Lake.

I found out they had an 8 a.m. service so I attended that service and felt right at home. There were about 300 members who attended the 8 a.m. service and Pastor Everett preached a powerful message with three points. I loved it. During that service, I learned that the lady who met me at the door the first time I attended the church was Lady Lynette Everett. Although it was a large church, it was a friendly loving church; I had found a home. I was part of the Lake Bethlehem family.

The amazing thing about Pastor Everett was that he knew most of us–he even knew my name. He was a great visionary; he was transparent and had a high level of integrity. He was an awesome business man who knew and lived by the Word of God. He walked the talk. His messages were direct and to the point, always in the word and always applicable. My co-workers would visit my office on Monday to find out what three things Pastor Everett spoke about on Sunday.

When I moved back to Texas, I missed my church school class and Pastor Everett's three point sermons. Pastor Everett, Lady Everett and the Lake Bethlehem family are very dear to me.

Rome Berg - *Finding a new church home that fits is always stressful but worth it if we go outside our comfort zone.*

Judy McCurdy Mitchell - *It's so important to find a good church home where we feel like that is where God wants us. I went through a similar experience when I relocated to AR. God has lead me to the best church home I have ever attended my whole life and I thank Him everyday!!!*

Carolyn Gray - *Judy McCurdy Mitchell, you are blessed. Every time I move, finding a church home is always on the top of my list and it requires constant prayer. I loved my Lake Bethlehem church home/family. When Pastor Everett did the purpose driven life--for 40 straight dsys-- several people from work joined me. In fact, they continued going while I was on travel. They sd they felt right at home.*

Judy McCurdy Mitchell - *Carolyn Gray That is awesome. We serve a mighty God!!!! My church family is an extension of my biological family and I absolutely love it!!!*

Day 114
Sandra Corbitt

Years ago, I saw the caption "each one teach one" on my niece's tee shirt from summer camp. I love the caption and decided I would teach others what I know if they wanted to learn.

Sandra Corbitt and I worked together in Dayton and she was eager to learn any and every thing anyone wanted to teach her. That anyone included me! I shared my knowledge with her and she grasped new concepts, how to research the regulations for answers to her questions, and writing responses to congressional correspondence.

Sandra was not afraid of work; in fact, she was so focused and detailed that she got more accomplished in two hours than most people did in eight. She loved feedback and acted on suggestions and recommendations from others "with the quickness" (that was one of her expressions).

I am grateful for Sandra's desire to improve personally and professionally. I told her she owed me for what I had shared with her. She enthusiastically asked what she owned. I told her she could pay me what she owed by continuing to learn and by sharing what she learns with others. The caption "each one teach one" came to mind. I had actually witnessed this full circle with Sandra. I shared with her and she shared with others.

Judy McCurdy Mitchell - *Sounds like you mentored another teacher--just like you!!! Great story.*

Carolyn Gray - *Judy McCurdy Mitchell, we have worked together so you know how we do...train, share, train...*

Day 115
Dr. Sistla Krishna

Moving is very stressful for lots of reason--in particular, you have to find a new everything: new church, new doctor, new cleaners, car wash and not to mention nail and hair salon.

I was fortunate when I moved back to Houston because my friend Sandra Byrd referred me to her physician, Dr. Sistla Krishna. I was able to get an appointment almost immediately. She told me he was straight forward and he is! The office staff scheduled me around my lunch period so that I would not have to use very much sick leave.

Dr. Krishna's office staff is awesome. When I fast for lab work, they have coffee and a bagel waiting for me. They do the nicest things for patients.

Dr. Krishna is extremely patient and he loves to educate. He explains everything on a level that I can understand. His office staff calls me if I am overdue for my follow up appointment. They also call me just to see how I am doing.

Dr. Krishna is interested in what's going on with me–whether I am speaking, presenting a workshop, reading a book or writing one. He is witty and compassionate. I love the care I receive and I am grateful that I didn't have to go to several doctors to find one I liked.

I drive 30 miles one way to be seen by Dr. Krishna and I don't mind.

Judy McCurdy Mitchell - *Sounds like a very good doctor w an awesome staff. Bagel and coffee--after fasting blood--now that is fantastic!!!*

Frances Johnson - *Good docs are hard to find...better stick with him.*

Day 116
Sylvia Lacey

I have had the privilege of working with some wonderful people over the years. Sylvia Lacey is in that category.

Sylvia and I worked together in New Orleans for a very short period–maybe three months because I transferred back to Shreveport. Sylvia teases me that she has not forgiven me for leaving her after such a short period. Although we stayed in touch via telephone, she proclaimed... that was not the same.

I transferred from Shreveport to Houston and Sylvia relocated to Houston after Katrina. We were back in the same office working together and I think I was beginning to see the light at the end of the tunnel with getting off of her list–I think she was trying to forgive me. We attended the same church for a while and I was making progress. Then, I retired! I was right back on her list.

Sylvia and I are friends. She is someone I look up; she possesses the best writing and speaking skills of anyone I can think of. Sylvia writes like a journalist, speaks like an evening news anchorperson and is extremely quick witted. Let me not fail to mention that she is extremely resourceful and has a heart of gold.

I have asked her if we can apply some type of statute of limitations on her not forgiving me for leaving her alone (twice). She is not budging. I am grateful for my friendship with Sylvia because we always have a good laugh about me leaving her and her not forgiving me.

Carolyn Gray - *Kendra Wilson-Hudson, Joleen Clark is an excellent person to have mentor you. She is extremely knowledgeable with first hand experience at the MC, VISN and Central Office level. Hard to find someone with all that.*

Frances Johnson - *Ms. Lacy was great to work with and then so were you.*

Carolyn Gray - *You were wonderful to work and carpool with. I am blessed to have people like you in my life.*

Sylvia Lacey - *Frances Johnson Thanks, you and Mrs. Gray made it easy to adjust at a very trying time in my life. I am grateful.*

Day 117
Linda Phelps

Be ye steadfast, unmovable, always abounding in the work of the Lord. This is a portion of the words to one of the songs friend, Linda Phelps sang so eloquently at church. When I hear it, I think about her.

Linda was my Mom's spiritual daughter which makes her my spiritual sister. She affectionately called my Mom "G" most of the time unless she was being formal then, she called her Mrs.... Garnett.

During Sunday service when Linda was not singing in the choir, she sat on one side of my Mom and I sat on the other. I think my Mom orchestrated that to keep us from talking. Linda loved my Mom and had great respect and admiration for her. She often called "G" for counsel or sometimes, she was called by "G" for counsel!

I am grateful for the love, respect and compassion Linda had for my Mom. She called my Mom regularly, took her to dinner and sent her cards to express her love. She made my heart glad knowing she felt the way she did about my Mom. We both miss her very much; however, we have each other.

Day 118
Val White

I am so grateful for Val White. Val is my sister's friend so that makes her my friend. Val and my sister are Registered Nurses and darn good ones.

When my Mom was hospitalized, we were spending time around the clock with her. Val packed her bag and prepared herself to spend the night with my Mom and my sister so that my sister could get some rest. That was remarkable but that was not the first time she extended herself. She did the same identical thing when my Dad was ill.

Talking about a friend sticking closer than a brother – Val was right there for us. After my Mom passed away, Val sent cards and called to check on us. Her cards and calls always arrived just when I needed them. She shared words of encouragement and wanted to know if there was anything she could do to help. She would drive from her home to my sister's – over 50 miles one way – to see how she was doing.

Family is wonderful and we sorta expect family to go the extra mile. However, when friends extend themselves like Val has done so many times, there is a very special place in my heart and thoughts for them. Her actions make me take being grateful to a whole new level.

Day 119
Nelson Ricks

A steady drip of water will wear a hole in a boulder! I was that drip of water and Mr. Ricks was the boulder.

My husband and I were on a waiting list for an apartment when we lived in Augusta. Mr. Ricks TOLD me it would be about 60, maybe 90 days before an apartment would be available. Well, I checked in with him every two or three days. At first I called the rental office and he was always pleasant as he told me "nothing available yet, check back in a couple of weeks." Then I started stopping by the rental office because it was near where I worked.

We were approaching the 30 day mark and I was getting impatient. We had one vehicle at the time and it seemed I was the one being dropped off! Moving to that location would allow me to walk to work in less than 10 minutes.

Mr. Ricks mentioned to me one day that he liked a particular chocolate so with chocolate in hand, I stopped by the rental office. I wasn't expecting to hear anything but "nothing available yet." However, to my surprise, Mr. Ricks told me he had good news–he would have an apartment available the following week. I jokingly said that's why I brought your favorite chocolate.

I was so excited and grateful at the same time. I am so sure I wore Mr. Ricks down. He probably moved us to the top of the list to keep me from bothering him every couple of days!

Carolyn Gray - *Tiffani Speller, I have plenty of that!*

Judy McCurdy Mitchell - *Remember our saying at work--the squeaky wheel always gets oiled*

Carolyn Gray - *Yep, Judy McCurdy Mitchell, I was squeaky!*

Judy McCurdy Mitchell - *Sometimes we must be "squeaky" to get things done*

Day 120
Bridget Turner-Jenkins

When I wrote All About ME* (*Manners and Etiquette for TWEENS and TEENS) I thought the local school districts would invite me in to teach manners and etiquette. I was very very wrong.

Since the school districts were not interested, I had to market the book differently. That differently was to spread the word through my website, at network meetings, church and through friends and acquaintances.

I met Bridget Turner-Jenkins at Sandy Lawrence's Networking Bistro. After I finished my intro, Bridget asked me if I had my book with me and I said yes, I do. She said I would like to buy one of each of your books.

Months later, Bridget contacted me because she wanted to purchase several copies of All About ME. She wanted to give them as gifts to her daughter's friends. She went on to explain that her daughter was turning 13 and she was having a different kinda birthday party.

I have had Manners and Etiquette birthday parties before but Bridget's was truly different. She gave the gifts – my book-- to each young lady invited to the party. That was not the highlight of the party. What she did was allow them to prepare a meal, set the table and serve themselves. I saw the video and it was phenomenal. Those little ladies were all about business in the kitchen.

This is a mother who wants to help build character, good manners and share a book (my book) with her daughter and her friends. I am grateful to have been a part of her daughter's 13th birthday celebration and for Bridget's support.

Judy McCurdy Mitchell - *How exciting! Carolyn -- u r one of the most talented and gifted women I know. I'm so thankful God allowed our paths to cross.*

Toni Trahan Shirley - *Carolyn, you have always been a gift in other people's lives; it will never change. You only get better at it!! Praise God!*

Cyndy Justice - *How refreshing! You are a special person, Carolyn.*

Day 121
Carol Gooch

Traveling to Conroe to attend a networking meeting is a tranquil drive. I hop on I-45 and head north away from traffic and in 20-25 minutes, I am there.

The first time I attended the meeting there were 110+ women business owners in attendance. That equates to 220 ears -- I talked until I was hoarse! I mentioned to Carol Gooch, Founder and Executive Director that I wanted to join Montgomery County Association of Business Women (MCABW). The group was very friendly and they were having fun.

Carol gave me an application to complete and the rest is history as the saying goes. I told Carol that I am not a bench warmer and that is what got me involved. I joined the Diplomat Team and the Education Committee. As a member of the Diplomat Team, I had the opportunity to speak with each member as I called to remind them of the monthly meetings. I love that job!

Meeting someone who enjoys having fun as much as I do has been awesome. Carol Gooch is like the life of the party; she is hilarious! I am grateful for the opportunity to serve as Co-leader of the Diplomat team. Carol has been supportive of the programs the Diplomat Teams has implemented. In fact, she purchased a beautiful crown for our Diplomat Queen of the Month.

I am happy to be a part of such a fun group that is extremely involved in the local community. MCABW is a great fit for me and I thank Carol for affording me the opportunity to serve.

Toni Trahan Shirley - *Good acknowledgement of Carol, Carolyn. Good recognition, too, that you are NOT a bench warmer!! Love you, my friend of the heart.*

Brandie Joy - *It was my first meeting last time and already I adore Carol and the group. It is so upbeat and fun!! Can't wait for many more meetings!*

Carolyn Gray - *Toni Trahan Shirley, you know I am no more a bench warmer than you are! Can you wrap your mind around me sitting still for 90 minutes --LOL! Don't answer that! Love you back.*

Day 122

Nancy Sides

My birthday is Dec 30 which means that for years I received what I called a Chribirthday present. The year I turned 13 my Chribirthday gift from my parents was a portable script typewriter. I taught myself to type and I typed everything. That was the coolest gift ever.

I couldn't wait to get to high school so that I could take typing because I already "knew" how to type. (An easy A) Well, I learned I had developed some very bad habits: I didn't position my hands on the keyboard properly, my posture was horrible and I had to look at the keyboard if I wanted to correctly type a 6, 7, or 8.

I knew all this about my typing skills because Miss Sides, my typing instructor, shared this with me and everyone in my typing class. Although she blasted me in front of the class, she took that opportunity to chide all of us. She told us we were slaves to our typewriters and she was going to do something about it. And she did! She made us move every other week to a different typewriter – IBM selectric or Remington or Royal manual typewriters. Talking about a challenge – going from a feather touch selectric to a pound the keyboard manual typewriter was no fun.

She made me do drills in an attempt to unlearn my bad habits. I had to do the drills during my lunch period or after school until I got it right. She was also kind enough to cover the keys on the top row of the typewriters in the class which forced us to learn the 6, 7, and 8 keys.

Why oh why would I be grateful for Miss Sides? After I cleaned up my act, Miss Sides and I were like this: X! (Fingers crossed) Just like she blasted me in front of the class, she complimented me in front of the class. She recommended me for a summer job with the school board and I when I was selected, she made the announcement in front of the class.

I am grateful that I learned early in life to accept feedback, corrective criticism or being blasted – I am a better person by making changes based on the guidance of people who wanted the best for me.

Carolyn Gray - *Robert T. Juarez, you should have been in Miss Sides class you would NOT have been able to look at the numbers! Just knowing the keyboard is very useful.*

Carolyn Gray - *Angela Hicks Campos sounds like Mrs Kilmer and Miss Sides went to the same school. I took Typing I and II as well as advanced typing as recommended by Miss Sides. I am so glad I did.*

Angela Hicks Campos - *And now I see my typo... I can't stand it. LOL. Yes, it sounds as if they attended the same school.*

Carolyn Gray - *Typos don't count any more! Per ME!*

Day 123
Mary George

When your neighbors don't know you, they make up stuff about you based on observation. My neighbor in Maryland had me pegged as a spy!

Seriously.

Mrs. George lived in the building next to me and she was always on her patio when I left for work and when I returned. My comment about her was that she slept on her patio. (Pegging works both ways.)

One day, I walked past her patio as the kids rode their bikes and she started a conversation. We chatted for about ten minutes and she seemed satisfied that I was at least normal – a normal spy. We started to chat on a regular basis because she was always on her patio. We got to know each other better and we both learned the truth about each other. I wasn't a spy and she didn't sleep on her patio.

Mrs. George was a wonderful little lady who was divorced after years of marriage and was lonely. Other they getting into my business afar, she was someone I became very fond of. She was my support system since I had no family within 1000 miles. In fact, when I found myself without after school daycare, she stepped up and helped me out. She kept the kids for about an hour and a half each day.

She and my daughter watched the soaps until my son was dropped off then they all watched cartoons because that is what he wanted to watch. It seems that Mrs. George favored my son. They also had whatever he wanted for snack. That situation got a little touchy sometimes and Chris always prevailed–she cared for both of them, she just cared more about him having his way.

I was very very grateful to have her in our lives because she took excellent care of them.. Other than having to referee a misunderstanding a time or two between my kids, it was like having a Grandmother nearby for them

Gayle Yess Fisher - *I thought you were a spy myself. Whew!!!!*

Judy McCurdy Mitchell - *Love reading your life experiences. Another good one.*

Patrice Eaton - *I scared my 1st Texas neighbor. He asked what I do since I seem to work a weird nightly schedule so I told him I do bank jobs. Last I saw of him. I worked at the bank in Data Processing from 6 at night till 6 in the morning 4 days on 4 days off so my schedule constantly rotated.*

Frederick Blackwell - *HI MRS GRAY STILL LOOK GOOD TAKE CARE*

Day 124
George Walker

Mr. Walker was from California and was way cool. The only time I saw him angry was the day I have a fight with a boy in my English class.

I had a real fight–no hair pulling, scratching, kicking or biting. Just raw fist! Tex was always picking on girls. I mean always. He was a bully. This particular day, my friend Judy asked him to pass some paper to me and he wadded it up and threw it at me. I got up, pushed him and he punched me on my arm. I gave him an upper cut. I hit him so hard and so fast that he really didn't know what happened and could not rebound.

It was a very quiet fight. The other kids were just watching. They were surprised to see me act like that and after it was all over, so was I. Mr. Walker entered the room and called us uncivilized heathens. I was so ashamed I just wanted to hide. I really came to myself when he mentioned he was going to contact my Dad. Mr. Walker told me that he was disappointed in my lack of self-control. I was sooooo embarrassed.

Mr. Walker made me stay after class. He told me again how disappointed he was and I cried and cried. He gave me the animals fight humans discuss speech. I was grateful for what he didn't do–he did not call my Dad. He said he would let me take care of explaining what happened to my Dad.

I got home, prepared myself for a l-o-n-g period of being on restrictions once I told my Dad. To my surprise, my Dad did not put me on restrictions. He heard about the fight from one of the other parents. I did however have to apologize to Mr. Walker and the class the next day. No more physical fighting for me. Being referred to as an uncivilized heathen was a serious blow and I never ever wanted to be referred to like that again in my life.

Sylvia Lacey - *Okay, to a new chapter in my book, Pearls and punches. You never cease to amaze.*

Day 125
Tina Fox

Networking has afforded me many wonderful opportunities to mix, mingle and meet some fantabulous people. I met Tina Fox at a networking meeting a few years ago. She is one of the friendliest people I have ever met.

We attended the same monthly networking meeting for some time as well as the party of a mutual friend. Tina is gracious, charming, poised and always looks like she just stepped off the runway. That probably has something to do with the fact that she is a former beauty queen and hosts local beauty pageants.

Tina contacted me one day and asked if I would serve as a judge at one of her pageants. I was honored to be a part of the event and excited to have the opportunity to witness some of the behind the scene action of a beauty pageant.

The participants were all beautiful, talented and well spoken. I had a grand time plus I received gifts for serving. I was extremely grateful for Tina inviting me to be a part of the pageant and to serve in such a wonderful community event.

Day 126
Mrs. J.

My husband and I delivered meals to senior through the Meal on Wheels program for NAM. My husband drove and I delivered the meals to the door of the participants.

We meet some wonderful people who were extremely appreciative for the meal and to have someone to chat with. Of course, I became too attached to some of the seniors. One lady in particular was Mrs. J. She was so sweet and always happy to see me.

When Mrs. J. opened the door and saw me, she would give me the biggest hug which made my day because I love to hug. One day she commented "you sure do smell good" and asked what fragrance I was wearing. I told her and she said she needed to get her a bottle.

After we finished our deliveries, I went to the mall and purchased a bottle of the cologne I was wearing just for her. On our next visit, I gave her a gift bag and she cried. I told her she was crying and didn't know what was in the bag. She said it didn't matter the fact that someone thought about here made her happy.

Watching her open that gift bag was like watching a child open a present. Mrs. J. smelled the cologne and immediately sprayed some on then gave me a bear hug.

I was grateful because I was to be able to make Mrs. J.so happy with such a small gift. She made my day.

Tanya Ann Furtado *Lovely story. My parents have been delivering since they retired yesrs ago. I want to start delivering myself.*

Carolyn Gray - *Tanya Ann Furtado, it is so very rewarding to give back to others as well as the community.*

Maria Bruederlin - *Beautiful story Carolyn, the little things we do can mean so much to people...random acts of kindness should a part of our every day.*

Judy McCurdy Mitchell - *I absolutely love this one. It really touched my heart.*

We never know what people are going through in life. An act of kindness, a big smile, a hug or just kind, loving words may make their day. God bless you Carolyn for your kind, caring and loving spirit!!!

Day 127

Crystal Washington Martin

In 1991, it took my co-workers dragging me into "the computer room" at work to get me started using the computer. I did not know how to turn the computer on. They told me I could not hurt the computer so just start typing.

Over the years, I learned to use the computer to my advantage – like drafting in the computer and using the internet. I got to where I stop writing anything on paper, I would use the computer. I considered myself proficient in the word processing area.

Then, there came social media! Just when I thought I had arrived, something else was thrown my way. But Crystal Washington Martin saved the day for me. I attended a workshop where she was presenting and OMG (osh) that was the day I became knowledgeable about Twitter, LinkedIn and the Facebook.

Crystal's presentation was obviously prepared just for me! She did not use phrases or terminologies that were over my head. She explained everything in such a way that I left her session feeling empowered. When I got home, I logged on the computer and opened a Twitter account. Still didn't know what to do with it but I had a Twitter account. I had a FB and LinkedIn account although I was not using them regularly.

With notes in hand, I was determined to make social media my new best friend. Before long, I had 500+ connections on LinkedIn and my goal for FB was to have 1000 friends. It took a while but I got there. I am so happy that I attended Crystal's workshop and grateful she presented the information at my level of understanding.

Frances Johnson - *We have all arrived............*

Carolyn Gray - *Frances, do you remember the computer room in ELR?*

Frances Johnson - *Not sure if I do..........was it in the old building? I had an antique computer in C&PA when I first started there. And boy was it an antique. And then I had the only word processor in the secretary's office and everyone would borrow it and I had to use the typewriter. Those were the days...*

Carolyn Gray - *The ELR computer room was the office next to the door going to the hall. We had two computers in the room w/ WordPerfect. Then we arrived, we all got desktops with Windows. Those were the days!*

Day 128
Jarlene Crawford

Some of the best food I have eaten was when I lived in New Orleans. Food at the mall in the food court is good in New Orleans.

The food was delicious and the people I met were wonderful. Jarlene Crawford was one of my biggest fans ever. She knew the city, the facility, managers and employees and didn't mind helping me shorten my learning curve. She was a great resource. If she didn't know the answer to a question, she knew where to find it. She was never too busy to help and always always did everything she did with a smile.

Jarlene made THE best hot wings you have ever eaten. She prepared a huge pan for our Christmas party and I ate more than my share. She offered to give me the recipe but that is not what I needed. I needed her to prepare the hot wing.

When I announced that I was transferring, Jarlene didn't say a word about "fixing" (Texas for preparing/making/cooking or anything else we want it to mean) hot wings for my going away party. Well, she didn't have to say a word, that gigantic pan of hot wings did all the talking.

Along with the hot wings, Jarlene and her husband, David, gave me a special gift; a book on friendship. Since I was leaving, I asked for the hot wings recipe. Jarlene gave me the recipe and I still have her handwritten recipe that I guard like it is a gold bullion bar. Her recipe has become one of my three or four secret dishes to fix for special occasions.

I am very grateful for my friendship with the Jarlene and David – they made my stay in New Orleans memorable.

Carolyn Gray - *Jarlene, thank you for reading the post. I am grateful for the experience. You were a source of encouragement for me. The hot wings were my little something extra (-:*

Nancy Medina - *I will be in New Orleans on May 31-June 2. What are your top 3 places I should stop in or great food?*

Nancy Medina - *Also did you say... "Gold bullion bar" smile! Music to my ears*

Kendra Wilson Hudson - *Nothing like Peanut Crawford and David Crawford hot wings!*

Day 129
Rosemary Behrens

Everyone should have a BFF who you can talk about anything with. Someone you may not always agree with but feel comfortable sharing your thoughts with.

My friend Rosemary Behrens and I met about seven year ago through SCA. We started talking about general topics and found that we could get deep with each other. Rosemary and I discuss some very sensitive subject. The beauty of our relationship is that we respect each other and we are both open and straightforward.

Together, we attempt to solve the world's problems – sometimes, we come up with some solid solutions to situations we face. We share like humor although I must admit she is wittier than I am. I love talking with Rosemary because we are able to follow each other's conversations no matter how many people or subjects are interjected.

When we call each other, we ask "gotta minute?" Sometimes the answer is yes, sometimes it's "no, can I call you back." The funniest call back exchange we had went something like this: Me: "Can I call you back, I am at the register and I need to pay attention." Rosemary: "sure." Several hours later, Rosemary called me and calmly said: "you still checking out!" I cracked up because she said it so seriously and both of us knew I had forgotten to call her back. I apologized.

I am extremely grateful for such a low maintenance and drama free friendship that has so much depth. Rosemary is a wealth of knowledge and loves to share with others. She's a keeper.

Day 130
Dean Kring

Starting something new generally makes me a little uncomfortable. When I started my business, I was fortunate to have great resources to help shorten my learning curve.

Connecting with Dean Kring made the road of my new venture smooth and short. After inviting me to the Business Building Breakfast, the very next thing he did was to invite me to become a member of the Service Cooperative... Association's (SCA) Womens Business Center Advisory Board. I was grateful because I was a newbie and he was giving me an opportunity to learn and grow.

When I "checked him out" I learned that there was not much he had not successfully completed. Dean knows the ins, outs and in betweens of business development for entrepreneurs and he doesn't mind sharing.

As a member SCA Business Building Breakfast, I served as Master Host, Program Chair and Business Showcase Chair. In each of these roles, I learned valuable tips on how to run my business. Immediate follow-up has been the most valuable tip and take away for me.

I appreciate and am grateful for Dean's straight forward approach to everything he does. He is an awesome resource for entrepreneurs.

Toni Trahan Shirley - Well stated! And it is so good to give credit to those who are awesome to us along the way. Good job, Carolyn. Immediate follow-up, a grand practice!!

Susan Downs I love it when a mentor shows up just when you are ready for the next step.

Day 131
Trecie Cruz

My daughter, Trecie was born on December 26 – a belated Christmas gift– my little doll. I thank God for my sweet daughter who is a real life Proverbs 31 woman.

Trecie has always been a nurturer. As a toddler she "had" to take care of her friends. When her brother was born, she appointed herself as his personal 24-hour on duty care taker. She is compassionate, respectful, loving and dedicated to taking care of anyone she feels might be in need.

I am grateful for her being the best daughter any mother could ask for. She was not any trouble growing up. She always held herself accountable, did her school work without supervision, went where she said she was going and didn't have to have curfew. Trecie always had a job; she took care of the preventive maintenance of her vehicle, a Nissan Sentra (her baby).

A quote I used for years during training sessions with employees came from my baby girl. She told me "you have to conduct yourself at work (everyday) like you are on an interview because you never know who is observing you." She was fifteen and had just started working at McDonald's.

I was extremely proud of her as a college student because she took responsibility for her scheduled classes, made good grades, worked part-time and took care of her beloved Sentra. She kept that Sentra until she got out of school, got a job and purchased a new vehicle.

She and her husband, Marco adopted a new born in January and they are proud parents of a precious son, Ian Zachariah. I am so grateful and honored to be her mother. She is my friend –she is totally awesome.

Carolyn Gray - *Toni Trahan Shirley, thank you and happy Mother's Day to you and my Tiffany Shirley Timms.*

Carolyn Gray - *Hi Phyllis Jenkins Isiminger, happy Mother's Day to you.*

Carolyn Gray - *Caryn Ayers, I am only on day 131! Lots more special people to express gratitude to.*

Happy Mother's Day.

Donald Reel - *That daughter had a great role model(s) in you and your husband. Thanks for being a great mother and role model.*

Day 132
Sonja Barnes

Planning a workshop requires finding a location, shopping, planning and more planning. When I decided to host a workshop, I ran into the problem of locating an affordable place to hold the workshop. That problem was solved by Sonja Barnes, Barnes Benefits in The Woodlands.

Sonja allowed me to use her conference room. She got up early on a Saturday to open her office just for me. In addition to allowing me to use her conference room, she offered to provide coffee, cups and everything to go with it. I thanked her and assured her I had that part of the workshop covered.

Sonja unselfishly gave of her time. She helped me set up my coffee maker and the refreshments for the workshop participants. I got more than I asked for–I was grateful for the use of the conference room and I got help from her to boot! Sonja and her husband, Bryan are two of the nicest people. I am so happy I met Sonja through my networking group: WOAMTEC, The Woodlands. WOAMTEC members are serious about helping others grow their business. It is not just about referrals, it is about "let me help you!"

Janis Ehrhardt Gebhart - *Sonja is an amazingly sweet, wonderful person! We are blessed by her leadership in the Conroe chapter of WOAMTEC!*

Susan Downs - *You have a knack for meeting the nicest people. How do you do it?*

Day 133
Tracinda Shipman

Tracinda Shipman and I met at church. We bonded and became sisters. We were typical church ladies: we sat on the left side of the church; second row from the front every Sunday.

One Sunday, the Praise Team sang "I Can Only Imagine" Traci and I were singing, then crying and dabbing each other's tears.

When the Praise Team sang the chorus: Surrounded by Your glory, what will my heart ...feel --Will I dance for you Jesus or in awe of you be still --Will I stand in your presence or to my knees will I fall --Will I sing hallelujah, will I be able to speak at all --I can only imagine, we were totally moved because we could only imagine.

By the time the Praise Team started signing I can only imagine when that day comes and I find myself standing in the Son- I can only imagine when all I will do is forever --forever worship You -I can only imagine -- we both had a huge ball of tissue in our laps. We were seriously crying – tears of joy.

I am so grateful to have a spiritual sister like Traci who prays for me, checks on me and loves me. She is my Sissy and my friend.

Tracinda Shipman - *Awhhh Sissy!!! Know your friendship and love are valued! You are the most beautiful example of a lady! A mentor to many! And that smile! I love you!*

Stacey DeMarco Jata - *Love, love that song! You're the best!*

Frances Johnson - *One of my favorites...and I can only imagine...*

Gwen Y. Gistarb - *Happy Belated Mother's Day to my friend. Love ya*

Day 134
Johnny Garnett

I am grateful for my brother Johnny for serving our country in the U. S. Army for 25+ years and for being a great husband, father, brother and uncle.

My brother and I shared time together when he was in college at Virginia Military Institute (VMI) since I lived in the Washington DC area, I was close enough to visit him and watch him play football. I have fond memories of traveling with... my kids to watch him play and my daughter chasing Moe, the VMI Keydets mascot, on the sidelines.

When my nieces and nephew were younger, they wanted "Dad" to tuck them in at night and to do things for them. That touched me and made me realize that my brother had devoted time with them. My sister-in-law was always there to take up the slack when he was away. She was the colonel in charge!

Together, they raised their children to be respectful, caring and responsible. My nephew followed in my brother's footsteps by serving in the U.S. Air Force. I am proud of my family members who have served and thankful that they all returned home safely.

Toni Trahan Shirley - *Love those who spent such significant parts of their lives in military service - and the families doing it with them! Especially Glad to read this one.*

Gail Ware Randolph - *Please thank him, his wife, children, you and all the family for the sacrifices they all have made to protect our freedoms. One of which is me being able to type this message to you and say without restrictions May our Lord God, Jesus His Blessed Son and the Holy Spirit continue to Bless and keep your brother and nephew safe during their service and protection over their families while they are apart.*

Brenda Lee - *Amen.*

Susan Downs -.*That is wonderful that they all returned home safely*

Day 135
The Dayton Mediation Center

Much gratitude to the Dayton Mediation Center. I signed up for mediation training to become a certified mediator; however, the class was full so they put me on the waiting list for the next class.

Somehow, some way, a slot became available! (I call that favor). The center director contacted me and I was in. The training was phenomenal. I was able to use the training in my position as HR Manager in resolving disciplinary and EEO issues. I developed an alternative dispute resolution program based on mediation. The program was well received by managers, the labor partners and employees.

After becoming a certified mediator training, I was afforded numerous opportunities to mediate community, family and juvenile issues. The juvenile mediations were court referred mediations – rewarding to witness the beauty of mediation with young people.

It was truly amazing listening to the facts as told by each party. There was very little difference in the facts; however, the perception of the facts was a totally different story. Serving as a mediator and a co-mediator helped me help others work through the issues and come up with their agreed upon resolution.

Mediation is a "tool" that I use regularly to help people resolve differences. The Dayton Mediation Center was a wonderful place to learn the art of mediation.

Susan Downs - *I think mediation is such a wonderful idea. I did not know you were an official mediator.*

Susan Downs - *That's cool*

Toni Trahan Shirley -*You are just about everything! And so dynamic, yet able to* *be silent and LISTEN....*

Carolyn Gray - *Toni....sometimes. LOL!*

Day 136
Mrs. Young

Back in the day, there was always someone at work who "mothered" us. They told us if our dresses were too short or tight, if we had on too much make-up, stop chew gum, get back to work and on and on.

The lady who "mothered" us when I worked in D.C. was Mrs. Young, the student employee coordinator. It did not matter to her whether you were a student or not, she treated every young lady... in the office the same.

For those of us who were regular employees, she didn't have to "get on us" as much or as often; however, when she felt the need to, she would. Although there was no official dress code, Mrs. Young had her own dress code. Her favorite comment was "cover those ham hocks up!" Translated: your dress was tooooo short. If she said that to anyone, you would not see that person the rest of the day. Talking about keep your seat –

Mrs. Young was everyone's confident, sounding board and defender. She would get all over us but did not want anyone else to say a word to us. She was firm but fair and very very nurturing. I was grateful to have her in my life to help me chart my professional course. She had worked for the agency for years and knew the culture like the back of her hand and did not mind sharing. Following her guidance helped shorten my learning curve.

Monya Robinson Coleman - *The world, the work force & the church NEED more Mrs. Young's.*

Sheila-Nate Blue - *Love this. My Mrs Young was a wise woman named Linda.*

Carolyn Gray - *Monya Robinson Coleman, as I was writing this I chuckled because I am probably someone's Mrs. Young!*

Carolyn Gray -*Sheila-Nate Blue, we are the wiser for having them in our lives. I catch myself saying "cover those ham hocks" (to myself) when I see someone out and about w/tooooo much showing!*

Judy McCurdy Mitchell - *Another wonderful story. I agree with Monya--this world needs more Mrs. Young's everywhere.*

Monya Robinson Coleman - *I am officially Mrs. Young.*

Frances Johnson - *We could have used a Mrs. Young in Houston.*

Day 137
Thelma Mason

I am grateful for friends who don't mind taking risk. My friend, Thelma Mason was right there with me trying to play tennis.

I mentioned to Thelma that I took tennis lessons and loved the game; however, I wasn't very good. Actually, I wasn't good at all. I looked like I could play! I had all the cute clothes, fancy tennis rackets, head and wrist bands and cute shoes and socks.

There was a tennis court at the complex where I was staying--Thelma came over and we were set to "play" tennis. She was dressed up too! Honestly, you would have thought we were ready for the circuit.

Off to the court we went. We served the ball and after the serve, it looked like we were playing baseball. We had tennis balls flying everywhere. Good thing the fence was REAL high otherwise we would have been running after every ball we hit. Of course we were laughing like crazy. I am sure the neighbors were doing likewise.

Other than getting a good workout, our tennis career was over. She was a good sport about it. Thelma had other things she could do because she is very artsy craftsy–me, well– I like to read!

Emma Yerby - *Carolyn I took one lesson and the instructor told me to save my money. I took his advice. lol*

Kendra Wilson Hudson - *That is funny!*

Carolyn Gray - *Emma Yerby, I blamed it on not having anyone to practice with. I should have saved my money and time. We should have thought about playing years ago...maybe we wouldn't have gained weight on our diet!*

Carolyn Gray - *Kendra Wilson-Hudson, it really was funny.*

Rome Berg - *Cute story, I tried playing once. Same outcome.*

Carolyn Gray - *Rome Berg, something else we have in common.*

Toni Trahan Shirley *Makes me think of you and golf....you were better at golf I think!*

Carolyn Gray - *Toni Trahan Shirley Shirley, I was better at golf...*

Saturday at 10:06pm *via mobile ∑ Like*

Susan Downs - *Funny story. I can identify. Hope you didn't let those cute tennis duds go to waste. Maybe you can take up Pickleball with me and Marian LaSalle and others. It's a lot easier than tennis, but you do have to be able to hit a ball with a racquet.*

Carolyn Gray - *Susan Downs, I can hit the ball, just have no control. I guess w/ practice I would learn not to hit it so hard.*

Where do you *all play Pickleball?*

Susan Downs Fonde - *Recreation Center near downtown. Saturdays from 10.30 to 1.00. It is free, and you don't need to bring any equipment. Just wear that fancy tennis outfit of yours.*

Day 138
Ronald Earl Wilsher

I am in a networking meeting and in walks this tall good looking guy with long hair – that got me attention. He speaks and I am listening because what he is talking about makes sense.

He posed a question to the group: "do you own your name?" In my smart head I said "of course I own my name." Ronald Earl "Note to self" Wilsher went on to share with the group that we should own our name ...and brand ourselves. He added that if we send him an e-mail request he would add us to his "waykwel" friends list. Of course I sent him an e-mail – I wanted to be on his friends list!

Ronnie also said "if you don't own your name, call me, I will help you." I took him up on that offer! He was serious, he helped me get my URL and e-mail set up and asked if I had any additional questions. I didn't because he did speak geek, h spoke on a level where I could understand the process.

My gratitude to Ronnie for bringing me closer to the 21 century with this technology stuff and for introducing me to the wonderful, smart and beautiful Ms. Cathryn C. Wheat!

Ronnie's Branding of Humans is waykwel. He is humorous, loves to share and is an energizing presenter.

Donald Reel - *Carolyn, aren't resource people and mentors wonderful!!!! I have had so many great ones that I cannot count them all. Remember to: "Ask Questions - and DEMAND Answers. Have a great weekend and keep on doing the things that you love to do.*

Day 139
Nonie Maloy

Good gatekeepers in an office are a great asset to a manager. Gatekeepers may tick people off but the truth of the matter is they are vital to managers.

Nonie Maloy was THE best gatekeeper any manager could ask for. Nonie interviewed for the position with her husband in tow. She told me she was punctual, dedicated, loyal and committed to doing her work. For me, that was music to my ears; I hired her on the spot. Her husband was in the waiting area; however, before I knew it, he was in my office hugging and thanking me for hiring her.

He explained that she had been on several interviews and felt that she didn't get hired because of her age. I became like family to them–they invited me to weddings, anniversaries, church programs, you name it and I was invited and attended their celebrations.

I was grateful for Nonie for a number of reasons. She rode the bus to work and was never late--not rain, hail or flooding caused her to be late. She did not call in sick, did not make personal calls during duty hours and was the go between for me and my children if I was not available when they reported in after school.

People trying to get in touch with me nicknamed her the Sheriff! The beauty of my relationship with her was that I had time to work uninterrupted because she took care of routine calls and visitors without appointments. For those she was not able to take care of she referred to the appropriate specialist. She was very efficient which help me to be more efficient.

Alane Bertrand Roberts - *Carolyn, I love these stories!*

Anita Hunt - *Carolyn, great story, we have a shortage of "Noni's" in the workforce today. Where have all the people with good work ethics gone?*

Susan Downs - *What was her age when you hired her? Sounds like she had a good head on her shoulders.*

Carolyn Gray - *She was in her late 50s.*

Phyllis Jenkins Isiminger - *Nonie was a treasure. She often helped me out after I left Houston and went to work at other VA's. And you didn't mention it, but she made the best cookies! Yes, she was a one of a kind!!*

Carolyn Gray - *OMGosh how could I forget those cookies!? Of course I had my own tin of cookies!! (-:*

Judy McCurdy Mitchell - *Great story. Sounds like she was one in a million.*

Frances Johnson - *Nonie was great and is missed by all of us. And yes, her ginger cookies were wonderful.*

Day 140
RJ Orphe

I have known RJ all of his life–he's four. RJ is the cutest happy go lucky little fellow who attends church with his Dad.

I am grateful to have this little guy in my life. After church, he looks for me and asks this question: "you looking for me?" He smiles; I pick him up and he gives me a big hug. It just warms my heart and makes me realize that it is truly the little things in life that really matter.

He usually has a snack that he is willing to share – from his little hands to my mouth. I can never get my own chips or goldfish. He has the sweetest smile. I love that little guy.

I am taking advantage of RJ looking for me to give me a hug because in a few years those hugs will probably turn into a quick handshake.

Susan Downs - *You are a Touchstone in his life as well, Carolyn.*

Sheila-Nate Blue - *How precious.*

Jan PurposeFilled Cade - *I think he will continue to look for you and give you a hug. He will remember you just as much.*

Toni Trahan Shirley - *From what I see in Tiffany's life, they often return to give hugs; I expect the same from RJ for you!*

Carolyn Gray - *Toni Trahan Shirley, you are right, Tiffany Shirley Timms is so loved and respected by her students. She is one teacher that students never forget.*

Judy McCurdy Mitchell - *Love this story. So glad God placed RJ and you in each others lives!! God has a plan and I'll bet it will be magnificent!!*

Frances Johnson - *Kids are so sweet...........enjoy the hugs while you can.*

Brenda Lee - *Amen. We have to enjoy them while they're young.*

Day 141
Leslie Ann Phillips

I shared an office with another specialist and Leslie Ann Phillips who was our clerk. Leslie was a go-getter, efficient, fast and a pleasure to work with.

Leslie answered the phone on the second ring, kept her Xerox box empty, didn't have a backlog of filing, and responded to routine correspondence without being asked. I was grateful to finally have a clerk who could take charge of work and me.

We had an encounter in the office that was the talk of the office for a long time. Someone brought a kitten to work for Leslie. The kitten was in a box which was fine. Where things went wrong was when someone took the kitten out of the box so it could walk around and the kitten walked into my office. I am not fond of cats (or kittens). I know they are cute but–

My feet were no longer on the floor – they were on the desk. Actually, my whole body was on the desk. Leslie thought I stepped on the kitten because of my loud scream. Leslie and several other co-workers thought they were coming to the rescue of the kitten. When they saw me on the desk, they forgot about the poor little kitten. They were trying to console me.

Leslie put the kitten back in the box, they got me off the desk and I locked my office door. Everyone but Leslie thought it was hilarious. That day, she was in charge of me.

Toni Trahan Shirley - *Love the story...I knew bout the cats, but first time I heard this story!! And I can just picture you screamin and on top of that desk!*

Frances Johnson - *Haven't thought of Leslie in a while..........do you hear from her? You are really bringing back memories.*

Carolyn Gray - *Toni Trahan Shirley, you know I was getting out of the way of that kitten.*

Carolyn Gray - *Frances Johnson, Leslie is going great. She works for the Air Force as a specialist.*

Day 142
Arnetta Yardborough

My book, WOO to WOW: 5 Stages of a Relationship (WOO, WHAM, WHOA, WHEE, WOW) was an adventure. It was not a dangerous adventure, it was me doing something that was fun and exciting not knowing what the outcome would be. A risky adventure.

I mentioned to a fellow coach and friend, Arnetta Yardborough that I had written the book and her first question was: "where is it?" I replied "in the car." She said "I would like to purchase a copy." Arnetta purchased the first copy of WOO to WOW and offered to have a book signing for me at her home.

Arnetta's offer was overwhelming because I wasn't expecting her to ask to purchase a book and certainly wasn't expecting her to offer to have a book signing for me. What I have learned about her is that she is generous and likes to help her family and friends succeed. I am grateful and appreciative for her support.See More

Toni Trahan Shirley - *Wow, what a kick-start to get you going. Such a generous-spirited offer from Arnetta. Thank you, Arnetta!*

Susan Downs - *How can I get a copy of your book today?*

Amy Leigh Thomas *Koesters - Yes, I would love to buy a copy too!!*

Toni Trahan Shirley *- Sell, Carolyn, sell!!*

Amy Leigh Thomas *Koesters - I just downloaded it to my kindle from Amazon. Look for "Woo to Wow" in the search box.*

Day 143
Mrs. Randle

I expressed my gratitude to Mrs. Randle because I want her to know I truly truly appreciated her kindness toward my Mom.

My Mom would not drive at night; however, she loved going to evening service at church and other social events. Mrs. Randle made it possible for her to attend evening functions because she would drive miles to pick my Mom up and bring her back home.

I am also grateful for Mrs. Randle thinking of me and sending me inspirational cards, Christmas cards and "just because cards" after my Mom passed away. Her cards always arrived when I was feeling a little down. The cards were a great pick me up. In addition to sending cards, Mrs. Randle also expressed her concern by calling me which helped me through the grieving process. Friends are awesome.

Dawniel Winningham - *Friends ARE awesome #includingyou*

Suezette Duncan-Kay - *Mrs. Randle sounds like an angel.*

Judy McCurdy Mitchell - *God has special blessings for compassionate and considerate people like Mrs. Randle.*

Susan Downs - *She must have really loved your Mom.*

Carolyn Gray - *Susan, she did. She went out of her way to help my Mom. My Mom could drive and would be all over the Houston area during the day. She would have that car in the garage before dark.*

Day 144
Cyndy Justice

It seems kinda scary meeting people in a chat room.

Not so with Cyndy Justice.

Cyndy and I met in a virtual networking chat room. We were to spend five minutes sharing with each other about our business. When Cyndy introduced herself, she told me where she lived and I added that we are almost neighbors. We decided to meet in person at a local sandwich shop for a face-to-face networking session.

We visited for over an hour and have been chatting ever since. Cyndy invited me to her networking group and I accepted the invitation. The group was dynamic; I met some new people and saw several I already knew.

Cyndy is an inspiration to all. When I heard her story, I was grateful beyond measure to have met her. She has a very gentle spirit and does not let anything stop her from doing what she wants to do. She expresses gratitude in a way that is unbelievable.

During our face-to-face meeting, I shared with her that I teach manners and etiquette for tots, tweens and teens and that I had written a book: All About ME* (*Manners and Etiquette for TWEENS and Teens). She immediately said "I have a referral for you." She went on to say "let me get a number for you and get back with you." A few days later, she called me with the name and telephone number. That was so sweet and thoughtful of her and a great opportunity for me. Cyndy is a remarkable lady.

Dee Toohey - *I have several friends that I met that way. Nice story!*

Kendra Wilson-Hudson *How do I get a copy of the book?*

Judy McCurdy Mitchell - *Another great story. Love reading your life experiences.*

Carolyn Gray - *Kendra Wilson-Hudson - my website (connectingheartscoaching. com). I offer the book after my manners and etiquette workshops. Believe it or not, teen males are my best clients.*

Carolyn Gray - *Dee Toohey, that was a first for me. I "attended" because I wanted to see if it would be a viable alternative to physically attending a networking meeting. I thoroughly enjoyed it.*

Carolyn Gray - *Judy McCurdy Mitchell, thank you. I have soooo much to be grateful for--along with soooo many people to show gratitude for what they have shared/given me over the years. Of course, that includes you. Thank you, thank you..you continue to support and encourage me. Some things just don't change!*

Day 145
Clifton Tate

When everyone started ordering books, clothes, gadgets, etc. from internet sites, I would not order anything because I was skeptical. My friend, Clifton Tate and I discussed books we were reading or preparing to read and he always had the latest books. One day I asked him where he purchased a particular book and he said Amazon.

This was before Amazon was cool and dial-up was it. Clifton "assured" me it was safe and that he had ordered several books and had not had a problem.

I took the plunge and ordered from Amazon and E-bay. I trusted his judgment and he had not had a problem. I received my items as promised and that was the beginning of me ordering from the internet. I am grateful that Cliff got me out of fear mode; however, he helped to create a monster. I started ordering from the comfort of my little office with a credit card specifically designated for internet shopping. Guess I was still a little skeptical.

Toni Trahan Shirley - *I love Clifton*

Susan Downs - *I hope you have learned to tame that shopping monster.*

Carolyn Gray - *Susan Downs, I have tamed the monster. I still order books from Amazon ONLY when I cannot find them at Half Price Books.*

Carolyn Gray - *Toni Trahan Shirley--everybody loves Clifton!*

Day 146
Rome Berg

I am somewhat technologically challenged; however, with friends like Rome Berg, my life is made easy.

Rome and I collaborated on a workshop that was too much fun. We met, decided what we would present then it was time to prepare the flyer. I looked at Rome and she must have been reading my mind because she said "I will do the flyer."

When I saw the beautiful flyer, I was excited and ...could hardly wait to conduct the workshop. I thought, maybe she can teach me to prepare a flyer for another workshop I was planning. I asked and she said "of course."

Not only did Rome prepare the flyer but she made a template and showed me, step-by-step, how to use the program to prepare future flyers. Well, the rest of the story is that I forgot a couple of the steps when I tried to go it alone.

I called Rome and she walked me through -- over the phone -- how to add my information in the template. I am so grateful for friends who have patience and don't mind sharing their knowledge. I got it!

Toni Trahan Shirley - *These technos are made even better when they take those patient steps to help, really help, those around them who are less skilled. Three cheers for Rome!!*

Toni Trahan Shirley - *Happy Memorial Day!*

Susan Downs - *Can you teach me how to create a flyer, Carolyn?*

Carolyn Gray - *Susan Downs, do you have publisher on your computer?*

Curtis R Smith - *Good to see an IT literate person being recognized for being helpful :-). Good job leveraging your resources Carolyn!!*

Day 147
Jolie Adams Hardeman

During a Bistro networking meeting the discussion was around banners for Facebook business pages. I was in the dark so I turned and asked Jolie Adams Hardeman "what's a banner?"

Jolie explained it and I asked her if that was something she could do. She replied "yes" and told me what I needed to send her in order for her to make the banner for my FB business page. The Connecting Hearts Coaching banner was delivered to my e-mail and all I had to do was upload it to my FB business page.

Grateful for Jolie helping me understand FB terminology and answering my questions about graphics. I am blessed to have patient people in my life to help me with my technology challenges.

Day 148
Rollis Fontenot

I had a linked in account for over a year with about 50 connections and I thought I was doing good. I met Rollis Fontenot III at an HNN conference and as we chatted he asked me if I was on linked in. I replied "yes but I only have about 50 connections." He asked me if I had just joined and I replied "no I don't know how to build my connections."

Right there, he gave a crash course on linked in and told me how to build my linked in account. (I followed his instructions and it worked.)

I asked him about his business and he told me he had a recruitment firm. Well, that caught my attention since my background is HR. After abou five minutes, I had to let him go but not before thanking him for being so helpful.

Rollis was knowledgeable, exceptionally polite and respectful, soft spoken and an extremely impressive young professional. Although we only spoke briefly, I felt we had established a relationship. I connected with him on linked in and Facebook.

I am grateful to have met such a wonderful young man who knows what he wants, works hard, helps others and treats them like a good friend. A truly rare find.

Day 149
Anna Ryan

My desire to become technologically savvy has been enhanced by Anna Ryan. Anna and I are co-team leaders of the Diplomat Team for Montgomery County Association of Business Women (MCABW).

During a conversation about ways to effectively communicate with the MCABW team, Anna introduced me to Group Me. I was still using e-mail and texting to share information with the team. Anna, a techno...logy wiz, encouraged me to download the Group Me app which would help make my tasks of notifying members more effective.

Using the Group Me app is like having a conference call in text form. It is one phenomenal tool because everyone in the group is in the feed. When my pastor mentioned that the team leaders at church would be using Group Me, I was ahead of the game – grateful that Anna had me using Group Me. I love learning and in this technology driven society of ours there is so much to learn.

Susan Downs - *A great tip. Who knew that existed???*

Carolyn Gray - *Susan Downs, try it!*

Day 150
Russell Johns

There are a number of people I am grateful for because they have guided me into the world of technology with very little pain. The blessing is that they were very very patient and understanding.

Russell Johns is all about IT and he shared do.com with me. I downloaded the app and started using it immediately. I use do.com for projects and for keeping notes. With this app, I am able to list things that need to get done with a due date and assign/share with people in my group if I choose.

I use this app more than I use my calendar. It is a life saver – I don't have things fall through the crack nor do I have a gazillion post it notes all over the place. I am really efficient–I scare me!

Susan Downs - *Sweet! I still prefer pen and paper for this task. Maybe I will join the tech world one of these days.*

Curtis R Smith - *You are evolving into a technology proficient woman:-) Congratulations on your efforts to actively seek to learn and encourage that in others through sharing your stories.. Keep on being a difference maker.*

Judy McCurdy Mitchell - *Wow!! You are a hi-tech lady. I've never heard of the things you talk abou. Keep learning and teaching.*

Day 151
Doris M.

Self-control is a great characteristic to possess. I have observed numerous people in my life display self-control regardless of the circumstances and some, well...

Doris M. was an engineer before there were very many female engineers in the workforce. Sometimes, she had to fight to be treated fairly and she did not mind fighting. I am grateful that I was able to observe her style of fighting. Whatever she fought for, she always said "I'll take care of this through the system." And she did!

She believed in documenting and I learned from her–document because documentation helps to support your claim. Although I never filed a claim, I did use what I learned from Doris to support EEO, disciplinary and adverse action cases presented before a third party.

It is not just what we learn by reading a book or sitting through a lecture but often by observing people around us.

Judy McCurdy Mitchell - *Another great lesson. Thanks for sharing. She sounds like a real professional and classy lady!!!*

Donald Reel - *Most individuals don't understand the importance of proper documentation in our daily lives. This concept along with "critical thinking" should be taught at every grade level in the public school system and in our college/ universities.*

Susan Downs - *Cool chick!*

Day 152
Florence and Marita Littauer

My gratitude today is for two phenomenal women I met first by reading their books and later in person when I traveled to California to attend their Personality Assessment Training Class.

There are numerous tools in my "tool box" that have helped me become the person I am today. One that I shared with others and promote often is one that Florence Littauer and her daughter Marita Littauer teach.

Once I understood my temperament and that I cannot change others, I have better relationships with people I interact with. I thank Florence and Marita for their passion about the personalities and teaching this subject in such a way that is easy to understand.

This is one *tool that I use daily as I communicate with family, friends, business associates and children. It is amazing how much better life is when you can get along with almost anyone realizing that we are wired differently. Florence and Marita, I appreciate you.*

Curtis R Smith - *Well said!*

Toni Trahan Shirley - *Sounds like an awesome tool!!!*

Liz Plaster - *Send the link!*

Day 153
Gene Daniel

I never imagined working with a group of engineers being fun. Well, the group I worked with was beyond fun. We worked hard but we played hard and I am grateful for the people who made my life away from home and family so enjoyable.

There was a Purple Phantom in the office, aka Gene Daniel! Gene wore a mask and a purple cape and was caught on camera (probably by his partners in crime – Margaret and Emma) fishing in the goldfish bowl and so many other crazy things.

That was the best group of guys to work with and I am grateful I had the pleasure of starting my career off on a fun note. They set the culture in the office which is why I have fond memories and smiles when I think of the engineers in 620.

Monica Olivares Hirvela - *Love it and Engineers can be a lot of fun. ;-) Married one. LOL!*

Margaret A. Volk - *Ahhh...the Purple Phantom...they don't make them like that anymore! :-) A great group of guys!*

Day 154
Ollie Williams

Ollie Williams and I have been friends since elementary school; she is very sweet, compassionate and genuine. I have never seen her when she wasn't smiling.

Life has not changed her and I love that about her. She is someone who sees the glass half full. Ollie is very encouraging and giving to everyone. She frequently sends me inspirational text messages which are received just when I need them.

She celebrated her birthday not too long ago and I was there to share in the festivities. It was wonderful observing her do what she does best: serving others and making everyone feel welcome.

I am very grateful to have known her all these years and for our friendship to remain close and caring. It is great to have friends you can be yourself with. Smiles back at you my dear friend.

Susan Downs - *Friends like this are so rare. You and Ollie are very lucky.*

Judy McCurdy Mitchell - *Another awesome story. True friends are like rare gems--and a gift from God!*

Day 155
Beth Doublin

My sister's ex-sister in law has a heart bigger than Texas; Beth D. is the sweetest lady. I am grateful that she is not just nice to my sister and my niece but to everyone in our family.

My Mom had surgery several years before she passed away and my sisters and I were in the waiting area wishing for some snacks and soft drinks. We did not want to leave because we were afraid we would miss the doctor. In walks Beth with a HUGE athletic size travel bag with chips, cookies, peanut butter crackers, nuts, water, juice, soft drinks and more stuff than all the people in the waiting area could eat.

Beth never misses an opportunity to give to others – not just family, anyone in need or want. She is someone you can't say I wish I had so-and-so because she is like Jeannie–she comes out of the bottle with it.

Everybody loves Beth.

Judy McCurdy Mitchell - *She sounds like an angel. The world needs more people like Beth.*

Carolyn Gray - *Judy, she is. Her husband (who was as giving) passed away a few months ago. I think everyone they ever spoke to attended his services. It was not held at their church...too many people. The comments ppl made about him were spot on. They both let their light shine.*

Judy McCurdy Mitchell - *What a wonderful testimony these two ppl shared. I hope she is doing okay after the loss of her husband.*

Susan Downs - *I just love people like that who can anticipate your needs and fill them without even being asked. We all have that gift within us--it's called empathy. Beth and her husband sound like very empathetic and kind people.*

Day 156
Dr. Thomas P. McHugh

Dr. Thomas P. McHugh and his gorgeous wife Katherine spoke at the luncheon meeting of WOAMTEC, The Woodlands today. Dr. McHugh is not only an internationally renowned board certified plastic surgeon, he is a dynamic speaker.

Dr. McHugh took time from his very, very busy schedule to speak to us about plastic surgery, Botox, and breast augmentation in terminology that everyone in the room could understand. He has a great sense of humor. I love his high level of integrity and his displayed passion for what he does.

My expressions of gratitude are extended to Dr. McHugh and Katherine

McHugh for unselfishly sharing with the group today. Thank you Katherine and Dr. McHugh.

Day 157
Frances Bryant

My guard is always up when I am asked "have you ever tried–" That question is generally a dead giveaway that someone is trying to get me to try something I don't recognize nor eaten it before.

I was in Little Rock and Frances Bryant asked me if I had ever tried alligator. Well, I had not but after watching her eat alligator, I decided to try it. It did not taste like chicken! It was not bad; however, I didn't care to try it again. When I say I don't care for a particular food, believe me I have tried it and I don't care to try it again.

The good thing about experiencing new things is that I don't have to wonder because I know firsthand. I am grateful that Frances made the alligator look so appetizing and that was brave enough to try it. Thanks for the experience, Frances.

Day 158
Texas Repertory Theatre

For several years my Mom and I attended every show at the Texas Repertory Theater here in Spring. Everyone knew her and doted over her and she loved every minute of it. Page Allen would engage my Mom in a conversation and tell her how happy she was to see her.

About three months after my Mom passed away I went to the theater and before anyone spoke to me, they all asked "where's Pheobie?" When I told them my Mom had passed away they were speechless and I was in tears.

Page, an artist/painter, made a beautiful sympathy card and presented it to me the next time I was at the theater. I was touched and very grateful that she took time to personally make the card and add her comforting words.

Susan Downs - *I always appreciate people paying special attention to the oldest and youngest in our society. It touches my heart as well. We are all one big family anyway.*

Judy McCurdy Mitchell *-That card was made w true love and compassion!! Those are the best ones!! Wonderful story!!*

Carolyn Gray *- Judy McCurdy Mitchell, you are so right. I was so touched.*

Carolyn Gray - *Susan Downs, I am very much the same way. Our youth and seniors should not be over looked.*

Day 159
Ann Houston

When you have a death in your family, people want to say something but often just don't know what to say. I am grateful that there were a number of people who comforted me after my Mom passed away. They all had just the right thing to say to me.

Ann Houston shared a story with me that helped her through her grieving process. Ann sent the story to my e-mail and I read it several times. The story – Here She Comes – helped me through a very difficult time in my life. I have shared it others they all told me it really helped them with their loss.

I don't think Ann or the author will mind me sharing the story--Here she comes.

(The following little story is by Henry Van Dyke and was in a pamphlet hospice gave Ann.)

"I am standing upon the seashore. A ship at my side spreads her sails to the morning breeze and starts for the blue ocean. She is an object of beauty and strength. I stand and watch her until at length she hangs like a speck of white cloud just where the sea and sky come to mingle with each other.

Then someone at my side says: "There, she is gone!"

"Gone where?"

Gone from my sight. That is all. She is just as large in mast and hull and spar as she was when she left my side and she is just as able to bear the load of living freight to her destined port.

Her diminished size is in me, not in her. And just at the moment when someone at my side says: "There, she is gone!" There are other eyes watching her coming, and other voices ready to take up the glad shout: "Here she comes!"

And that is dying."

Our Lord and Savior along with other loved ones are shouting "Here she comes!"

Thanks Ann for sharing Her she comes with me. It helped me through my deep pain.

Carolyn Gray - *Judy McCurdy Mitchell, this story helped me tremendously. Ann told me it would. So worth sharing.*

Karen Moore - *Great analogy and if fits perfectly with my thoughts on passing away. A loss on this side is a gain on the other. Sorry to hear your mom has passed but I imagine the happiness she must have felt to be in the presence of pure love of the Lord.*

Cyndy Justice - *So beautiful. Thanks for sharing it with us.*

Carolyn Gray - *Karen Moore, my Mom was excited as she entered the presence of the Lord. Her last words let us know how happy and excited she was.*

Day 160
Liz Plaster

After my Mom passed away, I was able to get through the grieving process through prayer and many many compassionate and caring friends. Liz Plaster was one who helped me through that dark period in my life. The amazing part about her helping me through my darkest moment is that she was working through her own moments.

Liz unselfishly gave of herself to help me and I am grateful for he...r friendship. Her calls and cards were timely and much appreciated. Liz listened as I talk through my Mom's quick passing away. I was numb and probably wasn't speaking in a coherent manner but that did not matter to her–she listened.

Although she was going to her own personal "moments" during the same time, she showed me that she was as concerned about me getting better through her acts of kindness. Thank you Liz - you are phenomenal!

Brenda Lee - *Friends like her are rare and I know you appreciate her.*

Susan Downs - *It was probably therapy for her too, just to listen.*

Roselyn Holub Sluis - *And in d end , The love u give is equal to d love u take.*

Day 161
Michelle Harden

I met Michelle Harden at a Powerful Women International (PWI) luncheon and she invited me to the live taping of her television show, Kingdom View. She was interviewing First Ladies. I arrived at the event to find excitement everywhere.

There were lots of new faces, vendors, food and a number of very impressive First Ladies scheduled to be interviewed by Michelle; there were some powerful, powerful women of God present in that room. The taping of the show was interesting to watch because Randy, Michelle's husband was making it all happen. He has a very gentle spirit and was fascinating to observe.

I was grateful for being invited and even more grateful to Michelle for making arrangements for me to be in the audience because I was not able to register prior to the show. She told me to "come on" and I am glad she did. Attending a live taping of a show is very different from being a part of a live show. It was a wonderful experience.

I have attended other tapings of her show and they were just as fascinating to be a part of as the first show. Michelle and her husband are a magnificent team.

Toni Trahan Shirley - *Sounds very uplifting for ever-active you!*

Day 162
Bishop Larry Brandson

Bishop Larry Brandon and I were classmates in Leadership Shreveport. He was well respected by the entire group.

I am grateful that Bishop let his light shine everywhere: in class sessions, on the bus, at restaurants–everywhere. I visited Bishop's church on many occasions and he was the same at church as he was as a participant in Leadership Shreveport.

I attended the 8 a.m. service at my church so I was able to often attend the 11 a.m. service at Bishop's church. I loved that he was all about winning souls, not how people dressed, walked or talked which helped people feel welcomed and loved.

His church, Praise Temple, was also concerned about the surrounding community and it showed by the church sponsored activities.

It was wonderful seeing all that Praise Temple gave to the community and how much Bishop gave of himself. An awesome man of God.

Susan Downs - *Wow! I love it when a church shares a common vision for being involved in the surrounding community. It is such a powerful testimony when you walk the walk and not just talk the talk.*

Day 163
Thu Nguyen

OMGosh, there is someone out there who is more social than I am–and I am grateful that she is my friend. Thu Nguyen – that's To Win!

Thu has supported me by purchasing "the whole series" (her words) of my books. I have told her they are not in a series but she still chooses to refer to them as a series. I can't stop her so I am grateful that I have a spokesperson out there.

Whether attending a gathering at her lovely home or attending a networking event, Thu is the same: friendly and looking for ways to help others.

Thu loves to travel and take pictures of her excursions and that makes me happy because her photos make me feel like I was on the trip with her. Some of my favorite photos of her are the ones where she has that little drum at a parade - way too cute and funny.

Toni Trahan Shirley - *I like her already!*

Judy McCurdy Mitchell - *Sounds like a fun loving lady*

Day 164
Terri

Expressing gratitude for favor shown to me is something I try not to overlook. Terri, the manager at a facility in North Carolina extended favor to me a couple of years ago.

I was contracted to work for a month in North Carolina. I had less than a week's notice so I was scrambling to find a place to stay and I didn't want to be in a hotel room for a month. I contacted Terri because I stayed at the extended stay facility before; however, she told me she did not have any vacancies but she put me on a waiting list. I reluctantly made reservations at a hotel.

The next day, Terri contacted me to say she would be able to accommodate me and since I left the unit spotless on my prior stay, she was waiving the deposit! I was grateful because she had a vacancy, she called me and she waived the deposit–I call that favor and warrants my expression of gratitude. Small acts of kindness matter.

Susan Downs - *And it also pays to leave your hotel room clean. You never know who will notice and remember.*

Carolyn Gray - *Amen Momma Susan Downs!*

Day 165
Sheryl Sitts

Sheryl Sitts shared a really cool tip with me several years ago as I was leaving a networking event that I will always be grateful for.

As I was leaving the event, people were coming in, I spoke and started to walk out when Sheryl suggested I exchange business cards with them and tell them something about the event. I did and that has started a new networking tradition for me. It is interesting that I always remember more about that person than I do about others I met. And for the person entering the event, it is like an icebreaker for them.

Not sure where she learned and "one for the road" in networking but I love it and grateful that she shared it with me!

Juslyn Woods Young - *Ms Carolyn Gray you're so full of wisdom.*

Deanna Ooley - *I love Sheryl Yancey Sitts. She always has good ideas.*

Toni Trahan Shirley - *Cast your net, you pretty fisherwoman of people, cast it far and wide!*

Sheryl Yancey Sitts - *Thank you Carolyn Gray and Deanna Ooley. :-)*

Curtis R Smith - *Awesome advice*

Day 166
Freddie Garnett, Sr.

I know how to spit shine leather shoes, pack a footlocker, play cards and cook liver and onions because my Dad taught me these things.

Dad taught me more than just these things; however, these are just a few of the unusual things he taught me. I needed to know how to shine shoes because that was important to him. His shoes were always shined–always. He loved to play cards and sometimes I was the only one around to play cards with him.

Although my Mom did the majority of cooking in our family, Dad liked to cook liver. I am so sure he taught me so that he could be relieved of that duty when he wanted liver.

My Dad taught us to work hard, be respectful, courteous and compassionate. He impressed the importance of getting an education to us on a daily basis. Dad (and Mom) did not allow us girls to use our gender as a reason or excuse for not advancing or achieving something. We knew to try harder if we didn't make it the first time.

Dad showed me how confident he was when he stepped out with a pink dress shirt and a pink and grey tie before it was cool for men to wear colored shirts. Dad was very social and I am told that I am just like him. In addition to being social, he was quick witted and a jokester – he always had a comeback as well as a hardy laugh. I do know that I inherited the laugh.

I am grateful for a fun loving father who was light hearted but could get very serious on short notice.

Judy McCurdy Mitchell - *Sounds like a very special dad. What a lovely story!! You r a very blessed woman.*

Curtis R Smith - *Spit shines, liver/onions and cards all bring back positive memories. Thanks for sharing! Have a blessed day!*

Carolyn Gray - *Curtis Smith, thank you. Wishing you a Very Happy Father's Day.*

Carolyn Gray - *Judy McCurdy Mitchell, my Dad was soooo much fun.*

Toni Trahan Shirley - *Carolyn Gray, it sounds like you fit right in with your dad - such a good thing to remember.*

Madge Fletcher - *I can remember you telling me that one of the first things you noticed about men were their shoes!!!*

Carolyn Gray - *That's why Madge Fletcher...my Dad did that to me!*

Susan Downs - *My Dad taught me how to play cards as well, and I got so good that I beat him frequently. He would always ask at the end of a game, "Do you want to play again?"*

Susan Downs - *My Dad also taught me the names of trees, plants, flowers and birds. He taught me to identify constellations. What would we do without our Dads?*

Day 167
Leadership Shreveport

As a participant of Leadership Shreveport, I was exposed to landmarks and the history of Shreveport as well as the capitol of Louisiana.

I am grateful for the opportunity to have walked the halls of the state capitol in Baton Rouge, personally meet my representatives and to participate in a real discussion on the floor. It was fascinating to witness the activity first hand.

I am very grateful that my Medical Center Director invested in me and allowed me to attend the activities offered by the program sponsored by the Shreveport Chamber of Commerce. I met a group of wonderful professionals that I am still in contact with.

Being a part of the program gave me a better appreciation of how our elected officials serve us. This was an awesome educational experience!

Day 168
Mitzi Norris

The first time I requested authorized absence to attend a national board meeting for The American Society for Microbiologist by boss summons me to his office for an explanation.

His specific statement when I walked into his office was: "I didn't know you were a Microbiologist." My specific response was: "I'm not!" He was speechless. I had to explain the whole story to him.

The story was simple, Mitzi Norris was a board member and they needed a nomination for a Public Member – she nominated me and I was selected as the Public Member for the National Board. I was so extremely grateful for her considering me as a nominee and even more grateful when I was notified that I had been selected and appointed to the board.

After he got over the shock that an HR Manager was appointed to a National Microbiology Board, we both had a good chuckle. We both said: there is always a first time for everything. He approved my absence and I was off to one awesome educational experience.

Susan Downs - *Smart boss.*

Day 169
Art Johnson

Having Art Johnson as an office mate for a short time was what the doctor ordered for me. Art was like a walking King James Version of the Bible. Well, he was actually a Presbyterian minister who really knew the Word and didn't mind sharing it with others.

He was calm, caring and easy going. Sharing an office with him actually caused me to study the Bible more and live what I learned.

As a Staffing Specialist, Art could recruit and fill vacancies faster than three specialists. In addition to sharing scriptures with me, he also shared his years and years of staffing knowledge.

I am grateful that he had me memorize scriptures and that he delivered the sermon he preached on Sunday again on Monday–to me! RIP my friend.

Judy McCurdy Mitchell - *What an inspiring story. Fantastic testimony!!!*

Frances Johnson - *Have not thought of Art in many years.............he was truly a great guy to know.*

Donald Reel - *Art was one great man. I really enjoyed talking to him and listening to his sage advice!*

Day 170
Bertha Johnson

True confession – never in a million years did I think I would be grateful for Aunt Bertha! Aunt Bertha was my great aunt who was well traveled, affluent, direct and very outspoken.

When we all piled into the car on Sunday afternoon heading to Aunt Bertha's house, we prayed that we wouldn't have to eat dinner. Why? Because she MADE us eat beets and all that green stuff on our plates, sit up straight at the table and ask to be excused when we finished eating. Even at home, we could sometimes get away without eating the green stuff, not with her.

I am grateful she MADE us eat our veggies because it gave me an appreciation and love for broccoli, okra, greens, spinach, asparagus, and anything else green as well as beets.

It is funny how things happen; I am considered the Aunt Bertha for my nieces and nephews. I had a great role model – Aunt Bertha.

Rosemary Behrens - *Beets, yuck!*

Melanie Dunn - *It's funny how things come full circle, huh? :)*

Janet Anne Watson *Stramrood - Beets are awesome :-). One if my favorite veggies.*

Carolyn Gray - *Melanie Dunn, I am talking FULL circle! How have u been?*

Rosemary Behrens - *Janet, I'll pass you mine under the table. . . LOL*

Carolyn Gray - *Rosemary did you not have an Aunt Bertha or a GiGi to supervise the eating of the beets?!*

Rosemary Behrens - *nope, just a Mama who had already done the raising of four kids ahead of me....and she liked beets so we had them often....I've come to discover that brussel sprouts aren't so bad if you don't start with frozen ones and overcook them...LOL!*

Tina Marie Spataro-*Eid - I must agree with Aunt Bertha, all of those things are worth eating!*

Carolyn Gray - *Rosemary Behrens, I love brussel sprouts. I have learned to prepare the frozen one to make them yummy. I'll share my recipe. Not necessarily healthy by yummy.*

Carolyn Gray - *Tina Marie Spataro-Eid, I agree w/her now but then, a whole nother story.*

Deborah Higdon - *Is that who taught you to make gizzards and rice? I still consider it a special treat!*

Carolyn Gray - *Oh no, not her! Deborah Higdon, I haven't had gizzards and rice in forever....think I'l make us some for lunch.*

Theresa Honeycheck - *Love that message!!!*

Toni Trahan Shirley - *And you are a great role model to many youngsters and adults. Thank you Aunt Bertha!!*

Curtis R Smith - *Thanks for the blessings of Aunt Bertha's. GOOD eating and now i appreciate the health value*

Michelle Mihalko - *Don't think I could ever do the beets!*

Carolyn Gray - *Michelle Mihalko, beets are delicious and soooo good for you. Have you tried them as an adult?*

Carolyn Gray - *Curtis R Smith, you are spot on...I appreciate the health more that I can express. Grateful!*

Toni Trahan Shirley - *Gizzards are delicious and good for you, too...just cook them low and slow so they get really tender!!*

Toni Trahan Shirley - *Add some to a chicken gumbo, too!*

Carolyn Gray - *Toni Trahan Shirley, I have...yum!*

Day 171
Toneal Jackson

Toneal Jackson, radio host and author interviewed me and I was excited. Toneal is from Chicago and I was officially being interviewed by someone outside of the great state of Texas.

I enjoyed chatting with Toneal as we discussed relationships and all that she does to help others have better relationships. Being on her radio show gave me a phenomenal opportunity to share and learn from someone who is committed (as I am) to helping others have better relationships.

During the interview, she shared some of her life challenges and how she has been able to overcome. Toneal is an inspiration to those of us who have had an opportunity to listen to her story. I am grateful that this young lady is authentic and transparent which allows her to help so many people.

Listening to her you might think she is well beyond her years; however, Toneal is just a wise Godly woman.

Day 172
Christine Alexander

I met Christine Alexander while attending Kingdom View Talk Show. She was sitting quietly minding her own business. She was not bother a soul and I walked over and introduced myself and asked her to move to the section where I was sitting so she wouldn't have to sit alone. Sometimes, you can't mind you own business and be left alone!

Chris allowed me to ask the question: what do you do? She told me all about the League of Extraordinary Women. I was not familiar with the League but found what she was doing intriguing. She devoted an enormous amount of time gathering helpful information to share online with others. While I like all of the topics, Marriage Monday and Think about it Thursday are my personal favorites.

She did all this in addition to being a Mom and completing her undergraduate degree. I was impressed and grateful that she allowed me to enter into her quiet space to learn about her and what she does for others. Kudos Chris.

Elizabeth Fazio Wisnoski - *That's my Carolyn Gray gotta luv you!*

Carolyn Gray - *Elizabeth Fazio Wisnoski, I had to do it. I tried not bothering her but something came over me!*

Elizabeth Fazio Wisnoski - *I know that feeling!!*

Carolyn Gray - *IF anyone can relate, it would be you Elizabeth Fazio Wisnoski!*

Day 173
Willie Barley

My paternal grandmother was the best. She was a storybook grandmother. We called her Gramps. She was a seamstress, an excellent cook and baker. Gramps allowed me to help her cook–I got to stir and I thought I was cooking! I still love to stir – not cook, just stir.

I would find dresses in the Sears and Spiegel's catalogs and Gramps would purchase the same fabric and make the item for me. I had Keds, black and white saddle oxfords and black patent leather shoes to go with my outfits. I loved loved wearing dresses.

Before my grandmother passed away, she told my grandfather to make sure I got her sewing machine. The joke in the family was: why would Gramps leave me her machine since I was the only one in my family who could not sew. I saw no need to rush over to pick up the machine but Pops kept asking me to get it and I finally did.

On day, I bought a pattern and some fabric and started sewing. Gramps would be so proud of me because I learned to sew–I taught myself. Grateful that my grandmother asked Pops to make sure I got the machine. On my own, I never would have purchased a sewing machine which means I never would have learned to sew. Gramps believed in me. Grandmothers are so awesome.

Day 174
Alex Nora

In this modern time of everything technological, I am grateful for Alex Nora preparing a cd of a recorded teleconference for me.

I gave Alex a recording of my teleconference and he turned it into an awesome piece of work. He added music between topics, faded out background noise and provided me with a professional sounding cd.

What I was looking for was a cd to offer as an "opt in" gift on my website. I did not imagine the recording I gave him would or could sound like the finished cd he produced. When I dropped the recording off, he asked me a few questions about the type of music I liked and that was all he needed.

Alex and his lovely wife Brandy made this a painless experience for me –they are both so giving and accommodating.

Brandy Nora - *He is pretty amazing isn't he? U r so sweet!*

Carolyn Gray - *Brandy Nora, yes he is and so are you.*

Susan Downs - *Now that is going above and beyond the call of duty. What a sweetheart!*

Toni Trahan Shirley - *Aren't people wonderful and generous! But then, you deserve it.*

Carolyn Gray - *Thank you Toni Trahan Shirley, you are in the generous group.*

Day 175
Dr. Greg and Azita Reger

The expression "we don't know what we don't know" resonates with me everything I hear someone speak at WOAMTEC, The Woodlands.

Dr. Reger and his lovely wife Azita Reger, presented at our last luncheon. Dr. Reger explained the causes and solutions of varicose and spider veins and other procedures and solutions. I was paying attention to what he was discussing because he made it very interesting. Actually what he did was explain in terms that I understood.

He removed some of my fears and concerns about the pain involved, the thought of having scars as well as how quickly you are able to resume your routine after a procedure.

I am grateful Dr. Reger made time to present to our group. His level of commitment to ensuring that we got information firsthand speaks volumes. Thank you Azita and Dr. Reger.

Susan Downs - *Love to listen to speakers like that. I think you have that ability as well, Carolyn.*

Sue Kittrell - *Wow! Did you send him a card letting him know this? Do busy doctors check their Facebook page? Send Out Cards is a quick simple way to get your thank you sent directly. :)*

Day 176
William Gray

I am not a picky eater; however, there are some things I have not eaten just because. One thing I will say is that I will try something before saying "I don't like it." When I say "I don't care for it," I have tried it and don't like it.

Several years ago, I told my brother-in-law, Bill Gray, I had never eaten duck. He was surprised and decided to prepare dinner for us one evening. He roasted the duck with all the trimmings and it was delicious. I can honestly say I enjoyed the duck. So when asked if I would like to have duck, I can say yes.

Telling Bill you have not eaten a particular food is like asking for it! He loves to give and serve others. I am grateful that he is not just my brother-in-law; he is a very good friend and one of my greatest cheerleaders. He is a genuine all around wonderful person.

Day 177
Steve Fenley

I can't act, sing or dance but I have a love and appreciation for those who can and I love seeing them on stage. My favorite place to enjoy some exceptional acting, singing and dancing is the Texas Repertory Theater in Spring.

I am extremely grateful to be a part of the volunteer group at The Texas Rep. I am not just a volunteer, I am an active part of the theater–after all, I know Steve Fenley, the Artistic Director at The Texas Rep and he knows me! (Just call and ask him if you think I am joking.) Steve is humble and can be seen doing a little bit of everything around the theater.

During some of our chats, Steve has educated me on all things theater. Steve loves loves the theater and doesn't mind sharing with others. I enjoy watching his face light up as he talks about his experiences and different productions performed at Texas Rep.

Every time I see Steve in a play, I tell him "that was the best ever." He can act, sing and dance and always out does himself. He is very talented. My gratitude to Steve for being so genuine and easy to talk to about the theater; he is totally AWESOME!

Day 178
Jimmie Long

My aunt, Tee, had five boys and my Mom had six girls (and two boys) so to get her "girl fix," she spent time with her nieces.

Tee was a good cook like my Mom – she makes the best oyster dressing and fries mouthwatering chicken. Yum! Tee was not as strict as my Mom. She let us get away with not going to bed on time, eating breakfast in our gown and for my sisters who did not like wearing shoes, she let them walk around without shoes. I think she did that because she does not like wearing shoes!

Tee is genuine, down to earth and straight forward. Never do you have to wonder what's on her mind because she will tell you. She loves to play cards and she can PLAY cards; it is hard to beat her playing cards. You can give her a rock and she makes a big deal over it. To this day, my sisters and I marvel at how grateful she is for really really small things.

After my Mom passed away, her role changed in that she gets more calls and visits from us. The only thing we can't do is interfere with her BINGO playing. We know not to visit on the evenings she plays BINGO because she will leave us sitting in her living room to entertain ourselves! Nothing comes between her and her BINGO.

Day 179
Deborah Wallace

Looking through our family photo albums a few years ago I noticed there were very few photos of me. I always stayed behind the camera for several reasons.

When it came time for me to provide a photo to one of my organizations for the member directory, I panicked and seriously did not know what to do. One of the members was able to get a great deal for us with Barfield Photography and that solved one of my problems.

My concern-- a huge concern was how the photo would turn out. No worries, Deborah Wallace took care of that for me. She took pictures of me until I got tired. Deborah had me turn, then lean forward, tilt my head up then down until she was satisfied with the shot.

She told me she would send the photo to my e-mail. True to her word, the photo was in my e-mail a few hours later. I was pleased and very grateful for Deborah being patient and persistent. She is very professional and passionate about her work. Awesome photographer who loves what she does.

Day 180
Minister Jackie Hill

My pastor has been a speaker at Minister Jackie Hill's Women's Conference for several years. We were blessed to have the conference at our church one year.

Minister Jackie is authentic and transparent. She has a testimony and she doesn't mind sharing it. The first year I attended the conference, Minister Jackie encouraged us to be courageous and bold and stop selling out for a car payment because we are worth more than a car payment!

She is a powerful woman of God who is direct yet compassionate.

Last year, she invited me to participate on the panel the first night of the conference. The topic was about relationships. I was grateful to be a part of conference as a panel member and honored that she invited me. I was in the company of so many awesome women.

Minister Jackie is a mighty prayer warrior–and I love being in her company.

Day 181
Johnnie Mae Curtis

I love pearls. I wear pearls with almost everything–dressy and casual clothes, sweat pants, t-shirts and everything in between.

My grandmother, Mime wore beautiful necklaces: single strands, double, triple strands and more. I admired the way she dressed; she was sharp – from head to toe. She wore hats, gloves and her shoes and handbags always matched. Mime was an elegantly and stylish dresser. I took from her what I loved most about the way she dressed and that was her accessories which included nice watches.

I love nice watches and necklaces, and rarely do I go out without them. I have been teased by many and called June Cleaver because of my pearls. I have been teased about clutching my pearls when shocked about something or if I am getting ready to express my candid opinion.

I owe that girly part of me to Mime. I have jewelry boxes of beautiful beaded necklaces in all colors. I hit estate sales, antique shops and garage sales looking for beaded necklaces.

My gratitude to my grandmother for helping me appreciate the beauty of beads and pearl necklaces and accessories.

Day 182
Kellie Mazzilli

My sister loves fresh flowers, so I stopped by Kreations by Kellie during Nurse's Week to order some for her. Kellie Mazzilli told me she would send something really pretty. She asked me my sister's favorite color, and gave her my sister's office number just in case.

The just in case turned out that Kellie was unable to deliver the flowers because my sister was not at work that day nor the next two days. I had to locate my sister; that was unusual. I found her at home, and she was very ill. At that point, she was in trouble with me for not calling to let me know she was ill.

Kellie told me she would deliver the arrangement the following week. I am grateful to Kellie for delivering a fresh arrangement the following week. My sister was elated to have beautiful flowers in her favorite color waiting for her when she returned to work from her illness.

My sister sent me a picture of the arrangement and it was beautiful. Kellie, thank you for going the extra mile (literally miles) to deliver the arrangement. Exceptional customer service!

Day 183
Tony Gambone

My friend is the host of a weekly radio show and she honored me by asking me to host the show for her. After I said yes, I realized I knew absolutely nothing about hosting a radio show.

She assured me it was easy and she was confident I would do a good job. Well, with my notes in hand that she prepared for me, I took the plunge. I contacted Tony Gambone, the producer of the show for further instructions. Tony walked me through the process and he also assured me I would do just fine.

It was show time and I was cool as a cucumber – really. I reviewed the note sheet and with Tony's crash course, I was ready. I was live–doing just fine then I forgot to say something and there went my coolness! I was nervous; however, I had to quickly regroup because I was on the air. I could hardly wait for the first break. I needed a drink of water and to catch my breath.

Tony came on the line and told me I was doing just fine. That was the longest hour! I am grateful for my friend and Tony holding my hand and the opportunity to experience the behind the scene operations of a radio show. I have a much better appreciation of what the radio host has to do to have a successful show, especially the part of being live. You don't have a "do over" opportunity. Truly, "is what it is." I enjoyed myself and was glad my friend was back the following week.

Day 184
D'Andra Anderson

Today was an awesome day. I attended a great networking luncheon where we celebrated the birthday of our chapter director; the second thing was meeting D'Andra Anderson.

I needed copies of some prior year documents so I contacted the financial institution and my mindset was–put on your boxing gloves. Well, D'Andra was extremely accommodating which made me shift from fight mode to nice mode. D'Andra was the honey and I was the fly! She located the documents I needed, printed them and I was all set.

Talking about bending over backwards, D'Andra provided exceptional customer service and I had to share with her my initial attitude. We both laughed. D'Andra is the type of employee everyone one would love to have on their staff. I am grateful she was there to serve me and offer further assistance if I needed it.

Lesson learned: don't enter the room with preconceived negative ideas about how you will be treated. You might be helped by D'Andra or someone just like her. Grateful for the small things in my life.

Day 185
Mills Brown

My maternal grandfather was sometimes the brunt of our humor. Of course our comments were said behind his back. The humor about Nampa was that he ALWAYS found something nice to say about everyone.

Our favorite thing to make fun of was his comment about our youngest sister. She would boil water for his morning cup of instant coffee and he would say: "my granddaughter sure knows how to boil water." We thought that was humorous because most people made the comment about others who can "not boil water." He had more substantive compliments about everyone else. She can now do more than boil water – she can really cook. As I age, I have come to appreciate Nampa's ability to find something genuine and nice to say about everyone.

He loved orange slices and offered them to everyone. I don't care for orange slices but I took them and when he left the room, I would put them back in the bag. I could not make myself say "no thank you" when he offered them because I felt it would hurt his feelings.

Blessed Assurance was his favorite hymn and he would crank that old hymn up any time of day or night and sing his heart out. He sang the entire hymn before stopping.

Nampa was a very sweet, loving and kind man who loved to share with others.

Day 186
Dr. Crystal Broussard

Telling me to lose 20 pounds was like telling me to walk to Austin from Houston. Just wasn't gonna happen. Not that I don't need to lose 20 pounds, my mindset was to lose 10 pounds but not 20 and at my leisure!

Dr. Crystal Broussard spoke at WOAMTEC, The Woodlands Chapter luncheon and convinced me that I should lose the weight. How did she do that in a presentation? She told how she lost 100 pounds herself and why she lost the weight.

Dr. Broussard explained how losing 5 pounds would decrease your blood pressure. I thought about that for a second and it hit me– is losing 5 pounds would decrease my blood pressure, 20 pounds would really improve me health. She encouraged us to take action before we developed health issues.

I am grateful for Dr. Broussard being transparent and for taking time from her practice to share her story about how she gained the weight and also how she lost the weight. I am on a mission to lose weight – 5 pounds at a time. I am on the road to better health.

Day 187
Sonia Moorthy

Sonia Moorthy is so much fun. On day, she stuffed me in the back of her vehicle with a bicycle. It was hot as I don't know what and I am glad I only had to travel about a mile under those conditions.

The story about being stuffed in her car was really a humanitarian gesture on our part. A little boy fell on the bike trail next to our house and banged himself up pretty bad. He was crying and I rushed to his rescue to render aid. Sonia drove up as I was trying to get the young man to let me take him home. To his credit and good teaching of his parents, he would not get in the car.

Quick thinking on our part made us decided to put the bicycle in the back of Sonia's SUV and take it home. One small problem – Sonia had "stuff" on the front seat so I got into the back and she closed the hatch! We laughed all the way to the little boy's house. It took him several minutes to limp home so I was in the back for a good while. When we met his mother to give her the bike I was relieved to get out of the back of the SUV.

When we re-told the story, it was even funnier as everyone who heard it wondered how we got involved. Sonia and I had a good time with that story.

I am grateful that Sonia has a wonderful sense for humor; however, I am most grateful that she completes my son. She is generous, caring, compassionate and loving.

Day 188
Barron Richmond

For a number of years, I have used an expression I learned from my Personnel Officer, Barron Richmond. The Barron as we affectionately referred to him was a southern gentleman and an optimist.

If I mentioned I could not do something because it would take too long, he would say "oh, you can hold a bear in a snuff can for that long!" Now, the funny thing was I had to hold that bear for a week or sometimes months. Regardless of the length of time, he always told me I could hold a bear in a snuff can. It was humorous as I imagined myself trying to put a huge bear in a snuff can. I have to admit that thinking about it helped me to temporarily forget about my problem.

I found myself sharing that expression with others and sometimes having to explain to some "what in the world is a snuff can." I recently told someone they could hold a bear in a snuff can and they had a hearty laugh.

It was a pleasure working with Mr. Richmond as he mentored and encouraged me. He also protected me from and shared with me how to tactfully and diplomatically communicate with aggressive managers. Grateful for mentors like The Barron.

Day 189
Leo Luka

Another expression I am grateful for is "don't be like the cow that followed the crocked path." This expression was shared with the staff during a staff meeting. It was not very palatable because it came from a supervisor who was somewhat acerbic.

The context in which this expression was used was not positive and I took it as an admonishment. The specific incident was someone (honestly, it was not me!) prepared a cut and paste document (literally) that had more than its fair share of incorrect information.

Lesson learned – if you cut and paste, read the document for accuracy before releasing it. Not a hard lesson but a very valuable one and I am grateful that I learned this one early in my career. I have shared this with others but with a softer delivery.

Realizing the supervisor who delivered the message was not the most pleasant person, I decided to take what I wanted from the comment and move forward. Sometime we learn things in adverse or unpleasant conditions. Still grateful!

Day 190
Slavyanka

There is a lady at the market where I shop who just inspires me. She is the hardest working person I have observed in a long time. She retrieves carts from the parking lot, cleans up spills on isle whatever AND bags groceries.

She is like a ninja! I see her in one area of the store and when I go down another isle, she is there. Honestly, by the time I get to the checkout she is there bagging groceries. Totally beyond me. Her name is Slavyanka and I am grateful that she is so engaged in what she does for all of us who shop there. Slavyanka is always smiling and offering to help. I don't know her story but I need to find out. I gave her a tip and I thought she was going to cry. She thanked me four times before I left the store. Then I wanted to cry.

As I backed out of the parking lot, I thought about a quote: No act of kindness, no matter how small is ever wasted ~ Aesop

I am grateful for Slavyanka's kindness and dedication to what she does... she would probably tell me she is just doing her job. Thank you Slavyanka.

Day 191
Naomi–Louetta Station of the Post Office

A visit to the post office general causes one to have some negative comments upon arrival and departure. Such is not the case at my branch of the post office.

Naomi is a postal worker at my branch who makes my visit to the post office pleasant. Although there may be a long line, she greets every customer with a smile and asks them how they are doing. She is knowledgeable, patient and extremely helpful.

Because I visit the post office regularly, I have plenty of opportunities to observe the postal workers at the counter and I must commend them for the exceptional customer service they provide. I am grateful that most of the time I am serviced by Naomi.

On the rare occasion when there is no one behind me, Naomi and I get to chat briefly. It is a pleasure to be service by her.

Day 192
Daniel at GoDaddy

I am trying hard to educate myself on technology related stuff; however I run into challenges all too often. When that happens, I call tech support for help.

I am grateful for Daniel at GoDaddy.com for bailing me out of a recent situation. Daniel was soooo patient as he repeated the steps a few times trying to help me. When he realized I was a techno peasant, he paused and said "let's start over." I could tell in his voice that he was not frustrated and did not mind helping me. That is not always the case when I call tech support for assistance.

Good customer service is important to me and I really appreciate the tech support representatives at Go Daddy. I have been truly fortunate to have a representative who does not mind helping. I suspect that Go Daddy has a phenomenal training program for their reps because they want us to keep coming back–and with customer service like that, I will keep coming back.

Day 193
MCABW Diplomat Team

When working on a team and the final project is awesome, sometimes we forget to thank and appreciate the entire team, not this girl!

As a co-team leader of the Montgomery County Association of Business Women (MCABW) Diplomat Team, I am grateful that I work with a wonderful co-team leader, Anna Ryan (Keller Williams Realty, Conroe). Anna and I work great together...like a tag team. However, this is not about me and Anna; this is about expressing gratitude for our AWESOME team.

Each month, the Diplomat Team is responsible for contacting the MCABW members to remind them of the scheduled monthly meetings. Once the diplomat completes their assigned calls, they notify me and their name is entered in the drawing for Diplomat Queen of the month.

We have had so much fun with crowning the Queen with a beautiful "diamond laced" tiara provided by Carol Gooch, MCABW's Founder and Executive Director. The Queen reigns for an entire month and her picture is placed on the MCABW website.

Grateful for KiKi Koymarianos (Keller Williams Realty, The Woodlands), Lou Barron (Waddell & Reed), Pat Brandt (First Choice Collision), Lisa Poppell (Upstream Investment Partners), Amber Provence (Link Magazine/GDFX Marketing), Rhonda Holst Redmon and Barb Salinas (GenuWine Tasting Room), Donna Rodriguez (Donna Rodriguez CPA, JD), Elaine Smith (Berry Hill BaJa Grill, The Woodlands), Beatrice Stair

(Love Me Bougie Boutique), Sondra Stewart, Laura Warner (Warner's Trading Post), Mary Sneed (Golden Moments Personal Care Home) and Linda Brown (Amber Springs Event Facility) for being the most amazing team to work with. The MCABW Diplomat Team Rocks!

Day 194
Kim Martin Goodall

I was introduced to Kim Martin Goodall by a mutual friend. Kim and I spoke on the phone and she invited me to be a guest on her show: Mommy to the Max.

Kim is a wife, Mommy and internet TV show host. I was honored to be a guest on her show where we discussed the importance of manners and etiquette. She asked me to plan on sending about 90 minutes with her and it took every minute of that to record the show.

Since I had attended a live recording before, I knew it would take some time. This time I was on the other side of the camera and it really makes a big difference. Just when we completed what I thought was perfect take, a dog started barking! So that was take 2. We got half way through another very good taping and the sound of a low flying airplane caused us to take 3. Ok, we were set and as the saying goes, third time is a charm and it was!

This was a great opportunity for me and the real plus was that I got to meet Kim and her lovely family.

Day 195
Davin Allums

It is very gratifying for someone to choose me to share personal matters with. My heart was overjoyed when a young man sent me a text and asked for scriptures because he wanted to be a better man of God. He said "I gave myself to the Lord and I want to go to newer heights."

I was elated for him and grateful that he wanted to share this with me. Later, we talked about his conversion further and what he shared with me made me cry (tears of joy). He said he has so much peace now and feels great. He said he apologized to his Dad because his Dad is the one who received the worst of his behavior. He also apologized to his Mom and girlfriend and asked for forgiveness.

I am getting all chocked up writing about this. My prayers are with him as I stand with him and I thank God that he has given his life to Him as a teen. He is a great young man who is now a blessed young man of God. Lord I am truly grateful that I was able to be a part of this joyous moment in his life. He is getting baptized and I will be right there.

Day 196
Christina B.

It seems I am always meeting a new BFF. Christina B. was from New York and we met at the first Women Who Win conference at New Light.

Christina's story blessed me because she "pressed" her way to that conference knowing she was going to be blessed if she could just get there. She shared with me how she heard about the conference one night while watching TV. She said she didn't have the money for trip but she registered anyway. Of course the rest of the story is she attended the conference.

I am grateful to have met Christina and share with her during the three day conference. For someone to want something so badly and to have their prayer answered the way it was answered was heartwarming–amazing! Her faith was strong and she did not waiver. She got her breakthrough and I found a new BFF.

Day 197
Jim Gray

My husband has been my greatest supporter for over forty years. He has loved, cooked, chauffeured, pampered, listened, nurtured and supported me in my many ventures. Truly opposites attract!

Jim is quiet and private and I am talkative and open, he loves calm and I am all over the place, he is very organized and I am too (in my own way!). We made a commitment to each other and have lived up to for better or worse. It has been about love, respect, patience, serving each other and forgiving.

I am grateful that I have someone who loves and cares for me. We have managed to work through our likes and dislikes. Jim doesn't mind doing the laundry; however he hates to fold sheets and I don't mind. He does not like to shop and I have gladly taken on that task. The biggie in our relationship is that I do not like to cook and he DOES. (That really works for me.)

We have this saying when one of us leaves the house – "I'll be here when you get back!" As simple as that may sound, it is comforting to know that I can look forward to another forty years with my boo!

Day 198
Curtis Smith

Curtis Smith and I are members of the International Coach Federation, Houston Charter Chapter. Curtis is outgoing, family oriented, wise, patient and compassionate.

Curtis and I have a common story – our Mothers have passed away. I have struggled with my Mom's death for a while and I am grateful to have met and chatted with Curtis. Curtis helped me to honestly give myself permission to take my time to grieve and heal. In that soft compassionate voice of his, he told me it is ok to be where I am and take as long as I need to move forward.

Sage advice from someone who knows firsthand what I might be experiencing and I accepted it. I value his friendship as well as his advice because I have been able to take baby step to get where I am today. I have been given advice and encouragement from many others and I am appreciative. I think I was ready when Curtis shared with me. I am in a great place and I thank those who have helped me get here.

Day 199
Jerry Seltzer

When I was ready to publish my book, I did an internet search and found Jerry Seltzer with DragonPencil. Jerry made the entire process so easy from the graphics to the actual printing of my book. I did not stressed over this project at all. I felt pampered and nurtured. I am extremely appreciative and grateful for the relationship I established with Jerry and the entire team at DragonPencil. They taught me "publishing lingo" which allowed me to discuss my printing needs with other printers and authors.

Day 200
Pheobie Garnett - my Mom

The darkest moment in my life has been the loss of my Mom. Through prayer and others praying for me, I have come this far truly by the grace of God.

My Mom and I were friends. We traveled together, shopped together, went to the theater together; we enjoyed each other's' company. I had the utmost respect, love and admiration for my Mom. She was a GREAT mother. She taught me to be confident, respectful, trustworthy, loyal, kind to others and to love and revere God.

She was very organized and I guess she had to be with eight children. Growing up, she cooked, baked, washed, ironed (yes, ironed) and cleaned house every day. In addition to doing all that, she was always dressed and ready to go. Her nails were perfect (never, never had chipped polish) and so was her hair. My Mom was very much the lady.

Mom gave advice to everyone "in love!" She was appreciative of her family and friends and showed it by sending thank you cards for every dinner prepared or purchased, gift or theater ticket purchased for her. It was wonderful going to the mailbox and finding a card from her.

When we came home for a visit, Mom prepared our favorite dish: macaroni and cheese and homemade lemon meringue pie for Sherrie, beans and barbeque for Johnny, spaghetti and homemade lemon meringue pie for Freddie, rice and gravy for Jan, fried pork chops for Pat and pound cake with no icing for me. Alicia and Deborah had what they wanted when they wanted it because they were within driving distance.

Mom loved to travel and visited all of us regularly which would take almost a year to make the rounds.

My Mom's prayer when we were small was to live to see all of us grow up. Her prayers were answered and she was blessed to see many of her grandchildren grow up. I am grateful that God gave us such a wonderful Mom. I miss hearing "Momma loves you; stay prayerful." I miss her terribly -- I am staying prayerful.

Day 201
Will Irwin

I am grateful for the people in my life who are willing to do what they can for others. Will Irwin, the founder of Broken Yoke Ministries, is always willing to serve. Will and I attend Embassy Church and I am forever calling on Will for something.

It does not matter if I ask him to pick up print material or banners from the printer, check the church to see if I turned all of the lights off or helping to put cds in my car when we are having an outing his answer is always "yes."

Will is active in disaster relief and is ready to go anywhere in or out of the country at the drop of a hat without question. When someone is in need, he is on his way to render aid. I love his giving spirit and how much humility he has. Thank you Will for having a servant's heart.

Day 202
Iona Alphonso

Iona Alphonso is the realtor who takes care of the buyers long after the closing. I learned how to take care of my customers from Iona through observation.

She knows the neighborhood and the surrounding area. On national holidays, Iona places a flag in our front yard. She sends cards throughout the year and will occasionally drop by to say hello. Iona was "missing" for about two months and I was concerned so I called her. She was doing fine; she changed her routine so we were missing each other.

Iona is a wealth of knowledge. When I needed to find a recycle center, I called her and she provided me with a list of nearby centers.

I am grateful that she has been a part of our "family" for the past eight years. It is comforting to know that we are not "someone she sold a house to" but someone she is truly concerned about. The special attention she gives us is so appreciated.

Day 203
Kinta Roberts

It is so gratifying to observe others as they interact with their mother. It is particularly gratifying when it is their spiritual mother.

Kinta Roberts and his spiritual Mom have had their mother-son relationship for about 20 years and that bond could not be any stronger had she birthed him. They love each other and have great respect for each other.

He is extremely respectful and caring in his actions toward his spiritual Mom, as he often goes the extra mile for her when she says: "Kinta, I need–" he is right there to get what she needs. Their relationship is not one sided at all, she is the say way with him.

It is a blessing to observe them as they chat with each other, and as she talks about praying for those things he has shared with her that he wants. I love their relationship – they love, respect and care deeply for each other.

Day 204
Freny McKay

I have had the pleasure of working with some wonderful volunteers and I have learned many valuable lessons from some very engaged volunteers.

Freny M. applied for a job as a volunteer and we gladly hired her. I express my gratitude to Freny because she was the ideal employee. She was very engaged, came to work when she said she would, completed every task assigned to her in an exemplary manner and scheduled her time off for appointments as well as vacation.

Freny applied for a compensated position and we hired her without reservation. Her work ethic changed–she was even more engaged! She was great to work with.

Day 205
Bev Childs

For the past several semesters, I have been blessed to be a part of the KinderReady class with Bev Childs at The Woodlands Children's Museum. Bev teaches the class of 4 and 5 year olds who are being groomed for kindergarten and I teach the manners and etiquette portion.

Being in that class is like attending a live taping of the Art Linkletter show! You truly don't know what to expect because kids really do say the funniest things. Bev and I work well together as we teach by observing the children and proceeding from there.

We have flown kites with the class, taught manners and etiquette, introductions, handshakes and eye contact, formal and informal place settings and common courtesies. The fun event that we enjoyed with the class last semester was journaling. Yes, they were seriously journaling. Bev and I spent quite a bit of time writing the narrative for the pictures and the words.

I am grateful for the opportunity to work with Bev and to learn how to best get and keep the attention of a 4 year old. Love those little guys and girls.

Ginny Chaffee Levenback - *What a wonderful experience!*

Toni Trahan Shirley - *Makes me proud of you two and the children!*

Judy McCurdy Mitchell -*You and Bev are giving these lil ones a wonderful gift. May God Bless both of you!!!!*

Daniel Perez - *manners and edequite very important but most are morals*

Day 206
Sally Guerrero-Redmon

I was invited to the Montgomery County Women's Council of Realtors luncheon by KiKi Koymarianos. It was a very interesting meeting and I met lots of new people. One new person I met was Sally Guerrero-Redmon.

As we prepared to leave the luncheon, it started to RAIN. Several of us were standing under the canopy hoping it would stop; no such luck! Since I had an umbrella, I made a run for it to my vehicle. I went back to the canopy area to give Sally a ride to her car.

Our brief chat birthed a relationship for us. I learned that Sally is devoted to her family and her faith. She is a committed prayer warrior–she can pray and she prays about everything. She started a prayer group – Praying Wives that meets every Monday, rain or shine. The group is open, compassionate, warm and nonjudgmental.

I am grateful that my path crossed Sally's. She is such a blessing as she shares her heart with anyone who wants or needs prayer or sage advice. Sally walks the talk.

Day 207

Pastor Allan Fowler

Sometimes we have to put our desires and wants on the back burner to serve others. I am extremely happy that I decided not to attend a meeting I was invited to and wanted to attend very badly.

Pastor Allan Fowler, New Spirit Ministries invited my grandson to a Top Shelf Event where they had poetry, comedy, Christian rap and jazz performers. I struggled with attending my event or taking my grandson to the Top Shelf Event.

I decided that I could attend my event next month and headed to the Top Shelf Event. My grandson who enjoys writing poetry and Christian rap had a fabulous time. He was impressed with the ladies who recited poetry. One poet was so moving that I was mesmerized! Afterwards, my grandson told me he learned so much about her just listening to her. I can't say that I was that deep.

I am grateful that Allan invited my grandson to the event and thankful that I was willing to take him. I will attend my meeting next month. I think I help a young poet get a jump start on something that is near and dear to his heart– for sure he learned something about reciting poetry.

Day 208

Martha Davis and Cathy Drobinski

I had the pleasure of sharing lunch with Martha Davis. Cathy Drobinski and Martha Davis invited me; however, Cathy wasn't able to join us. Martha and I had an opportunity to catch up because we have not seen each other for about a year.

Martha introduced me to some people who have achieved senior level status in their organization. One gentleman shared that he has retired his wife and she gets to stay home with their young children. He also said his wife is going on vacation for four weeks – he will be joining the family the last week of the trip.

It is absolutely awesome hearing stories of how people are generating residual income, improving their standard of living and then helping others to do the same. It shows me that the system works if you work the system.

Grateful I ran into Cathy and that she invited me to lunch. Since we have reconnected, we plan on meeting for coffee soon to see how we can collaborate. I can hardly wait as these ladies are passionate about what they are doing.

Day 209
Destiny Batalla

You hear of young men accepting the call to preach at a young edge. At my church, Embassy Church, we have a young lady who can preach. I know a number of female preachers (my pastor is one) but this is the first time I have met a young lady who has surrendered to the call.

I have heard Destiny B. preach and she is phenomenal. She is poised, confident, and gracious and has excellent stage presence. Destiny is beautiful inside and out–she displays the fruit of the spirit in her every day walk; she is so sweet. Destiny will be preaching at a national competition in a few weeks. I am grateful that I have the opportunity to witness the spiritual growth of this young lady. Destiny is only 13 years old and is wise beyond her years and a wonderful role model for young people.

I am extremely proud of Destiny and thankful for her parents (our youth pastors) for encouraging and nurturing her. This is one young preacher who is committed to serving the Lord.

Day 210
Angela Colton

I was introduced to the Angela Colton, Executive Director, The Woodlands Children's Museum because my friend wanted her to see my book All About ME* (*Manners and Etiquette for TWEENS and Teens) and hear the Manners and Etiquette program I offer.

Angela and I met and spoke for an hour about the program the museum offers for children 4-5 years old entitled KinderReady. The program prepares children for kindergarten. Angela liked the modules in my manners and etiquette program and invited me to participate with the KinderReady students.

This is a phenomenal program where the students learn social as well as academic skills. I am extremely grateful to be a part of this awesome program. Angela, the staff and the children in the class are always eager to see what I will be discussing.

Being a part of this class is an experience I would not trade for anything. When I knock on the door to the classroom, I am overjoyed by those little voices yell, it's Ms. Carolyn!

Day 211
Mr. and Mrs. Lane

We sometimes forget the small things that other do for us. However, reflecting on the some of the people who have entered my life, I am grateful for many many different gifts I have received over the years.

The gift of a smile, a hug, a cup of coffee/tea/soft drink, a book or the times the parents of my son's friends who gave him a ride home from school or activity can't be overlooked. Mr. and Mrs. Lane wherever you are, I remember your kindness and I appreciate you treating my son like your son-- sharing your wisdom and love.

It takes a village to raise a child and I am grateful that you were part of the village that helped raise my son.

Day 212
Dawn Mitchell

We can learn if we would just listen carefully to what others are saying. As a big talker (yea, I have to call ëem like I see ëem) when I quiet myself and pay attention I learn so much from others.

I was on a call with four other ladies after missing the call for several weeks and Dawn Mitchell mentioned she got some advice from her Dad regarding being a successful salesman. After the call, I quickly called Dawn because I wanted to know more about becoming a successful salesperson. I was focused on what Dawn was sharing and both of us acknowledged that her Dad knew what he was talking about.

The next day, I set out to put my new found knowledge to the test. I had to make the information work for me. I am grateful I was on the call and that Dawn did not mind sharing what she had learned–talking about divine intervention.

Day 213
Johnny Garnett

My younger brother attended Virginia Military Institute (VMI) and every year my children and I traveled from Maryland to Lexington, VA for family weekend at the college.

The kiddos loved the trip and I loved the drive.

The Thompson family "adopted" my brother which meant he had family in the area. They also "adopted" me and my children. Every year, they opened their home in Buena Vista, VA to us. They rolled out the red carpet–they cooked, cleaned and transported us around like we were tourist at a resort.

That part of the country is beautiful, especially during the fall. The foliage was a sight to behold and the snowcapped mountains in the distanceóbreathe taking. I enjoyed the four years my brother was there and always looked forward to that four day weekend trip because it was so relaxing.

The Thompson's made it so special. I am grateful and blessed to have so many wonderful people touch my life.

Day 214
Shelly Hogan, Melody Seals and Donna McMullen

Working with dedicated volunteers is such a pleasure. There are several people from my church who volunteered to serve on our pastor's dream team and they are awesome.

Two of the ladies get up at 4 a.m. for work and they stayed at church until 9p.m. preparing products for our pastor to sale at a conference. Shelly, Melody and Donna, I am grateful to have the opportunity to work with you. Love your commitment to excellence and the fact that you all work extremely good together. Your hands are blessed.

I can't wait to get our shirts made for the dream team. They are going to be off the chart cute!

Pastor Robert Johnson, thank you for making the team a priority. I think you should be a part of the dream team. There you go; you are officially a member of the dream team.

Day 215
Bryan and Nancy H.

Hurricane Ike left our area of town without electricity for two weeks. We were fortunate in that we were able to prepare a few meals because we have a gas cooktop.

We are truly blessed by Bryan and Nancy H., friends of our daughter, because they loaned us their generator. We were able to use our refrigerator and my husband was able to watch a little television and tinker on the computer. I was excited that we had ice and fans!

I am grateful for Bryan and Nancy loaning us their generator. Far too often we take the conveniences of everyday life for granted. I appreciate that I can flip a switch and have light or adjust the thermostat and the A/C keeps me cool. Pausing right now to again appreciate the kindness of Bryan and Nancy.

Day 216
Anthony Wingate

There is something about being surprised that makes me overjoyed for days, weeks, months or years when I reflect on the gift I was surprised with.

My nephew, Anthony Wingate, had one of those whirlwind weekend trips and I was on the agenda! I didn't know he was even in the state so when I looked out of my kitchen window and saw his legs, I actually thought it was my son; however, in full view, I saw it was Anthony James. I opened the door and gave him a couple big bear hugs. It has been over a year since we have seen each other and the element of surprise made the short visit wonderful.

This is the little nephew who allowed me to occupy his room when I visited them in Arizona. He gave me instructions on what I could and could not touch. I returned the favor when he visited me by telling him what he could and could not touch at my house.

When I visited them in Arizona, I had the opportunity to watch Tony play soccer. He made sure I noticed how hard he was playing by showing me the sweat on his face that he did not want wiped off.

Grateful to have been on the short list of people to visit on a three day weekend from Arizona to two Texas cities. I am going to return the favor and surprise him soon.

Day 217
Missy Harris

Great friends are our life line. You don't have to talk every day or see each other often to be considered great. However, when you need them, they are only a phone call away.

My daughter and her friend Missy Harris met the first day of orientation at college YEARS ago. They were both two sheltered high school graduates leaving home to be on their own. They started chatting and the rest is history.

They were not roommates but they should have been. Missy lived close to the college so she frequently invited my daughter to her home where her family treated my daughter like family.

They are both married and their husbands have been brought into the fold. It is wonderful seeing four people enjoy each other when they do visit. Missy, her husband Ronnie and two sons are very loving. I am grateful that they are still good friends and that they don't let distance keep them from visiting each other. It is a true blessing to have great friends.

Day 218

Cecilia Engquist and Gina Fernandez

I needed to get to a Bed Bath and Beyond and I had 25 minutes to find the one nearest to the Galleria area. This was not a life threatening situation but an important one. I did not want to have this task facing me in the morning.

As I left the meeting I saw Cecilia Engquist and Gina Fernandez so I asked them "where is the nearest Bed Bath and Beyond." In a split second, Gina pulled her tablet out and found several in the area. Cecilia knew exactly where one was and told me we could get there in about 15 minutes.

Cecilia did stop there – she told me to follow her and I did. Although the store might have been near her home, she probably went out of her way to make sure I got there before the store closed. It took a bit more than 15 minutes because there was construction on Westheimer (imagine that!)

Two minutes before the store closed, I walked in, grabbed four boxes of coffee and made it to the check out just in time to hear "it is 9 o'clock and our store is now closed." I am grateful for Gina and Cecilia saving the day for me.

Day 219

Pastor Monica Haskell

Pastor Monica Haskell, Prevailing Church International in New Castle, Delaware shared her Kingdom Millionaire Faith Confession with instructions to say it daily. I read the Kingdom Millionaire Faith Confession when I received it and immediately share it.

The prayer outlines things I should and should not do. It tells me fear has no place in my life because it cancels out faith and I know without faith it is impossible to please Him. I especially like the sentence that jealousy has no place in my life because He is big enough to afford everyone's dream. This is something I believe and have shared with many many others over the years.

I love the short paragraph about favor stalking me everywhere I go and God is at this very moment raising up somebody somewhere to use their power, influence and ability to help me. The last few sentences tells me that what I make happened for others God will then make happen for me.

I am grateful for being in Pastor Monica's address book and I thank her for sharing this prayer. I do not read it–I say it out loud every morning and I am telling you, my position has changed and I have stepped into my Kingdom Millionaire Status in Jesus name! Pastor Monica thanks for sharing.

Toni Trahan Shirley - *Compelling...*

Day 220
Kimm Mast Dwyer

The first WOAMTEC luncheon I attended Kimm Mast Dwyer was the speaker. After her presentation, she gave the book The Four Year Career (how to make your dreams of fun and financial freedom come true or not–) to those of us who wanted it and said we would read it.

I got a copy and I read it; however, it did not change my mind about network marketing–just being honest. I have read portions of the book twice and it still did not change my mind about networking marketing. What did change my mind was seeing Kimm in action and observing her. Her commitment to succeeding at network marketing is evident as she shares information about It Works with others.

Kimm has her "mobile office" and she heads off to have a wrap party when and where you want to have one. This girl knows what she wants and knows how to go about getting it. She is enthusiastic, authentic and committed. These characteristics, her established goals and those big warm eyes of hers make you listen and pay attention to her as she shares valuable information --

I am grateful that Kimm shared the book The Four Year Career, her belief and her drive with those interested in having financial freedom and fun. I got it Kimm.

Day 221
Marlene Pugh

Since both of us are too old to get into trouble for what I am about to tell, I am extremely for the friendship of Marlene Pugh. As a new student with no friends, I was excited when Marlene and I met.

Marlene had her license and access to her Mom's convertible push button Plymouth. We thought we were all that! Both of us loved the beach and not because we could swim. We just liked cruising along the beach with the top down looking like we owned the world. We would occasionally park, take our shoes off and walk in the warm sand.

Of course that would not get us in trouble; however, skipping the last period of school would! I wrote my excuse and signed my Mom's name. I always had a dental appointment. (The mind of teens) The hour we were supposed to be in class was spent at the beach. She would drop me off at home and beat it to her Mom's job to pick her up.

On one of our excursions, Marlene pushed the "Drive" button and it went too far – all we could see was a hole; we panicked. I was thinking about how I was dead meat because I was going to be late getting home and she was going to be late picking her Mom up. Saved by a couple of guys who knew how to repair the button. She got me home and got her Mom picked up. That stopped us from skipping class.

I am smiling thinking about how blessed we were that those guys came out of nowhere, I got home on time and Marlene was not late picking her Mom up. Divine intervention for real!

Day 222
Magic Gray

Today I express gratitude to my nephew Magic Gray. He is a wonderful nephew and I appreciate him so very much.

I needed a graphic for a book I wrote and based on my vague verbal instructions he was able to give me exactly what I wanted.

When I completed the next book, I called him again and he took what I told him I wanted and created a very appropriate graphic -- a Hot Chick with a red boa for my book: Hot Chicks and Attentive Dudes.

Magic is talented, creative and one great photographer. He is soft spoken, hardworking and has more patience than ten people. He is a blessing to everyone whose life he touches.

Toni Trahan Shirley - *Sounds like Magic has a touch of magic, and that is a good thing. So glad you are recognizing him!*

Judy McCurdy Mitchell - *Such a talented and gifted young man!*

Day 223
Rita Santamaria

I had a wonderful workshop for TWEENS and Teens at a location that was perfect for them–a class room setting.

I was fretted over a location that would be ideal for my Pancakes and Personalities workshop for TWEENS and Teens. I approached Rita Santamaria as she was leaving a meeting to ask her if I could use one of her conference rooms and she said sure. She referred me to Teresa who scheduled my workshop on the day I wanted to have it and as they say, the rest is history.

I had to call Teresa back because I forgot to ask if food was allowed in the conference room. Again, I was told yes. What was initially a planning disaster for me turned into an absolutely wonderful workshop for the TWEENS and Teens thanks to the generosity of Rita and Teresa.

The workshop was educational and fun. The pizza was delicious and was delivered on time. Grateful beyond words for Rita and Teresa saving the day for me.

Day 224
Tracy Ray

It pays to have friends in high places! Tracy Ray handed me a copy of The Woodlands Lifestyle and Homes at one of our luncheons which I promptly stuck under my arm and went off chatting with a couple of other ladies.

When it was brought to my attention that our WOAMTEC, The Woodlands Chapter has submitted a photo of to the magazine, I said that's "nice – we made the happenings section." Tracy asked my in her ever so jovial manner "princess, did you see your picture!" I said no. I thought you were just making sure I had my very own copy of the magazine.

She directed me to the Happenings Section and there it was a picture of me and three other members of our networking group. It's official, my step into stardom. (-: Well, maybe not but we all had a great time joking about being stars. Thanks Tracy for letting the thousands of readers of the magazine learn about WOAMTEC.

So grateful that Tracy presented information on and helped us with our marketing pie at the monthly WOAMTEC, The Woodlands educational session. A funtabulous session!

Day 225
Patricia Barnes

We refer to some people as angels or sweet angles and they are just that: sweet angels. Pat Barnes was a sweet angel. Pat and I worked together and had lots of laughs. She was from Washington, D.C. so we had a number of things to talk about since I worked in D.C. for a number of years.

I never say her when she wasn't smiling or helping someone. She was always dressed for the runway and had an infectious smile.

Pat and I occasionally chatted on the phone after I moved to Ohio. When I came home for a visit, Pat was the first person to locate me, no matter where I was in the building. We would embrace and find us a spot to catch up on what had happened since the last time we saw each other. Of course there was a lot of laughing going on.

She touched my life in a very positive way. Pat was very easy to talk to and we would talk about anything. She was the most resourceful person I had the pleasure of working with. No matter what –Pat could (and would) find a way to get "it" done.

Pat passed away eight years ago; however, that sweet angel's memory still lives with me. A very precious precious lady.

Day 226
Kathy Brandon

I love learning and if I am not careful, I will have to upgrade my technological status to almost competent because I have learned about Google Hangout.

I am grateful for my crash course by Kathy Brandon, the Happiness Chick, on getting on Google Hangout on my desktop as well as my mobile device. Kathy was ever so patient in walking me through the process. She shared with me that it was easy but that is what everyone tells me. Kathy was right, it was easy.

Hangout on my phone is really cool. After I pushed and clicked a few things, I surprised myself when my photo appeared. Not sure if I was surprised because I was successful in getting on Hangout or how I looked on the screen. The clasp on my necklace was showing, my badge was caddywhompus, my hair was–well, let's just say I have seen it look better and

I didn't have on a drop of lipstick. I quickly logged out of Hangout and "fixed" all that was wrong with me. Lesson learned: do a thorough mirror check before signing in on Hangout again.

Next time Kathy tells me something is easy, I will listen to her. Thanks Kathy, you are a great teacher.

> **Kathy Brandon Happinesschick** - *let's reschedule your interview...so glad you got the tool loaded and working...can't wait to see your GORGEOUS face and personality on video sister!! let's reschedule, can't wait to introduce you to the Happy Peeps!*

Day 227
Karen Webb

I had a one-on-one with Karen Webb that was absolutely wonderful. Karen called me to ask if we could meet and of course I responded in the affirmative. Karen and I are members of the International Coach Federation, Houston Charter Chapter.

Karen is extremely positive and ever so encouraging. I love that she is someone who likes to systematize and make things simple. When she told me that, I shared with her that I am like Sniff and Scurry in the book Who Moved My Cheese by Spencer Johnson. We both got a chuckle out of that.

We discussed our niche, our websites and the client/customer appreciation system that I use. Because it is simple and automated, Karen gave her seal of approval with a smile and "I like it!"

I left our meeting energized and grateful. Grateful that Karen called to ask if we could meet and energized because she shared her positive outlook with me.

Day 228
Abigail

A TWEEN who attended my Pizza and Personalities Workshop for TWEENS and Teens called to thank me for having the workshop.

She went on to say that she is changing and wanted to let me know that she noticed it herself. She told me her mom even noticed she has changed. This was a moment of gratitude for me for a several reasons: 1) I am excited that she learned about herself and is making improvements–she is 10 years old; 2) her mom acknowledged the changes and complimented her and 3) she took the initiative and the time to call me to share the good news with me.

This young lady, at the age of 10, realized she needed to make some changes and is working on those things that she identified needs to be changed. I suspect she heard from me some of the same things her mom has told her and she had an "aha moment." Whatever the reason, I am grateful she has learned it at the tender age of 10. Blessing my little friend. I am proud of you.

Day 229
Ann Reed

Ann Reed was the coolest teacher because she was young, hip and could relate to high school students. Years later, she taught my son in Vacation Bible School and he stole her heart.

Being the coolest teacher and being fond of my son is not what I remember most about Ms. Reed. I remember that she spoke at our What Happens When Women Pray prayer group about praying to pray.

She explained how to enter into prayer by first praying. She said don't just run up to God and start talking. Ms. Reed taught us how to pray that night and I still remember her instructions as if she was here speaking right into my ear. I am grateful to have had someone like Ms. Reed who was so instrumental in my life from high school to adult and motherhood. Ms. Reed walked the talk.

Day 230
Darlene Powell

My Mom had many wonderful friends who treated her more like a mother than a friend and. Darlene Powell was one of those people. My Mom had knee surgery and had to have physical therapy three days a week. Darlene offered to take my Mom to therapy to keep me from driving from my residence to my Mom's then to the facility for physical therapy, 165 miles round trip. She did this once a week the entire time my Mom had therapy at the facility.

Once the therapy at the facility was completed, Mom had in-home therapy and Darlene was there to "supervise" every time the therapist came. She also prepared meals for my Mom and chauffeured her around until Mom was released to drive.

I am grateful that my Mom had Darlene there to help. I was at ease when she was there–it was like me being there. She was good to my Mom and our family.

Day 231
Debbie

When I take my bag of clothes to the cleaners, I am greeted with "hello Mrs. Gray how are you today" and a smile from Debbie, the clerk at the counter.

I appreciate Debbie being there because she brightens my day. She works in the cleaners which is not the coolest place to work, she is not sitting down and she handles our dirty laundry all day. Does this cause her to have a scowl on her face–no, no indeed. She is pleasant to everyone who comes to the cleaners.

When I get back to my car, I ask myself if I could do her job and the answer is yes, of course I could. How long would I last is a whole different story. I am grateful for those who serve me and particularly those who serve with a smile.

Day 232
Cheryl Patterson

I met Cheryl Patterson, CEO & President at Universal Xperience when she was arranging for my pastor to be a guest on Kelly Crew's show.

Cheryl blessed me by connecting me with Susan Jones, Editor in Chief of Impact Detroit Magazine. Susan featured my book WOO to WOW: 5 Stages of a Relationship (WOO. WHAM, WHOA, WHEE, WOW) in Impact Detroit Magazine. Truly, we have not because we ask not. Well, I asked and Cheryl and Susan made it happen. I would not have been featured in Impact Detroit Magazine had I not asked.

I am grateful that I met these ladies and thank them for their support. They did not initially have a category for self-published authors; however, because I asked, they decided to establish a category just for us – self-published authors.

Cheryl and Susan are making things happen for others and God is making things happened for them. Much success ladies and thank you for the opportunity to be featured in Impact Detroit Magazine.

Day 233
MiMi

Looking back over the past eight years, I realize I have lots of stability in my life. I moved to Houston and had to find new everything–including a nail tech.

Less than one mile from my home I found a nail shop tucked away in the corner of a shopping plaza. I went in and was met by MiMi. She is a chic, friendly, petite, sassy professional who loves what she does. She does my eyebrows and my pedicure and along with those services, I get caught up on what goes in between visits.

There are other ladies in the salon and I know them all. They are all professional and very good at what they do. If I get busy and miss seeing them regularly, when I do go in I get the third degree. I thoroughly enjoy my relationship with MiMi and the other ladies and grateful that I have not had to find another salon for eight years. There is no drama in this salon, no loud music and no soliciting-- just good friendly service.

Day 234

Barbara Bush Library

It would be a great honor if I personally knew Barbara Bush; however, the closest I will probably every get to know her is to frequent the library named in her honor.

The Barbara Bush library is one more thing that is stable in my life. The day we closed on our home, I left the title company and went straight to the library to get my library card. I tried to get it the day before but was told I had to have proof of my address.

The library is a vital party of my life – I often walk to the library, check out books and cd and hike back to the house. The staff there is extremely helpful. The children's library has been a frequent spot for my grandson who loves to read.

I have used the library conference room for seminars and conferences at no cost. The library is a resource that has enriched my life and I am grateful that it is within walking distance of my home. Grateful for the Harris County facilities that are available to me, especially the Barbara Bush Library.

Toni Trahan Shirley - *You are so fortunate to have this blessing and to take advantage of it.*

Markett Russell Harkinson - *I saw Barbara Bush speak at a SPCA luncheon a few years ago. She loves dogs.*

Madge Fletcher - *How fortunate you are to live close to the Barbara Bush Library. I read about it all the time in the paper and the many activities they sponsor!*

Ginny Chaffee Levenback - *Love your post! I wonder if you wrote Barbara Bush a letter letting her know how much her libarary means to you it may mean a lot to her as a champion of reading.*

Day 235

Tawni Haynes

Observing people who have a successful business interact with others is fascinating. Some are humble and down to earth while others are full of pride and self-importance.

Tawni Haynes is in the first category: humble and down to earth. She is a well know fashion designer from the Dallas area. Actress and Recording Artist Tamela Mann is one of her clients and so is Tasha Cobbs.

Lady Stephanie Sparks was wearing aTawni Haynes bow dress and I do mean she was wearing it. Some of the ladies at the conference purchased Tawni's fashions one day and had them on the next day. Tawni was there personally taking measurements of ladies as they ordered her custom made fashions. Tawni is so humble and gracious–her light shines bright and not at all for her glory!

I was blessed and grateful to be in her company and watch her do what she loves doing–helping women look good. She had breathing taking fabrics in all colors, patterns and designs and her signature bow blouses were gorgeous. Tawni Haynes is professional, super talented, warm and friendly.

Day 236

Sherrell Straker-Valdezloqui

I am grateful for being featured in Promoting Purpose Magazine. My interview with Sherrell Straker-Valdezloqui is in the August edition of Promoting Purpose Magazine. The interview is an easy to read conversation between the two of us. She included my photo and a photo of the cover of my book: Hot Chicks and Attentive Dudes.

I met Sherrell through Cheryl Patterson and I tell you these ladies have been a blessing. Cheryl, Sherrell and Susan Jones are extremely supportive, encouraging and fun to work with. Thank you ladies for your kindness.

Rebecca Montgomery-Nelson - *No one better can do this but "She"...my mentor, Carolyn Gray*

Bev Steele Childs - *Congratulations, you deserve it!*

Angela Hicks Campos - *Congratulations Carolyn! Now I need to order two copies of your book Hot Chicks . . . Attentive Dudes, one for my newlywed soon and one for me.*

Toni Trahan Shirley - *So happy to see you in print!*

Day 237
Jay Garnett

Having little arms wrapped around my neck and kisses on my cheeks is a memory I am grateful for and will cherish.

My nephew Jay was a very affectionate youngster; he loved to hug and snuggle and tell me he loved me. Of my three older nephews, Jay was the prankster. He laughed harder at his pranks than anyone else. He was a smooth operator and I was putty in his little hands.

When the nephews were all in town, they enjoyed spending the night at my house. We would race each other, watch movies, pop popcorn, tell jokes and before turning in for the night, Jay would always get his bid in for breakfast: French toast.

After breakfast, he would wrap his little sweet arms around my neck, give me a kiss and tell me how much he loved me and that I made the best French toast in the world. As the story goes, every time my brother transferred from one base to another, Jay would tell his new friends about my French toast. I think he is still telling that French toast story as he transfers with the Air Force. As an adult, he still gives those good warm hugs.

Judy McCurdy Mitchell - *Carolyn--you are a very loving and giving person!!! It certainly shows in all of your postings!!!!*

Frances Johnson - *What a great story.........everyone has a favorite Aunt.*

Day 238
Kathy Logan

Kathy Logan, a teacher and stay-at-home Mom was my daughter's tutor. Kathy was a reading specialist who was referred by a friend of a friend.

My daughter was told by her teacher that she could not read based on a standardized test she took on the first day of school. New home, new school and one of Houston's floods is enough to keep anyone from making a passing score on a test

When I got the news, I was at the school the next morning before they opened the doors. I could not understand how all of a sudden she could not read. I was told about the test and asked if she could be re-tested and the answer was no, not until the next semester.

Kathy tested my daughter and said she was not sure what test the used because she could read and comprehended very well what she read. Kathy worked with her twice a week for two weeks and told me I was paying her for nothing because my daughter could read and in fact was reading on a grade level above her current grade. I am grateful for her level of integrity because she could have kept tutoring my daughter; Kathy helped my sweet baby girl (who was in fifth grade) get her self-confidence back.

Day 239
Discount Tire

Having a flat time is at the very top of my list of things I HATE! I got in my car, drove about a mile and the tire pressure indicator came on.

I drove to my local Discount Tire and asked if they would put some air in the tire and they gladly obliged me. As I backed out, the young man stopped me and told me there was a screw in my tire. He said they could repair it; however, there was a wait of about an hour. I did not want to wait; however, he convinced me with what could happen if I did not get the tire repaired– I decided to wait. I had magazines with me so the wait wasn't too bad.

About 35 minutes later they were calling my name; my tire was repaired and I was on my way. I am grateful for the excellent customer service I received and the concern the technician had for my safety. As I drove away, I said "that's why we buy tires from Discount Tire.

Day 240
Frankie McNutt

My son was eight years old when he started playing little league football. He loved the game, the coaches and his fellow players.

Frankie McNutt's positive influence on my son has lasted for years. Coach McNutt's nephew played on the same team and called him Uncle Frankie. My son took it upon himself to refer to Coach McNutt as "Uncle Frankie!" I tried to convince him to call him Coach McNutt but he told me that the coach's nephew said it was OK. Mind you, the nephew was probable eight years.

Coach McNutt instilled values that my son still talks about. He corrected them when they got out of line, taught good sportsmanship, respect, self-confidence, team work, safety as well as the fundamentals of football. Coach McNutt always encouraged them and was fair. My son was sharing with his son something that Uncle Frankie taught him over thirty years ago.

Just goes to show the impact someone outside the family can have on a child's life.. It is said that it takes a village to raise a child – well, I am grateful that Coach McNutt as I refer to him and Uncle Frankie as my son still calls him was part of the village because my son is a very responsible young man and a great Dad. Thanks Coach McNutt for being a vital part of my son being who he is today.

Day 241
Helen Callier

I was leaving a workshop when I notice Helen Callier entering the room. I smiled and said to myself "there's Helen Callier – I haven't seen her in about three years."

I spoke and introduced myself to her because I was sure she did not remember me. She was gracious, warm and friendly. We started to chat and I mentioned that my presentation was on gratitude. Helen and I stood there for at least five minutes sharing our thoughts on gratitude with each other. Both of us expressed the important of gratitude when Helen told me about an interesting book she had read and invited me to contact her to get the title and author of the book.

We were not connected on social media; however, I have corrected that! I am grateful for Helen taking the time to share her thoughts and feelings about gratitude with me. We realize, acknowledge and value the importance of expressing gratitude to others.

Day 242
Jan, Half Price Books

Yesterday, I was told about a great book on gratitude. Today, I called Half Price Books to see if they had it. I spoke with Jan who was extremely pleasant and helpful. Jan checked the computer and said it showed there was a copy of the book in the store. She asked me to hold so that she could check to see if the book was on the shelf–it was.

I went in to pick up the book and as luck would have it, Jan had left for the day. She held the book for me and I purchased the book and headed home to start reading. I am reassured that gratitude is a simple act with huge rewards for the giver as well as the receiver.

John Kralik, the author of A Simple Act of Gratitude, shares about writing 365 thank you notes in one year.. This is inspiring because I am on a similar journey–expressing gratitude for 365 days. I am on day 242 of 365 days of gratitude and I must say that I am truly blessed.

Day 243
Jane Warner

As I was leaving an event, Jane Warner stopped me and asked if I was ok. I told her I was fine and she responded that I did not appear to be my usual self.

I explained that I was giving a presentation the next morning and I was concerned that I was not as prepared as I would like to be. I told her I needed to get home to finalize the presentation.

The next day, Jane sent me a message to ask how the presentation went. I was happy to report that it went well. Jane noticed that my facial expression was saying something that my mouth had not conveyed. I appreciate her being concerned enough to check on me the next day.

Saying thank you to a friend for being concerned seems so small. I am grateful for people in my life who notice when something is awry–Jane noticed and I am grateful she did.

Jane Warner - *Love you too*

Gayle Yess Fisher - *Yeah, that Jane Warner, and you should see here with Special Needs Sibs - SNS. Someone said, "She's the mother I wish I had."*

Kiki Aristidou Koymarianos - *It's the cancer in her That makes her the mother of all I too love Jane Warner!*

Dianne Buck Jane is great!

Day 244
Jan Johnson

Before I modernized myself, or should I say "came up to the 21st century", I wore a certain brand of pantyhose. At one point, I could not find them anywhere so I wrote to the manufacturer to see if I could purchase them directly. The manufacturer responded and gave me the name and phone number of a distributor.

I contacted Jan Johnson, the distributitor, in Chicago and shared my challenge with her. I ordered two dozen pairs of pantyhose and told her I would send her a check. Jan told me she would send the pantyhose and include an invoice. She explained that she was confident I would pay her since I went so far to find the pantyhose

Jan and I have maintained a close relationship for over ten years. Although I don't order as frequently as I once did we still communicate and catch up with each other. I am grateful she was a distributor and took care of my orders when I needed them and for trusting me to pay. This reminds me

I have not spoken with Jan in several monthsócalling her in the morning.

Toni Trahan Shirley - *And I remember Carolyn chasing those pantyhose, I really do!!*

Carolyn Gray - *Toni Shirley, I bet you do! I was in crisis mode until I hooked up w/Jan. She sent them priority mailed and I received them (just in time) before leaving on travel to Birmingham...she saved the day! Then there was a little calm in the office (-:*

Phyllis Jenkins Isiminger - *Love your story, but girl, I haven't worn panty hose since 1992.*

Carolyn Gray - *Phyllis Isiminger, you know I am slow to catch on!*

Day 245
Allen Miner

As I searched for a convenient location to hold the Pancakes and Personalities Workshop, I spoke with Allen M., owner of Another Broken Egg- The Woodlands about using the private dining at Another Broken Egg.

I shared with Allen what I wanted and we worked to negotiate a fair cost per person. Allen is very supportive of small business owners and networking groups. I frequent Another Broken Egg because I love pancakes and they have GRATE pancakes as well as excellent customer service.

It is refreshing to find a business owner like Allen who genuinely wants to help small business owners succeed. I asked to use the private dining area and was told yes. We have not because we ask not–I am grateful I asked and that Allen said yes.

Jane Warner - *when is the date?*

Carolyn Gray - *OK guys, I can spell GREAT...sometimes!*

Day 246
Lori Burns

Having someone remember what I like and don't like makes me feel great. It also makes me wonder how they remember what so many people in their circle like.

Lori Burns, my Silpada consultant/lady/rep/friend has my number. Lori noticed that I love all things pearl; she always has an eye out for pearls for me. There was a Silpada item I really really wanted; however, I never uttered a word to Lori. One day, Lori mentioned that Silpada was having a sale and there was a three strand pearl necklace she knew I would love. Well, she was right!

Stalking might not be the right word to use but I was almost stalking Lori and blowing her phone UP trying to catch up with her to get "my necklace." It worked! Lori was in a hurry when we finally saw each other so I made sure there was a quick exchange. She left me with "enjoy sweet girl" and I want her to know that I have enjoyed the necklace as well as the compliments I have received.

Expressing gratitude to my WOAMTEC sister for thinking about me. Lori has tried to interest me in other beautiful Silpada items; however, I go back to my pearls. Thank you my sweet friend for remembering that I love pearls.

Lori Mansour Burns - *Carolyn Gray - I couldn't imagine you, such a classy lady, in anything but beautiful pearls. I love that when I see pearls, I immediately and will always, think of you.*

Judy McCurdy Mitchell - *I love pearls. They go with everything!! U can dress them up r down.*

Day 247

Jennifer Stewart Booth

Keeping my home office organized has been a bit of a challenge for me over the years as I maintain balance with family, church, clients, networking, and conducting workshops.

Jennifer Stewart Booth, Thirty One, donated a door prize at the MCABW Christmas party and I won her donated items. There were many practical "mobile office" items and I was sure this was THE beginning of how I would stay organized--this time. I thanked Jennifer for the door prize and followed up by order a tote bag from Thirty One for all of my new stuff.

When the tote bag arrived, I organized the modules for my KinderReady manners and etiquette class by removing the material from the file cabinet and placing each module in its very own slot in the new "mobile office." WOW, that portion of what I do is so organized (still) that I decided to use the same system for the other workshop that I conduct.

I am grateful for Jennifer donating that generous door prize and for helping me select my tote bag "mobile office." Life is grand with things well organized – thanks Jennifer.

Elizabeth Fazio Wisnoski - If anyone can conquer the challenge you can! After you perfect it please come help me! God has put you as my friend and I am very Grateful!

Dianne Thomas - *Carolyn, You need my help:-)*

Carolyn Gray - *Thanks Dianne Thomas--I probably did but w/my mobile offices*

(I have three) I am very organized.

Jennifer Stewart Booth - *Thank you Carolyn. I was so excited when you were selected for that door prize. And even more happy about being your friend and knowing you. One more reason I am thankful for Thirty-One in my life, All the awesome people I have gotten to meet and have in my life now.*

Day 248
Ian Zachariah Cruz (grandson #2)

Having spent the past several days with my GS-2 (Grandson #2) I am bubbling over with gratitude.

I hugged and kissed him; rubbed his little head, listened to him "talk" and have him bite me with those two sharp new teeth of his were so joyous. He fell asleep in my arms and if that is not the most precious site I don't know what is. I am counting the days until I am able to spend time with him.

Grateful that God has blessed my daughter and son-in-love and the rest of our family with that precious little boy. As a grandparent, I loved on him but did not spoil him too much. Proverbs 17:6 tell us Grandparents are proud of their grandchildren just as children are proud of their parents (Good News Translation). I am proud of my darling GS-1 and GS-2.

I can no longer rock my GS-1 to sleep but I love on that precious young man just like I love on GS-2. I am proud of both of them -- Gigi loves those guys.

Day 249
Robert Adams

Expressing gratitude to Brother Robert Adams, a man who praises God from the very depth of his being. We affectionately call him BA (Bro Adams). BA loves to Praise the Lord.

Being in his presence on Sunday at church or during the week at his shop, you will experience praise like David praised! BA is a man after God's own heart and not only praises himself happy, but he gets the congregation stirred up. He ushers in the very presence of the Lord and I am grateful for the public display love he has for his relationship with the Lord. He is a blessing to me and I say thank you to him for walking his talk.

Day 250
Tammy Golden

Having my own CAbi consultant is awesome. My consultant is the Tammy Golden, who is always CAbi cute!

This year Tammy saw an item and claimed it for me. I tried the skirt on and fell in love with it. Tammy suggested I get the top and the skirt. Well, I didn't take her advice–shame on me. Tammy walked in with the outfit on, I told her to order the top for me and she did.

When she delivered the order, I wanted to change clothes right then but I didn't. I could not wait to wear my shirt and top and of course I had my pearls and I was set. Tammy knows CAbi and she knows what looks good on everyone. I am grateful that she is honest and straight forward. She is passionate about what she does and she makes it enjoyable to test drive the new fashions when the seasons change. One fabulous lady.

Day 251
Paul Barela

Paul Barela and I have served on the same advisory board for seven plus years. Paul knows taxes and financial statements and I have learned from him just being in his presence. I don't just take from him--I often give him a pen with my company's name and phone number on it. He really likes those pens and I am sure he considers it as a fair exchange. (-:

I spoke at a workshop where we were both presenters. After my presentation, Paul reminded me of a presentation I gave about five years ago. To my surprise, he remembered the topic and had to remind me. In addition to that, he sent me a very complimentary email message regarding my most recent presentation.

I am grateful and offer many thanks to Paul for taking the time to send me an email regarding my presentation. He's just that kinda of guy.

Day 252
Marco Cruz

My favorite son-in-love, Marco, has a special place in my heart. He is kind, compassionate and loving. In addition to being a great husband, he is one awesome Dad. Observing him take care of his son is an amazing site. He changes diapers, makes formula, reads to his son and showers him with love.

Marco is talented, creative, has anointed hands and loves to help others. He does not meet a stranger–everyone is his new best friend. He enjoys grilling and with his "Texas Crunch" he makes the best ribs.

His company, Anointed Arts, is appropriately named. He has a spirit of excellence and works as unto the Lord. He remodeled their home and it is absolutely beautiful. Those anointed hands built a deck for his neighbor that makes me want him to build one for us.

I am grateful that my daughter has such a loving and caring husband. He is a gentleman and is always doing something to please her. It is wonderful to have a son-in-love who treats me like a mother. Marco, you are my favorite son-in-love and I say thank you for letting your light shine.

Day 253
Nicole Finkbeiner

Do you know Nicole Finkbeiner? Neither did I before attending the Tomball Chamber's luncheon.

Nicole is the Executive Director, College Relations at Lone Star College, Tomball. She spoke on Effective Marketing using the Broken Window Theory as an introduction. Her presentation was brief, concise and very effective.

She gave a new meaning to the saying "a picture is worth a thousand words" as she use simple pictures to make her point about branding and marketing. I am all about good customer service and she pointed out that we can advertise all we want, but without good customer service it will not matter.

I almost didn't attend the luncheon because I felt I was not dressed for the occasion; however, my girlfriend told me what I was wearing was appropriate and it was. Grateful I attended because the material presented was timely, easy to understand and apply, and the presenter was excellent!

Day 254
Elizabeth Wisnoski

Elizabeth Wisnoski re-launched the Cypress Chapter of WOAMTEC in style at the Steamboat Steakhouse. You are off to a great start.

Elizabeth was excited and had lots of energy. The meeting had a wonderful speaker and lots and lots of door prizes. There were also men in attendance and they didn't mind being in the company of all those powerful women.

I am grateful to be a part of the re-launched group and for the support from sister chapters. It is extremely gratifying to be a part of an organization where women help women to succeed. Elizabeth, thanks for your dedication and service to the rest of us.

Day 255
Breanna Pair

Two of my friends and I posed as Charlie's Angels at the WOAMTEC, Cypress Chapter luncheon and Breanna Pair shot a picture of us!

Breanna and I sat next to each other and my challenge was: what do I want to order. Bison burgers were on the menu along with a couple of other things. I mentioned to her that I would like to try the Bison burger and she shared with me that someone she knows said the burgers were good.

Based on the feedback of her friend, we both ordered the Bison burger and it was delicious. Actually, it was so large that I could only eat half–not to worry; I ate the other half for lunch the next day.

Grateful for Breanna joining in on the fun my friends and I were having and for the menu recommendation.

Day 256
Shelly Roth

It has been a couple of years since I have seen Shelly Roth so I was excited to say hello to her at a networking meeting.

I mentioned to her how much I appreciate her quick tip videos posted on Facebook She put those videos together for people like me! Shelly gives without looking for anything in return and she does what she does with a smile.

Shelly gave a presentation that was concise and delivered with perfection. Her presentation had just enough data and white space to hold my interest. I am also grateful that she came to my side of town to share with us. Thanks Shelly.

Day 257
Cathy Mogler

Cathy Mogler and I met up for a one-on-one that was so much fun. Cathy is outgoing and a fun person to spend time with.

Cathy and I visited for over an hour; however, it did not appear to have been that long. Grateful for her taking time to meet with me and sharing about her business with me. When I called to remind her about a function,

I did not think it would develop into a nice long one-on-one session.

Both of us are outgoing and talkative thus the reason for the long meeting. We didn't plan our next meeting but there will definitely be one and it will be my treat!

Day 258

Jessisa, Grace and Kevin

Expressions of gratitude to Jessica, Grace and Kevin of Mardel's Christian Bookstore for their excellent customer service.

I went in to pick-up a donated item for a conference. Grace called Jessica who immediately tried to locate the donation and apologized for the delay. Jessica sent the manager a message.

While waiting for Jessica to get a response, I browsed around the store. Kevin was in the Bible section so I asked him if they re-bound books. He said no, but he could refer me to a company that does. He provided me with the name of a local and an out-of-state company. I left that section and headed back to the front of the store.

Jessica took care of the donation and I was ready to go. It is always so refreshing when I received excellent customer service–I could not let this opportunity go by without saying a special thank you to them and Mardel's. Thank you, thank you.

Day 259

Tina Giles

Grateful to be a part of the 2013 Women of Wisdom Conference and to share with so many wonderful women of God.

These women are committed and dedicated to serving and winning souls... I am blessed to be a part of the committee. Tina Giles, the conference chair is hard at work coordinating and keeping things on track. Kudos to her and everyone on the committee for devoting their time to ensure nothing falls through the cracks.

The scheduled breakfast meeting was phenomenal. We prayed, ate breakfast, made formal introductions, took care of the agenda items and the meeting was over, as scheduled. Talking about doing things decently and in order (I Corinthians 14:40) – thank you Minister Jackie and Tina. I am ready to serve.

Day 260
Nakia Laushaul

Attending the Bistro is always educational and inspiring; today was no different as Nakia Laushaul shared with the group today.

Nakia spoke on blogging, gave us many many resources and some great marketing tips. Nakia loves to write which is apparent to anyone who engages in a conversation with her or just be in her company.

Nakia shared a tool with us today which fascinated me. She told us about paper.il. I have seen paper.il for some time; however, I did not know it was so easy to create. I mentioned to Nakia that I was going to get a paper.il account today and I did. She told me she would be checking in with me to make sure I follow through and she did!

Grateful for having met Nakia at a book signing a while back and for being in her company because she is on fire. Her passion has flames that are felt when I am in her company. She is not just passionate – she is enthusiastic, creative and down to earth. Nakia, thank you for sharing; your presentation was awesome.

Day 261
Minister Shaye Bradley

As a member of the Women of Wisdom Conference team, I have been assigned to Minister Shaye Bradley's team. Minister Bradley has a soft voice but is a powerhouse for the Lord.

After going through my email messages looking for the conference call information without any luck, I decided to send Minister Shaye a message. She responded and told me she would call me and fill me in on what I missed. As soon as the call was completed, she contacted me and updated me as well as gave me the conference call information for future calls. Grateful she went the extra mile for me and I look forward to serving on the team with her during the conference.

Day 262
Dr. Lauren LeRoy

I have a new best friend – Dr. Lauren LeRoy. Oh, I forgot Dr. LeRoy, I can call you Lauren.

Lauren was a guest at WOAMTEC, The Woodlands Chapter luncheon. I am grateful that Lauren was early because that gave us an opportunity to chat before others started to arrive. Since she was early, she offered to volunteer to work (my kinda new best friend); however, I really didn't feel that was any way to treat a guest so I invited her to sit at the table with me. I don't think I was too bossy –well, maybe a little bit but she didn't seem to mind.

As a guest, I wanted her to meet some of the other members – I'll put her to work next time. Lauren is a Chiropractor and a very friendly one at that. She shared with me that today is her birthday so I wished my new best friend a happy birthday and invited to the next luncheon.

Day 263
Barbara Ann Odom

Another day and another new best friend! Barbara Ann Odom is a fascinating lady who I met at Secret Expressions open house.

We ate some of the most delicious dips, chips and cookies. Barbara and I chatted for a good while about traveling. She shared that she has traveled to every state in the country – my kinda girl. Actually, we "drove" a couple of thousand miles just talking. She knows every highway and short cut you can think of.

One thing Barbara shared with me was how long she can stay behind the wheel–nineteen hours! I thought I could drive long hours but I met me match. Fourteen hours is my record and twenty four is Barbara's.

She loves life and her family. Grateful to have met Barbara and to have traveled with her on some of my favorite highways: I-20, I-40, I-65, I-85 and I-95. I can't wait until we meet again so I can hear more about her road trips.

Day 264
Ralph Lewis

Ralph Lewis and I were members of a breakfast networking group several years ago. We have been connected through social media; however, we have not seen each other until today.

I am grateful that Ralph remembered me well enough to refer me to someone in his circle. Ralph contacted me several days ago to see if I could meet with him because he wanted to introduce me to someone. I was able to meet and I am happy I did.

Networking is such an awesome way to get to know like and trust people. Glad I was my authentic self and that Ralph thought his friend and I would be a good fit--he was spot on!

?#?gratitudeenthusiast?.??

Ralph Lewis - *It was great to see you again, Carolyn. Thank you for squeezing time out of your busy schedule to spend with us. I really enjoy introducing two people I know and I know it was successful like this was when they get along so well I almost feel like I'm eavesdropping*

Carolyn Gray - *Ralph Lewis, you did good on this one!*

Day 265
Mark Ashley

I am grateful for having meet Mark Ashley in person today. He is everything his wife said he is. He gave me a hug which made his stock go up by many many points with me–I like to hug.

Mark is authentic and has the best sense of humor of anyone I have been around in a long time. I don't know that he realizes how genuinely funny he is. He is just as helpful and resourceful as he is funny.

I know why his wife likes to "pass" things by him – he analyzes things almost before you ask him a question. Totally amazing guy. Now that we have met, I will start "passing" things by Mark as well!

Getting to know Mark and being a part of my friend's very special project made for an awesome day.

Day 266
Regina Cruz

My daughter married into a family of love. I am so very grateful for the love Regina Cruz has shown toward my daughter.

My husband and I lived about 1100 hundred miles from our daughter and I often fretted about not being closer to home especially when she had a health issue. I stayed on the phone getting up dates on her condition and was told not to come because she was ok.

Telling me not to come was not what comforted me– Regina telling me that my precious daughter was the daughter she never had (she has two sons) and she would take care of her just like I would. Hearing those words did help and before I could make arrangements to come home my daughter was back to her old self.

Regina along with my son-in-love took care of my baby girl and I had nothing to worry about. I will never forget Regina telling me how much she loved my daughter. Nor will I forget that she really does love her as the daughter she never had.

Day 267
Tremisha Allen

Today is devoted to the ASRs at Kelsey Seybold facility in Spring because they are very professional, courteous and helpful. There is very little turnover in that area which speaks well of the ASRs as well as Kelsey Seybold.

I am grateful for one ASR in particular: Tremisha Allen. Tremisha had a baby a few years ago so my conversation with her is to ask about the baby. One day I asked about her and she informed me she wanted to complete her college degree. That opened the door for me to ask what she was doing toward that goal and she had an answer for me. I told her I would hold her accountable and she smiled and said ok.

Months later, I saw Tremisha and I asked her if she had enrolled in college and she said "yes I am." That was a proud moment for me because she is completing a goal that she set for herself. It is not easy to work fulltime, take care of home and family and go to school. She seems to have all of the "balls" in the air!

Day 268
Dawn Candy

We have not because we ask not. When it was mentioned to me that we needed tote bags for the women's conference I said, "I have no idea where or who to get them from."

Dawn Candy, owner of I Promote You, and I were in attendance at the same networking meeting so I decided to ask her and another member if they had any tote bags they would like to donate. They both said "yes" and they both said they would call me to let me know how many bags they would be able to donate.

When I spoke with Dawn, she had the exact amount I needed so I went by her place to pick them up. I called the other member to thank her and to let her know that I had what I needed. She said if I need more just call her and she would get them to me.

I am grateful I opened my mouth and asked and for Dawn's generosity. Women helping women is the motto of the networking group and we have lived up to our motto. Thank you Dawn Candy I appreciate you.

Day 269

Sheila Carter

Small acts of kindness are so heartwarming. I was serving as a greeter at a networking function and did not want to leave the door to get me a drink. (My throat was dry – from all of the talking I was doing!)

Sheila Carter, Carter's Bookkeeping Solutions, was heading to get her meal and as she walked through the door, she turned and asked me if she could bring me something. I did something I don't usually do and said "yes, would you bring me a coke when you come back." Sheila smiles and said "sure."

About a minute later, Sheila returns with a class of coke and a straw. I commented "you did not have to make a special trip to bring this to me" and she replied "I thought you might be thirsty." Well, she was right. I was grateful for her bringing me the drink but I was impressed that she thought about me above herself.

I am sure she thought nothing of what she did and did not consider it a big deal; however, it was a BIG deal to me. Thank you Sheila and maybe someday I will be able to return the favor–I was really really thirsty!

Day 270

Erica – Methodist Hospital

Erica at Methodist Hospital gets the BOB award – bending over backwards – from me. Driving to the medical center from where I live is no joy ride. Driving to the medical center to find out my husband's appointment was two hours earlier was really a very unpleasant thought.

Erica shifted into action. She got permission from the next patient to move her appointment up and the doctor to see him. Although I was a bit anxious, Erica wasn't – she was working her magic. As it worked out, the next patient was called at her given appointment. That was good old BOB customer service at its best.

I am grateful for employees like Erica who don't mind going the extra mile to help a patient out (her customer) and avoid rescheduling an appointment as well as the patient who didn't mind having her appointment moved up helping out in this situation. FAVOR!

Day 271

Nikki Potts

Grateful is all I can say. I had the opportunity and pleasure of serving the beautiful and talented Nikki Potts, (The Kurt Carr Singers) at the Women of Wisdom Conference. Humility is all over Nikki Potts. She is gracious and was appreciative for everything I did for her – giving her a tissue or a bottle of water.

Nikki sang "It ain't over till it's over" from the depths of her soul and I was mesmerized – seriously. She is amazing. Expressions of gratitude to Nikki Potts for being so pleasant, appreciative and friendly. What an awesome opportunity to be able to serve her.

Day 272

Pastor Cassandra Scott

The Saturday morning session of the Women of Wisdom conference - Don't Waste Your Pain -- was P-O-W-E-R-F-U-L!

Pastor Cassandra Scott told us to put our eyes on the promiseónot the pain. She is a dynamic speaker. I am grateful that I was able to attend; I would have missed the word she had for me. I was blessed being in the presence of so many powerful women of God.

Nikki Potts sang and shared a bit of her testimonyóWOW! What a story. I am grateful, so grateful.

Susan Downs - *Thank goodness that these wise women are sharing their stories! We can all benefit from hearing them.*

Day 273

John Kralik, Author *"A Simple Act of Gratitude"*

A month ago duing a quick conversation I mentioned to someone that I am on a journey to complete 365 gratitude posts for 2013. She asked if I had read a particular book on gratitude and I said no. She told me about the book which she herself had read and that it was a good read.

The book: "A simple Act of Gratitude" by John Kralik is a phenomenal book about his 365 Thank You Notes project. John tell how being grateful for what he had really changed his life. After reading "A simple act of Gratitude," I feel like I know John Kralik – that we have a connection.

When I first started reading the book I wished I had read it before I started my gratitude post; however, I quickly abandoned that wish. I am grateful to have read his book, loved every story he wrote about but that was his project.

My journey thus far has been uplifting and rewarding. I am excited about what the next few months will reveal. I am already so grateful.

Ginny Chaffee Levenback - *I will miss your posts after you've completed your 365 days! Thanks for the book recommendation, I'll check it out.*

Carolyn Gray - *Ginny, I think you will enjoy the book. I enjoyed it and felt connected with the author. Check it out and let me know what you think.*

Curtis R Smith - *Your daily posts have been inspirational, up lifting and created a personal increased awareness of the power and benefits of acts of gratitude. Thanks for your leadership and being a true role model!!*

Day 274
A four year old

A couple of weeks ago, a young man (all of four years old) was acting up and I decided to speak with him about a comment he made. We had a nice long chat – maybe 5 minutes-- which resulted in him apologizing.

His Mom was there listening and as much as he wanted her to "save" him, she didn't. The next time I saw him he greeted me and said "I have been real good!" I was excited to hear that unsolicited comment from him. I am grateful that I now have another new best friend! A real cute new four year old best friend!

Toni Trahan Shirley - *It takes a village - so glad you participated!!*

Susan Downs - *Was this at church? Most parents will not let their children talk to strangers in the shopping malls or restaurants. I am glad he paid attention to you and learned some valuable lessons.*

Frances Johnson - *Sometimes all it takes is a word or two from someone other than a parent to talk with them.*

Day 275
Nicolette Hines

I experienced so many things by being a part of the Women of Wisdom conference. The first thing I experience was attending a breakfast meeting that started on time; we ate, took care of the business at hand and ended on time.

For starters, that was great; however, that breakfast meeting pales in comparison to my experience at the conference. Being surrounded by so many might women of God in action was awesome. Nicolette Hines, blessed me as she prayed–I am talking she was seriously praying. I did want to interfere as she prayed in several different positions; however, I didn't get too far away.

Minister Hines is an obedient servant who has such a sweet sweet spirit and is extremely friendly and humble. I am grateful for the opportunity to have been part of the 2013 Women of Wisdom conference -- I am still meditating on all I learned, heard and witnessed.

Day 276
Joshua McCulloch

I called me sister to say hello and my nephew Joshua answered the phone. He was excited to hear from me and told me he had been thinking about me and wanted to call me. I assured him that it was okay to call me anytime.

A couple of weeks later I decided to text him to say hello and ask about football how he was doing in school. He responded that he was doing fine and told me when, where and the time of his next game. I made it my business to arrange me affairs around that game and I am so happy I did.

Nothing like being at a Junior High football game at kickoff! Cheerleaders, fans and parents were making a little noiseóactually a lot of noise. It was a great game. My nephew made several really good plays and I got some video and pics of him in action which I sent to his phone as I captured them. I wanted to prove I was at the game! His team won so he left happy.

A couple of hours after the game, I received a text from Josh thanking me and expressing how much it meant to him to see me at his game. So grateful that I made my way to that game and even more grateful that my sweet nephew was thoughtful enough to let me know how much he appreciated me being there. Sometimes small things to us are big things to others.

Day 277
Cathy Wilson and Selinda Simpson

I had the pleasure of traveling to Montgomery, Texas where I found a well keep secret – Hotsie Totsie Boutique.

Cathy Wilson and Selinda Simpson own this cute little boutique that is chocked full of fashions and trust me you will not meet yourself coming and going. They even have shoes! I found dressy, casual and fun clothes. I will let others know about Hotsie Totsie and since there is a tea room right next door, that is reason enough for us to travel to Montgomery for lunch and a little shopping.

Cathy and Selinda helped me select a few pieces and gave me their honest opinions about what looked good and what look "just ok." It was refreshing to be able to shop without feeling rushed and to meet two wonderful business owners who know how to treat their customers.

I teased them about being so far away; however, I must admit I enjoyed the drive. It was very tranquil and the scenery was beautiful.

Day 278
Erna Nimr

Erna Nimr is a volunteer at the professional building where my primary care physician's office is located. Erna was crocheting an infant hat and I commented how much I liked it. She told me she makes about 40 a months and donates them to the nursery at the hospital across from the professional building.

Erna said she made up the pattern and adds a cut little ruffle on the hat for little girls. She asked me if I could crochet and I proudly responded "yes ma'am I can." That opened the door for her to invite me to her monthly crocheting class which she holds once a month in her home. She gave me her card and "instructed" me to call her to get her address.

Talking about a labor of loveóthose newborns and their parents probably don't realized the tender love that Erna puts into making those little hats. I am grateful for meeting Erna and for being invited to the monthly crocheting class. Thank you to Erna for freely giving of her time and talent to people she will likely never meet (never say never - probably never).

Day 279
Bobby Lee

Grateful for the butcher at Kroger for helping me out. My husband asked me to purchase a particular cut of roast and I didn't want to get the wrong thing so I went straight to the meat department and asked the butcher for the roast.

Bobby Lee, the butcher, stopped what he was doing and cut the roast the exact weight I needed. He brought it to the counter, handed it to me and smiled as he asked if there was anything else he could help me with. That was all I needed.

It is such a pleasure to be served by someone as pleasant and accommodating as Bobby Lee. Kudos to Bobby Lee and to Kroger–Bobby Lee provided exceptional customer service.

Day 280
Vickie

FedEx is a business I frequent often because I am in need of good quality printing. On my most recent visit, I needed to print five copies of five legal size documents and I was having a difficult time getting the color right.

I asked Vickie, the representative for assistance and she had the same problem. She did not however stop there; she said "let me try something else." Her something else worked; the copies were excellent! She apologized for the problem and gave me credit for the bad copies.

Employees in that particular FedEx store have always been eager to help and I am grateful for their assistance when I need it. Vickie was exceptionally accommodating and had the best attitude. I am not just grateful but I want to share with others how I was treated.

Day 281
Natasha Wade

At the ICF Houston Chapter monthly meeting I usually meet someone new and tonight was not different in that regard. What was different was that I saw an old friend at the meeting this month.

I was not in the room when Natasha Wade came in and that is a good thing because we probably would have been doing the "girlfriend scream" when we saw each other. When she stood up to introduce herself I knew immediately it was her before she said a word. Not wanting to be too disruptive, I waited until she sat down before tapping her on the shoulder and giving her a big hug.

It has been well over a year since we have seen each other. I was happy to see her and grateful that she is doing well. We had a nice long chat; in fact, I think we were the last ones to leave the room. Can't wait for us to do lunch so we can really catch up.

Day 282
Pam Schied

Pam Schied spoke to our group on Gain Insight with Foresight. Very interesting presentation and although it may have looked like I was texting while she was presenting, I was actually taking notes. I wanted to capture those nuggets for future reference.

Grateful for several wonderful take-a-ways like "cross pollinate knowledge" and "futurist pay attention." I also loved that she stressed staying well rounded because it will be important in the future. Pam also shared with us that we have to be flexible which I feel is crucial; however, admittedly, we don't focus and apply being flexible nearly enough. Her presentation was timely and much appreciated.

My gratitude also goes to the Programs Committed of the ICF Houston Chapter. They have presented excellent speakers and interesting and applicable topics.

Day 283

Dolce, Banquet Captain

In my opinion, being a server is not an easy job. I observe servers carrying multiple plates of hot food and I am amazed. My thought is that I would drop food all over everyone and everything!

Dolce is a Banquet Captain at the H.E.S.S club. She is extremely accommodating and always has a smile. She served our Advisory Board Members as she ran back and forth to the first floor of the building serving another group. When a member asked her if she was working alone (because she was doing everything) she responded "yes I am."

She served the food, refilled the beverages, cleared the table and when someone asked for extra gravy, she delivered that. She was pleasant and provided exceptional service. I am grateful that Dolce is so engaged in what she does and want her to know that I appreciate her spirit of excellence and exceptional delivery of customer service.

Day 284

Patsy and Scott Johnson

My neighbors across the street and I don't see each other often nor do we speak with each other on a regular basis. There is a reason: I rarely am outside; I go from the house to the garage.

Although we don't see each other often, we each know the other is there and ready to step in to pick up packages left on the porch, retrieve papers out of the yard and keep an eye on the property. Patsy and Scott Johnson are great neighbors and I am grateful they are only a few steps away.

When either of us is going to be away from home for more than a day, we make sure to share that information. Patsy and I catch up when we are both outside. She is outside more than I am as evidenced by her landscaped lawn.

Scott and Patsy are two of the nicest people I have had the pleasure knowing. Grateful.

Day 285
Alberto

Well-maintained deep green grass is something I like especially when it is my yard. For the past six years, Alberto comes by weekly to keep the yard looking good.

One year on a dare, I "landscaped" the flowerbeds in our front yard (my husband said I couldn't do it) and it really did look nice– after Alberto spread the mulch. I won the dare on a technicality. I did not agree to spread the mulch! Alberto came to my rescue.

I "paid" him back for helping me spread the mulch by spreading the fertilizer while he was on vacation. He didn't ask me to-- I wanted to return the favor. I am grateful that Alberto faithfully grooms our yard and always offers to help with any projects that I come up with.

Day 286
Paige Williams

Reconnecting with an old friend is always so enjoyable for me. Paige Williams and I have not seen or spoken with each other for a while. That changed, we saw each other on Facebook, sent a couple of messages then she decided to cut through all that and call me.

Let me not fail to mention that it was around midnight. We were on the phone for well over an hour catching up. I am proud of Paige because she has done extremely well in her not so new position. She did this as a result of hard work. This girl is like a machine plugged into the wall. She has a spirit of excellent and her work production proves that without a doubt.

I have seen her in action and I am grateful to be a part of her circle. This is a young woman who will work her way past her peers. Congratulations Paige, I believe in you and better than me believing in you, I am happy you believe in yourself. Girl, you rock!

Day 287
The Gratitude Enthusiast on Paper.li

A friend of mine has an online newspaper that I read almost every day. I find it informative and fresh like in super current.

While attend a networking meeting, I learned from a well known local author (Nakia Lunshaul) that I could have my own online newspaper through paper.il. She instructed me on how to create the newspaper and I committed to creating my paper that night. She told me she was going to hold me accountable and she did. She sent me a message letting me know she could not find my newspaper. I assured her I had created the paper and would go over the instructions.

After backtracking, I found the mistake and there it was-- The Gratitude Enthusiast was live! It is articles about gratitude and more articles about gratitude. After reading it, I was excited to learn more and more people around the world are trying this "gratitude thing" and liking it. Here is the site for The Gratitude Enthusiast: http://paper.li/f-1379392521. Check it out for yourself.

I am grateful for Nakia Lunshaul sharing and holding me accountable. I enjoy reading The Gratitude Enthusiast–so enlightening.

Day 288
Linda Dingledine

Linda Dingledine was pursuing a degree in psychology and one of the books she was required to read was Manchild in the Promised Land by Claude Brown. It was a paperback with very small print and it was not short.

Linda mentioned the book to me and commented that it was a good book and thought I would enjoy reading it. She was correct: it was a good book and I did enjoy reading it.

Actually, it is one of the best books I have ever read. It was graphic and educational because that was a lifestyle I knew nothing about. I don't remember every detail about the book, but I do remember the author describing his early/teen years of his life in Harlem and how he was able to get away from crime, drugs, and violence through education and faith.

My gratitude to Linda for sharing "her school work" with me and some of the discussions we had about the book. Reading that book helped me to have more determination and a desire to be a lifelong learner. Education is essential.

Day 289
Nicole Parsley

Nicole Parsley, Executive Director, SBC Business Network, Spring, thank you for inviting me to speak at the Spring, SBC Business Network luncheon.

Sharing about the personalities with SBC was great and I received lots of positive feedback. The group was engaged and that made the delivery of my presentation so rewarding. I am grateful for the opportunity. As I prepare for a full Personality Assessment Workshop, my presentation to your group was very beneficial and helped me fine tune the presentation.

You and your group made me feel very welcome. Thank you Nicole for allowing me to share with y'all.

Day 290

The W.I.S.E. Conference

Today was a wonderful day and I am so very grateful to be a part of the AWESOME groups of ladies and gentleman who: sponsored, donated to, participated in or attended the Women Inspiring Supporting Empowering (WISE) Conference.

The conference was professionally organized, the banquet hall was beautifully decorated, the speakers were inspiring, the fashion show was "fashion week" ready, the many many vendors were an exceptional selection of entrepreneurs, the food was delicious and the networking was phenomenal.

Thank you to everyone for making this conference The Conference to have attended. Thank you Cynthia DeLandro for traveling ALL the way up north to attend the conference! This conference was a true example of how when we work together we achieve an awesome outcome. What a team effort. Congratulations to the planning committee for an exceptional job.

Day 291

Jerome Duran, David Winters, Darrell Arrant and Charles Beasley

Expressions of gratitude to Jerome Duran, I-deZineit.com; David Winters, the Spanish Instructor; Darrell Arrant, Heaven's Best Carpet Care and Charles Beasley, First Choice Loan Services, Inc. for your support of the WISE Conference. These are the few good men who are part of WOAMTEC!

Jerome thank you for the graphics for the conference. The WISE Conference mascot graphic "the owl" is too cute. Charles, I saw you working hard helping with the set up and anything else you were asked to do–thank you so very much. David had a vendor booth and Darrell was all about encouraging us with his "ladies first attitude." These guys are the best and I am grateful to have them in my circle of friends.

The WISE Conference was a great success due in part to your much appreciated contributions.

Day 292
Reshonda Kelly

Friends come and friends go, but a true friend sticks by you like family. Proverbs 18:24 (MSG). Reshonda Kelly thank you for being a true friend sticking by us like family.

When situations arise, people often say: us to call when/if we need anything. I am grateful that Reshonda walked her talk – there was a family need and she said I can help and here is what I can and will do.

Thanking God for your kindness and praying for thousand fold blessings for you and your family.

Day 293
Walter Weaver

I have had some of the most caring and nurturing mentors in my life. Walter Weaver was a wonderful mentor to our entire office.

As I reflect on those times, I appreciate him more because he had his work cut out for him and met the challenge head on and worked with each of us to help us developed professionally. Mr. Weaver was very patient and soft spoken; however, he meant business. He was a gentleman; he was wise and shared his wisdom and professional knowledge with everyone.

He lead by example and truly walked his talk. I loved that he was never ever so busy that he would not stop what he was doing to speak with us. When I left that office, he reminded me that I was representing him and that he was there if I needed him. He gave everyone that same reminder.

I am grateful Mr. Weaver took the time to share his wisdom and professional knowledge with me. I am the person I am today because of people like Mr. Weaver.

Day 294
Nicole, Family Dollar General Store, FM 1960

If you haven't noticed, there are new corner stores in town: Family Dollar and Dollar General.

I frequent them because I can get in an out in minutes. The drawback is the employees are not all that friendly. That is not true for the Dollar General Store on 1960 and Sugar Pine. Nicole, one of the customer service reps smiled, greeted every customer and said thank you as she finished checking them out.

The manager is getting a call from me. I think he would enjoy hearing a compliment vs. a complaint. When I got to the register, I complimented Nicole for providing exceptional customer service. So grateful there are still caring service providers out there. Kudos to Nicole.

Day 295
Mike and Dena Fessler

There are some wonderful people in my church; people who unselfishly give of their time and talents.

Mike and Dena Fessler are greeters and always willing to serve in whatever capacity asked of them. They volunteer for any and everything that needs to be done at the church. They work well together on projects. I am grateful to be surrounded by spiritual brothers and sisters like Mike and Dena. They also give the best hugs–and I love hugs.

Day 296
Alana Padgett

Recently, I participated in a fashion show at a conference. I wore a beautiful jacket, lovely jewelry and cute shoes. The problem that day was my hair. I was having a horrible, awful, very bad hair day!

Alana Padgett to the rescue! Alana had her curling iron which she plugged in and put some curls in my hair. She was concerned because I was off the chart concerned about me hair. I am sure I thanked her but I don't know if she realized how grateful I was for her taking the time to help me out.

The fact that she was getting ready for the same fashion show was not her top priority– she was concerned about me having a "mini fit" over my hair. Alana was so patient, graceful and kind – thank you Alana for helping me "do something with my hair!"

Ethel Branch O'Dell - *You are always beautiful, inside & out!*

Lori Mansour Burns - *Girl...you are SO wrong! You looked, as you always do, fantastic and so classy that day Carolyn Gray. With that said, don't you love sisters that are ready to come to the rescue with curling iron in hand! Love it!*

Sylvia Lacey - *Please send pictures of what YOU consider a bad hair day. Thanks.*

Carolyn Gray - *Sylvia Lacey, sure will...give me an opportunity to get to my desktop.*

Day 297

Evelyn Bush

Mrs. Evelyn Bush and I were neighbors – good neighbors. We chatted over the fence, exchanged Christmas cards and checked on each other if we went too long with seeing each other.

Mrs. Bush was retired, 80 years old and a true "stepper." She played bridge, had lunch with friends several times a week, had a standing hair appointment (weekly), attended a weekly Bible study and shopped often. Since I was still employed, she was idol!

When I moved from Shreveport, I visited her on return trips and called her regularly. Two years ago I stop by to visit her and she told me she had to slow down and didn't get out much. (I couldn't tell – her car was in the driveway, she was dressed and her hair was freshly done!)

On a recent trip to Shreveport, I drove by her house and did not see her car. I called and someone answered the phone. I introduced myself and asked to speak with Mrs. Bush. The lady told me she was Mrs. Bush's caregiver and that Mrs. Bush was still in bed. I asked her to tell Mrs. Bush that I was passing through and wanted to say hello.

The caregiver insisted that I stop by and I am so grateful that I did. When I walked in, Mrs. Bush was excited to see me and we gave each other a big hug. She told me she had to slow down. She looked great, her hair was beautiful as ever and at 90, her mind is as sharp as a razor. I am glad I stopped to say hello.

Mandy Wilburn Rubio - *I'm sure you made her day! So nice to be thought of.*

Day 298

Believers Faith Fellowship (BFF) Church

Believers Faith Fellowship (BFF) Church members have been extremely kind to my daughter and son-in-love as my daughter recuperates from surgery.

I am especially grateful for the hospitality committee of BFF as that committee has provided meals and gift cards for them to purchase meals. Being an active part of a church family is so important especially when you are hundreds of miles from your family.

It is comforting to know that BFF members pray with my daughter, call to check on her, visit her and offer to "do anything" to help during her time of recuperation. Thank you BFF family for the many acts of kindness and the love you have shown to my children.

Angela Hicks - *Campos What a joy it is to know that your daughter and son-in-love are part of such a loving and giving church family.*

Toni Trahan Shirley - *Ditto, such a joy!'*

Judy McCurdy Mitchell - *Awesome story. How wonderful to belong to a church family who demonstrates the Love of Jesus by their actions!!!! What a blessing!!!!*

Allen Green - *At North Gate Christian Ministries Inc. we have a saying.... THE ATTITUDE IS GRATITUDE! Love that you guys are doing this!*

Day 299

Gary Wayne and Valencia Hail

Preparing a meal and delivering it is truly a labor of love. Gary Wayne and Valencia Hail wanted to help my daughter and son-in-love so they delivered dinner to them.

The meal was delicious and the corn was "off the chain" yummy. I have never have corn flavored with a hint of cinnamon before–I will be trying that next time I prepare whole kernel corn.

Randall and Jennifer Harvey, DeAngelo and Laura Waldon, Adrian and Kara Folmar and Gloria Scales-Johnson visited them, brought gift cards, offered to clean as well as help with my grandson.

Jeremy and Nikki Frazier and their sweet children visited and gave lots and lots of hugs and kisses. I was in on the hugs! Their son Dawson was super attentive as he picked up the toy my grandson dropped 999 times! Their smaller children were relieved that my daughter was better after being in the hospital.

I am so grateful and in awe of how loving and compassionate their friends are– they are truly blessed. It makes returning home a little easier.

Toni Trahan Shirley - *God blesses these awesome people for their giving, loving souls and I am so glad of it. Where do the kids live now? God's good graces fall with continued abundance upon this little family and those whose outreach has helped and is helping them!*

Kara N Adrain *Folmar - If you could only imagine how much we love Trecie, Marco & Ian....they are the most FABULOUS family I believe we have ever met.... God truly created them just for us. They have been an incredible inspiration in our lives, marriage & then some. We love them all more than words....so you are now included in all of the above*

Day 300
Sarah Szczepaniec

When I hear of someone having an alias my red flags of suspicion come out. I automatically assume something is not right or that the person is trying to hide something. Well, I have to change my position on that line of thinking.

My friend Sarah is contemplating using an alias for business because her last name has eleven letters and seven of those letters are consonants. That many consonants make it very difficult for most people to pronounce her last name.

As she rapidly approaches her personal, business and financial goals, we joked about her becoming famous and people having difficulty pronouncing her last name. Witty as she is, she came up with a quick fix: using an easy to pronounce last name like Smith or Jones!

I am grateful she shared the alias she is considering which is not "Smith or Jones" and that she also shared a couple of great tips on how to train the brain to retain new information.

Sarah Szczepaniec - *Thanks, Carolyn!*

Cyndy Kendall Justice - *What a wonderful friendship.*

Day 301
Success for Teens Magazine

Grateful for being given a copy of Success for Teens (Real teens talk about about using the Slight Edge). Personal development resources needed to help teens reach their potential.

Attitude is everything... There is no such thing as failure!

Laura Cope Taylor - *Missed you at church yesterday*

Day 302
Sonya Boney Warner

Mom, Dad, hundreds of pairs of shoes and FOUR daughters! This is a short description of Sonya Warner's family. Oh, there is more I am sure but four daughters means four different personalities.

The similarities: they are all beautiful inside and out, thoughtful and they all love Mom and Dad.

I know this about the Warner girls because they attended my Personalities and pizza workshop. They all had opinions about how to make things better "around the house."

I am grateful I had the privilege of sharing with these young ladies and their parents. The Warner family is amazing and I am blessed to have had the opportunity to witness sisterly and family compassion, love dedication and concern. Sonya, thank you guys for letting me have a peek into the wonderful life of an awesome Mom and Dad and four spectacular young ladies.

Sonya Boney Warner - *Carolyn Gray what a nice surprise to be featured on your daily gratitude! I can't wait to show my girls your post tomorrow! They truly learned so much from spending time with you. They are all distinctly different but their love for life is the same. Thank you for being a blessing in all of our lives! We look forward to spending more time with you!*

Carolyn Gray - *Sonya, you guys are awesome parents with four awesome daughters.*

Toni Trahan Shirley - *This is a mutual love-festa*

Toni Trahan Shirley - *This is a mutual love iofest brought together God's awesome planning. Y'all are blessed to have encountered one another.*

Day 303
Katrina, Subway

I stopped at Subway, purchased a foot long sub, chips and a bottle of coke. I asked Katrina, the sandwich artist and cashier if I could have a cup because I wanted to get some ice. She smile and said sure but it will cost the same as a drink.

I asked her if I had my own cup if I could get some ice. Katrina turned, smiled and handed me a cup and told me she appreciated my business. I was so grateful for that plastic cup! I was also impressed by Katrina's actions. She quickly decided that I did not have to go to my vehicle to get my cup – she was a position to make that decision and she did. I let the store a grateful and happy customer. Small things really do matter.

Day 304
Bobbie Carter

My heart is bursting with joy because I am so very happy for Bobbie Carter and I am just as proud of her. Bobbie had a list of "things" she wanted to accomplish and the foundation piece has been completed. There is no limit to what this determined young woman will do.

I am grateful that I witnessed her making her list of "things" she wanted to accomplish and now to witness her checking them off – done! I have watched her grow in her Christian walk, personally and professionally and I am humbled to see what God has done in her life.

The step she has completed was probably the hardest because it was the one thing she needed to do to lay the foundation for the rest of her goals. She will soar–I know she will because she wants to!

Day 305

Robert Johnson

There are people I my life who are: compassionate, kind, gentle, helpful and always giving, and then there is Robert Johnson.

Pastor Robert is humble, has the sweetest spirit and is kind to everyone-. especially to his wife, Sister Shirley. I am sure he gets frustrated and even angry sometimes; however, I have not witnessed that behavior in him. He has something positive to say, and even in his firm admonishing state he is gentle. I appreciate him and am grateful that he displays the characteristics of Christ in his everyday walk. He is an inspiration to everyone whose path he crosses. A GREAT and wonderful man of God.

Day 306

Joe, Meat Department, Food Town Market

I went to the market to purchase several packages of meat because it was on sale. When I looked at the price, I noticed it was not priced with the sale price so I asked the butcher, Joe, about the price. He apologized and asked me how many packages I wanted and I said two.

He re-priced the packages and I quickly realized that I should have gotten more than two packages. I asked him if he would mind re-pricing two more and he said "NO ma'am" I sure don't. He said "my goal is to make you happy and if you want two or ten, I will do what it takes for you to be happy."

I am grateful to encounter employees with that type of attitude. I wrote a thank-you note to the manager because he needs to know that Joe is representing them in an exemplary manner. I left the store happy!

Day 307

Live Happy Magazine

Everyone knows that I get excited when I get gifts. My girlfriend sent me a message and told me she had a gift for me–that was so wrong! (I had to wait for over a week before could get my gift!)

When I saw her at the WISE conference, she was smiling and I wanted her to stop smiling and give me my gift. She handed me a Premiere Issue of Live Happy. OMGosh, that was like THE best gift. It is about the Happiness Movement and my friend is an Ambassador of Happiness, a title that she wears well.

Live Happy is such a wholesome and inspiring magazine and in line with the journey I am on. I am getting a subscription because I don't want to miss any information about the Happiness Movement.

Spreading happiness is what my friend does best and I am grateful that we met a couple of years ago as we happily introduced ourselves to each other. She was a Happiness Ambassador back then!

Day 308
Mandi Shipman Garren

I am filled with gratitude when someone wants to volunteer, hunt you down and leaves a note that they want to help.

That is exactly what Mandi Shipman Garren did–she was standing at the door waiting for me to get to church but somehow I managed to slip in without her seeing me. She was on the hunt because she wanted to help with printing the sermon note sheet.

Mandi has the sweetest spirit, wonderful to work with and I must mention that she is always smiling. I love her tenacity and her positive attitude. That along with her gift of helps will take her a long way. Blessings and thank you Mandi for your dedication and determination to serve I am grateful and happy that our paths have crossed.

Day 309
Larry Lipton

I can't believe I failed to vote during the early voting period but I did. I was mentally preparing myself to get up and be there when the polls open at 7 a.m. No, that won't work -because I just know it won't.

I gave up on that getting up early and started to scroll through my Facebook page when I noticed a post from Larry Lipton with the link for me to find my Election Day poll location and to view the voter specific ballot.

I am grateful to Larry Lipton for all that he does to keep us informed and for his community involvement in the Cypress Creek Parkway area. Larry made my life easy by posting the link which allowed me to access the sample ballot and review the propositions. I will be in an out of my polling location in a flash. Appreciate you Larry.

Day 310
Mary Harlan

Being around people energizes me. I love to talk, laugh, listen, share and of course hug.

I am grateful for having met Mary Harlan several years ago at a conference in Sugarland. We both decided that it was not our first meeting although neither of us could remember where we met before the conference.

Mary is friendly, genuine and has the warmest smile. She told me she reads my gratitude post every day. That really tugged at my heart strings because she could do so many other things; however, she chooses to spend time reading about the people, things and places I am grateful for and to.

So blessed to have someone like Mary follow me on this journey that has been so rewarding and enlightening as I reflect on my good life. Actually, it doesn't matter where we first met. What matters is we are now connected and I am grateful that we are.

Day 311
Todd Moore

Facebook is a tool that is truly what you make it: Good, bad or indifferent!

I have chosen to make it a good tool in my world. Facebook has allowed me to connect and reconnect with a number of people I lost contact with over the years and for that I am grateful.

Each time I connect with one of my long lost friends, I reflect on the good times and smile or laugh (out loud) depending on what I recall. Connecting with my former co-worker and friend Todd Moore was no different as I laughed out loud about some of our chats and encounters.

My absolute favorite Todd Moore story is actually not about him but about a comment his darling son Brandon made when he was about five years old. I am laughing right now and every time I see or hear Cher's name mentioned, I think about Brandon.

Todd, I am so grateful for you reaching out and connecting with me– Thanks Facebook for another one in the good column.

Day 312
Mercedes Palacios

The Woodlands Children's Museum is a place that I frequent. Not to play with all the fun and educational stuff but to teach a Manners and

Etiquette Class to the KinderReady classes.

The museum staff and teachers are very creative and enjoy seeing the children learn and develop. Fortunately for me, they are not just interested in seeing children learn!

I noticed that Mercedes Palacios was working on a flyer so I decided to ask her a question about how to change the graphic on a marketing post card. In less than five minutes, she had given me a crash tutorial along with a website for free graphics.

I am grateful to Mercedes for the quick tutorial on a "very easy" way to prepare and edit my marketing post card. What a productive day–had a great time teaching my class and learned how to edit my marketing post card. Thanks Mercedes!

Day 313
Brenda Themis

When someone makes a rough day smooth, I am grateful. Brenda Themis, Community Print and Copy in Kingwood deserves the excellent customer service award AND an award the size of Texas for patience.

On a very, very, very short notice, Community was able to complete our print job. When I spoke with her, she told me she was swamped; however she would do her absolute best to get the printing done but it would be late afternoon before it would be ready.

Of course there were a couple of hiccups but she worked through each one and never once did I detect she was "not happy." I have asked for favors before but this was really a huge and very special favor. I am grateful there are people like Brenda and Deborah who are at work to serve their customers.

I called to see if the order was ready for pickup and was told it was on the counter waiting to be picked up. I was all smiles and grateful. Thank you Brenda, Deborah and Community Print and Copy you are greatly appreciated.

Day 314
Tequila Coleman

This week has been one THE best weeks. I am extremely grateful and overjoyed because three people I lost touch with have reconnected with me. One found me through Google, one found me on Facebook and I sent one an IM on Facebook and she immediately responded.

The most recent connection was with my "niece," (we adopted each other when she was very very young!) Tequila Coleman. She has been a part of our family for almost 30 years and I am excited to reconnect. As a child, she was my husband's favorite subject to prank by telling her there was a BIG green frog with golden eyes under our bed.

When Tequila visited us, he would look under the bed and give a quick scream and start the frog with the golden eyes prank. One day he persuaded her to look under the bed and behold, she said "I see it, I see it, I see his eye shining! We all laughed-- out loud.

She is all grown up with children of her own and this is still one of our favorite stories. Tequila and I made an agreement to stay in touch and I know we will. I am so extremely proud of her and love her dearly.

Day 315
Rylan Landrum

Today, before church, Rylan flashed her sweet little smile, gave me a big hug and told me "I love you." As if that didn't warm my heart, after church she found me flashed that sweet little smile a-g-a-i-n and gave me another hug. I am grateful for the genuine love of that adorable little four year old. Love you too Rylan.

Day 316
Angela Campos

When someone gives you step by step instructions on how to do something and you don't follow through for six weeks is just crazy and idiotic.

Well, that's the label I have to put on my back "crazy idiotic!" Angela Campos sent me a text to let me know there was a problem with my profile on the WOAMTEC site. I was polite – I said thank you and had every intention of making the correction (when I got home); however, I didn't make the correction.

After one of our luncheons, she politely mentioned that I still had not made the correction and again I said "when I get home I will make the correction." She gave me yet another gentle reminder today; I stopped what I was doing and made the correction. Maybe I can remove the label tomorrow!

It appears that Angela was more concerned about my profile not working properly than I was. Grateful for her continued persistence – thank you Angela for not taking what I needed to do off of your "to do" list. You are wonderful my WOAMTEC sister.

Day 317
Katie Slater

I appreciate it when business owners don't mind sharing information, situations and ideas to help others.

Often times, some business owners are reluctant to share because in some strange way they feel it might take business or revenue from them. Katie Slater does not fall in that category. In a discussion with Katie and another coach, about charging what you are worth, Katie offered to share an article she had with us.

She told us she would e-mail the article and true to her word, I received the article the next day. I am grateful that Katie did not mind sharing but more importantly, I am grateful for her promptly sending the article. I imagine she didn't give what she did a second thought because that is how she naturally and normally operates. It is very refreshing to associate with someone so willing to help others.

Day 318
Djena Diallo

A friend of mine contacted me to see if I would agree to being interviewed by a student who needed to interview an author for her class project. Of course I said yes.

When Djena Diallo called, she asked me if I would like to answer the questions in an email or over the phone. I opted to answer over the phone and I am glad I did. Djena and I had a very nice two part interview/chat.

She made me think way back when she asked "why I like to write and what inspired me to start writing." I told her my junior high English teacher gets credit for that because that lady made us read and read and write and write! I learned that Djena likes to write and might have a book waiting to be written.

I am grateful to have been able to assist Djena with completing that portion of her project as well be able to stay in touch with her through email. Thank you Djena for allowing me to be a part of your project.

Day 319
Bea Stair, Carolyn Gerken and Anita Turnbow

Love Me Bougie is a totally awesome and fun boutique in Magnolia. When I left home, I did not plan on purchasing anything because I told myself I did not need anything (that never stopped me before).

Well, let's just say I didn't get out of Love Me Bougie without making a purchase. A small purchase but a purchase nevertheless. It is entirely Bea Stair and Carolyn Gerken's fault for sponsoring the MCABW mixer. (Gotta blame someone!) I am grateful that I got my hands on that bracelet before anyone else saw it – it had my name all over it.

Kudos to Bea and Anita Turnbow for having a wonderful affordable boutique where there is something for everyone.

Day 320
Crown Financial Ministries

I am grateful for the small group that I am a member of at my church. The group is half way through Managing Our Finances God's Way and some of us have set new goals and established accountability partners.

The Crown Financial Ministries Small Group Study Guide and Workbook along with a resource CD are excellent tools. The resource CD is very user friendly (that means I am able to use it!) Studying the Biblical truths about money is an eye opening and rewarding experience.

Although this is not my first time going through managing my finances with my church, this is an excellent refresher and I am grateful that I signed up. I am enjoying exchanging with the other members of our small group and as one of the facilitators; I have been spending more time studying.

Day 321
Personality and Pumpkin Muffins Workshop

The Personalities and pumpkin muffins workshop was fun and eye opening. Learning to give others what they want in order to have better relationships is different from how we may have operated in the past; however, it really does work.

I am grateful that the participants came in with an open mind which made it easy to share the Personalities with them. Awareness is the name of the game and that is what we all did in this workshop–raise our awareness level.

It is awesome when people from different backgrounds, cultures and gender learn the Personalities. When they learn about themselves and begin to look at how they can change in order to be at peace with and have better relationships with others.

One participant suggested that this would be a good tool to help job seekers find a work environment that is a good "fit" for them and their personality. I am grateful the participants spent their morning with me becoming aware of their personality and how to give others what they want.

Day 322
Adriana Pelissari

I am so grateful for all of my new best friends. I seem to meet a new best friend each time I attend an event. The MCABW Mixer was no different; I met my latest new best friend: Adriana Pelissari.

That was her first MCABW event and I wanted to make sure she knew she was welcome and we appreciated her taking the time to visit the group. When Adriana walked in, I introduced myself to her, chatted a little bit then introduced her to other members as they entered. I actually introduced her as my new best friend and she was such a good sport.

Now, my old best friend Bree Kidd said "I thought I was your new best friend!" Well, Bree was right–she was my new best friend when we met a few years ago. I am very grateful for my new and old best friends. Although Bree has shot me without my knowledge, she is still on my list of old best friends. Let me not forgot to mention that I shot Bree once!

I enjoy networking with the ladies in MCABW because it is such a fun group. Adriana, thank you for networking with us like you have known us for years. Welcome to the group – we are glad you decided to join us.

Day 323
Glyn, FedEX Champions

As I put the finishing touch on my presentation, I realized I did not have enough copies of my handout. I drove to FedEx in Champions hoping someone would be able to help me. I was printing my handout on heavy cardstock and it would not easily go through the copier.

Glyn, the customer service rep asked if he could help and I said "yes sir, you certainly can." I explained my problem and he tried to print the copies but was unsuccessful. He said let me take this to one of the other machines and get this done for you.

While he was doing that I asked him if they had a paper cutter and they did. He gave me instructions on how to use the paper cutter. Glyn had the best sense of humor with a Dr. Seuss twist!

I cut the copies I had while he printed more copies for me. Well, as luck would have it, I broke the paper cutter – or so I thought. I got the attention of Sandy, another rep and confessed. She said, "Oh, I can fix it" and showed me what I had done to make the cutter jump off the track. With Sandy's help, I was back in business.

Receiving good customer service is always very important to me. I am grateful that I have very few encounters with service reps who do not meet my expectations. Like Glyn and Sandy, some exceed my expectations and that makes me extremely happy.

Day 324
Courtney Gilmore

Today was a funtabulous day. For starters, I got up at 4:50 a.m.; however, the fun did not start then. (Apostle Blanche Barley-- that is not a mistake–I really did get up at 4:50 a.m.!) Talking about being on a mission, I was on a mission.

I had to be at Westfield High School for the Girls Summit by 7:00 a.m. The program was phenomenal; each person on the program did an excellent job. Those are some very talented students at Westfield.

After the summit, I had the privilege of personally meeting Courtney Gilmore, KPRC, Channel 2. I was not able to hear her present because I was conducting a breakout session. However, I sat next to her during lunch which meant I had an opportunity to chat with her. She is very genuine and gracious. There was a photo op session with the summit presenters and Courtney. She shared with us that she has to be at work before 5 a.m. My hat is off to her because that would be a challenge for me!

I am grateful that I was able to spend time chatting with Courtney. I will follow her on Twitter and Facebook. OMGosh, this was an awesome day.

Day 325
Andre Samano

As a guest at Westfield High School for the Girls Summit, I say thank you for the warm welcome extended to me by the faculty and students.

Thank you to Andre Samano, the student assistant who helped me during the presentations. He was exceptional!

The faculty went out of their way to make sure everything ran smoothly. I am grateful for educators like Mr. Fagan, Ms A. Turner, Ms P. Oliphant-Smith, Ms D. Stowers and Ms Y. Brown. There were many many more involved in the success of the summit - these were the ones I worked directly with.

The young ladies were eager to learn and some students took notes. ..I was impressed. Several students wanted to purchase a copy of my book: All

Abour ME* (*Manners and Etiquette for TWEENS and Teens) which I did not have with me.

Kudos to the Duchess, De'Sha and Diamond Perkins, Ashuria Thompson and Jannell Hughes for their positive interactions during the presentation. I enjoyed being surrounded by so many intelligent and optimistic young people who serve as positive role models for their peers.

Grateful beyond measure for the opportunity to be a part of the Girls Summit. Thank you Ms Gistarb for inviting me.

Frances Johnson, Lillie Gooding, Carleen Su George and 12 others like this..

Susan Downs - *Yay! It sounds like a win/win!!*

Toni Trahan Shirley - *Glad you are reaching out to these students to provide them with positive life-changing tips!!*

Margaret A. Volk, Frances Johnson, Lillie Gooding Lori Mansour Burns, Carleen Su George, Ken P. Marsh

Day 326
Cy-Fair Women's Express Network (ABWA)

Grateful for the opportunity to speak to the Cy-Fair Women's Express Network (ABWA) group about the Personalities.

The speed networking format they used was a phenomenal way to network. I made some wonderful connections and will schedule one-on-one sessions with three of the members. It is all about building relationships and the way for me to do that is to meet with the ladies one-on-one.

Thank you Casey Cargle you for coordinating my visit to CYFEN and for the gift from the group. Please know that I enjoyed presenting to the group and of course for all of the hugs (freely given or taken!). I had a fun time.

Day 327
Donald Eugene White, Jr.

Today is November twenty checkin'! That's how my now thirty something nephew Donald Eugene White, Jr. said November twenty second when he was a toddler.

He loved to sing and would have his Mom call me so he could sing "I ja called to shay I love you, I ja called to shay I care and I mean it from the bottom of my heart." Then he would ask me to come pick him up so he could spend the weekend with me.

During the weekend visit, he would read his favorite book, "Goof off

Goose" tooooooo many times! Actually, he was picture reading–sometimes with the book upside-down. His reading was always followed by "don't you want some cookies and milk?!"

Grateful for the memories D. Love you and I hope your day was wonderful.

Day 328
Donovan Green

I find it extremely difficult to stay on an exercise program for any length of time. I have always been able to fine an excuse to skip that part of my schedule.

Now, thanks to Trainer Donovan Green, Dr. Oz's trainer, I have to stop the excuses! He posted five simple 30 second exercises I can do anywhere. I don't need any special equipment, I just need to do it!

I can't convince myself no matter how hard I try that I don't have 5 minutes a day to exercise. I am grateful that I met Jo Mousselli, Xtreme Lashes and saw the video on her Facebook page.

No excuses - Five simple 30 second exercises...I can do this. I will do this. Thanks Jo and Donovan.

Day 329
Maria Bruederlin and Guillermo Mendoza

Thank you Maria Bruederlin and Guillermo Mendoza for inviting me to be a part of Impact Coaching Solutions Final Assessment on Coaching Skills.

This was a phenomenal opportunity and I am grateful to have been a part of such an amazing experience. I was invited to be a participant in the Final Assessment; however, I received so much insight as an evaluator. Coaching is so very powerful.

Listening to everyone share their why, when and how they became involved in coaching was inspiring as we were "welcomed to the circle." Maria I was "that close to tears" as you spoke. Thank you for sharing and I am elated that I was there to hear your touching story. Much success my friends and thank you for allowing me to be a part of the journey.

Day 330
Jason Fleeks

My service advisor, Jason Fleeks is the best in the business. He is patient, knowledgeable and very personable. I have never heard him complain nor have I observed him wasting time. His level of integrity is above reproach. He is someone I would hire without reservations.

When I need to have my vehicle serviced I speak directly to Jason. I explain what's going on and he listens to my non-mechanical explanations about my vehicle.

I am grateful that I met him years ago when I had my vehicle serviced because he has been there to explain every small detail about my warranty and all repairs that are done. When I leave the dealership, I have been educated thanks to Jason, my personal service advisor.

Day 331
Sophia Jata, The Butterfly Princess

As a Diplomat, I eagerly welcome members and guest to our networking luncheon and I was on my job when I spotted Sophia, the Butterfly Princess. She waved and came over to where I was standing.

The Princess gave me the biggest hug– and yes, she made my day. Having those little arms wrapped around me made it worth getting out in the rain. I haven't seen the Princess in a while so I was excited to see that she now has her two front teeth!

I certainly didn't expect to see her at a network luncheon which goes to show I never know when or where I will have the pleasure of seeing the Princess. I am extremely grateful that her Mom and I are friends and this little sweetie is so genuinely loveable. She is of course a very pretty child but her real beauty is what radiates from the inside out. She is so precious.

Day 332
Randalls Food Market

When my husband asked me to pick up a brining bag while I was out I thought I would run into our neighborhood supermarket, pick up the bag and run out. Not!

After "running" into three different markets and Wal-Mart, I decided to "run" into Randalls. I am grateful that Randalls had the bag. I was about to give up and head home without the bag which would not have made the mister very happy.

Although Randalls is not on my direct route home, I can always count on Randalls to have those hard to find items. I really am grateful for so many small things – Thank you Randalls.

Day 333
Kirsten Berger

Today we celebrate Thanksgiving Day as a holiday–I say every day is Thanksgiving Day.

As I reflect just over the past week, I am grateful for a coaching session I had with Kirsten Berger. Kirsten coached me through a challenge I was experiencing in such a smooth and impactful way that it was magical.

Kirsten helped me changed the way I look at my challenge by having me change one word. I now reward myself and as Kirsten told me: "you will not talk yourself out of a reward!" She was correct. I have been rewarding myself since my session with her on other things and it feels great.

Coaching is so extremely powerful and as a coach, I know that. Even coaches need a coach!

Day 334
Angie Vargas

I am grateful for Angie Vargas, Legend Oaks-Katy for her warm smile and professionalism as I entered her office. We chatted about the holiday and how hard we worked as well as how much we enjoyed the day. Angie, was at work the day after the holiday and she was there just as chipper as if she was out shopping.

I explained what I needed and she took care of me and I was out of there without a hiccup. Although I was calm, I was actually in a hurry and she did not prolong my visit. It is wonderful to be serviced by people who at work to workówith a cheerful attitude.

Day 335
Nolan Hoyt, RN

Nolan Hoyt, RN, Memorial Hermann is one awesome nurse. Nolan was assigned to care for my relative and I am beyond grateful for the care he provided.

He has a very gentle and compassionate spirit; just the type of nurse you want to care for you when you are on the mend. Nolan gets kudos from me and a gold star because I asked lots and lots of questions and he had answers for all of them. He answered my questions in terms that I could understand. I now know what all those numbers represent on the monitors!

I admire him for pursuing a career in nursing because it is his calling.

Day 336
Larry Hayes

Rearranging your schedule to accommodate others is oftentimes not easy; however, we make the necessary adjustments in most cases.

I am grateful for my cousin, Larry Hayes because he makes adjustments in his schedule to accommodate my aunt. When she wants to do something or go somewhere, she says "let me check with Larry" and Larry is always there for her.

Because he acts on her request, my cousin will not find himself saying what he should have or could have done. I appreciate what he does for his Mom, my aunt.

Day 337
Deshon Burton-Essia

I was expecting a message from someone so the first thing I did this morning was to check my messages. Well, as things go, the message I was expecting was not there; however, there was a FB poste from Deshon Burton-Essia.

Deshon's post read: "please check your inbox ma'am" which I did. I did not see a message from her so I asked her to call me. Deshon called me and sure enough, she had sent me a friend request a l-o-n-g time ago. I accepted the friend request and we chatted for about 30 minutes.

I am grateful for Deshon getting me to connect with her because she helped me jump start my day. She shared inspirational messages and how she has personally developed and improved herself. She was in fact trying to get in touch with me to get information about a new networking group in the Sugarland area: WOAMTEC.

Deshon is on a mission to bring in 2014 with a BANG and she not waiting until January 1 – she has already started. She inspired me.

Day 338
Stephanne Davenport

I have always been told to avoid talking about politics and religion and I generally do. However, after working with Stephanne Davis Laviolette in my networking group, I have to abandon that line of thinking in this case.

Stephanne and I have served together in MCABW and I appreciate her willingness to share and help others. I am grateful to personally know a local political figure who is committed to serving and giving back to the community. As the Montgomery County Treasurer, Stephanne displays a sincere desire as a public servant to deliver the best service to Montgomery County. Stephanne, thank you for serving.

Day 339

The Joy of My Heart by Anne Graham Lotz

My morning meditation starts by reading the daily passage from The Joy of My Heart by Anne Graham Lotz. I have read the December 4 "One Life" devotion many many times; however, when I read it today it made me more grateful for my walk with Christ.

I am grateful for this devotional and the wisdom I have glean from reading it along with the book of Proverbs. Thankful that entertainers, athletes, and celebrities have not been my role models and that I have not compromised my integrity or my character for "stuff" or positions.

It is extremely gratifying to know that I can be that "One Life" that has the courage to stand for godly convictions in the mist of moral compromise. Grateful beyond measure.

Day 340

Chelsea Stormes

Xtreme Lashes Studio in the Woodlands had one awesome open house. I learned some very good skin care and makeup tips from Tammy Hunter.

Chelsea Stormes and Xtreme Lashes Studio staff rolled out the red carpet: great food, complimentary waxing and hydrating strips. Tammy made up an actual client – the before and after view was an amazing transformation.

I am grateful that Tammy convinced me that I can wear coral colored lipstick. She applied the lipstick without using a lip liner because I have a natural lip liner so I now have a new look!

Chelsea completed my complimentary waxing in a flash as I relaxed in the Xtreme Lashes Studio. The entire staff extended a very friendly welcome to everyone. I had a funtabulous time.

Day 341

Kathi Boyd

Walking into the Grand Palace, I knew I was welcome and there was going to be a celebration. Kathi Boyd left no stone unturned as she and the Grand Palace staff prepared for the MCABW Christmas party.

There was plenty of everything: delicious food, snacks, desserts, beverages and good music. The DJ was fabulous with videos to accompany the music. Everyone had a grand time dancing, mixing and mingling and enjoying the food.

When Kathi mentioned that Grand Palace was sponsoring the Christmas party, I did not envision a party like that! Kathi and Kristin Van Hauen I am grateful to "run" in the circle with such wonderful, thoughtful and creative ladies.

Thank you Kathi Boyd for an amazing evening.

Day 342
Michelle and Derrall Gustafson

As a member of the financial management small group at my church, I am grateful for the "bonding" that has been developed with the participants of the group.

Michelle and Derrall Gustafson are members of this small group and I am happy they decided to participate in this particular group. They are energetic and don't mind sharing their time and talent with the group.

I had the opportunity of visiting them at their home and I was entertained as I drove up. Derrall has a Christmas light show in their front yard that is connected to 88.9 FM radio. When you drive up and tune you radio to 88.9 FM, the lights "dance" to whatever song is playing. I was fascinated–so much so that I stayed in my car until the song that was playing finished before going inside.

I am grateful that I got to know them and learn about all the really cool stuff they can create. The special part about Michelle and Derrall is that they love, love to share with others.

Day 343
Cynthia St. Dennis

While sharing with someone about being a part of Toastmasters, I reflected on my transition from another Toastmasters district to the very warm welcome I received by Cynthia St. Dennis to Toastmasters in Houston.

As I searched for a Toastmasters club, I found one very near my home – in the home of Cynthia. Cynthia had a spacious conference room in her home and that is where our club met. Cynthia was busy busy; however, she made time to make the club members feel welcome and the meeting very enjoyable.

At the time, she was a student, worked full time, held a district level position with Toastmasters International and held club meetings in her home. Cynthia and I both love to talk and we often found time after the meeting to do just that: talk.

I am grateful for her sharing her home with us and especially for welcoming me of the Houston Toastmasters family where I served as Area Governor and District Chief Judge. Just in case I did not say thank you then, I will now: Thank you Cynthia St. Dennis for your generosity as well as your friendship.

Day 344
Roscoe Knight, RN

I am grateful to Roscoe Knight, RN, Kelsey Seybold Spring Clinic for providing excellent care for a family member. Roscoe was patient, professional and compassionate as well as an awesome educator.

It is extremely gratifying to leave a medical clinic empowered because the nurse has explained things in such a way you don't have any questions. Roscoe was thorough and spoke in terminology that a child could understand.

The Director of Nursing will hear about this first thing in the morning!

Day 345
Gloria Copeland

In most organizations, you have some people who are committed and can be counted on to do their share and more. In MCABW, that person is Gloria Copeland.

Gloria is a "working board member." She arrives at the meetings early to get things set up every month. Gloria is very accommodating in that she volunteers to make calls for the Diplomat Team when a Diplomat is unable to make her calls.

She donated door prizes for our Christmas party–talking about a labor of love-she made fudge. I know the ladies who won that prize were happy.

As a member of MCABW, I am grateful to serve with Gloria and thankful for all she does for the organization. She is a quiet shining star in MCABW; however, she can whistle very loud when she calls the meeting to order! Thank you Gloria for all you do. You are appreciated.

Day 346

Nick, RoseMary, Heaven and Nick, Jr. Flores

The Flores family is very special to me. I love and appreciate their commitment to their relationship with the Lord, each other, their "church job," their family and friends.

Nick, Sr, Rosemary and Heaven are so loving, kind and caring and I am grateful they are a part of my life. Nick, Jr. or Bubba as he is affectionately referred to has his very own gratitude spot with me.

Bubba does not have a lot to say; however, when he speaks, he is like E.F. Hutton, everybody listens, especially me. He is respectful, caring and has great compassion for his familyó serious compassion. Bubba is an awesome role model and I am grateful that we are friends.

Day 347

Constable Robert Avila

Receiving a summons for jury duty was not necessarily the highlight of my day especially knowing that I had 1001 things to do. I showed up as scheduled and I am excited that I did. Not showing up was not an option.

Being in the courtroom with Constable Robert Avila, the Bailiff, was worth being called to jury duty. Constable Avila educated us on Texas history, court procedures and other terminology. I learned what COP stands for: Constable on Patrolóactually never gave it much thought before today.

Constable Avila made waiting very interesting as he was extremely entertaining. The order of selecting jury panels was rather fascinating to observe. I am grateful I had jury duty because it actually made me come home and brush up on my Texas history.

When he, Constable Avila retires, I am sure he will pursue a career in comedy – he has an arsenal of good clean jokes.

Day 348

St. Luke's Radiology Department

Today was a crazy busy and borderline stressful day. The day started off way too early for me at 4 a.m. plus I had a 2 p.m deadline and I was working remotely without good reception on my mobile device.

I am grateful that I was served by wonderful staff members at St. Luke's main campus. The receptionist in the Radiology Department was smiling and acting like it was time for them to get off. The same was true for the doctor, the nursing and the radiology staff. They all made my day brighter and less stressful. Although I was borderline stressed, I quickly got over that and worked on my deadline.

Meeting the deadline with time to spare allowed me to focus on the "home nursing duties" I was assigned with the discharge instructions. I managed to let go of the fact that my day started at 4 a.m. The day was actually a good day thanks to the dedicated staff at St. Luke's.

Jackie Hill - *Praise The Lord! #4AM!*

Carolyn Gray - *Minister Jackie Hill, I know. Praise Him.*

Susan Downs - *Cool! Love it when things work out like that!*

Day 349
Isabella Cummins

When someone goes above and beyond to help me, I am always grateful. Isabella Cummins at Bullritos went out of her way to help me.

I was trying to contact Bullritos at Cypresswood and Stuebner Airline; however, I contacted the one at Cypresswood and I-45. Isabella answered the phone and when I asked if I had reached the Bullritos on Cypresswood and Stuebner, she said "no." I asked her if she had the number for the one on Stuebner she said "no, but if you don't mind waiting, I will get it for you."

Isabella came back to the phone and asked if I was ready for the number – I was. She was extremely pleasant, cheerful, and polite. She closed by saying "thank you for calling and have a nice evening." Isabella may have been reading from a script but it did not sound as though she was. I love it when service reps go above and beyond–Isabella gets my BOB Award: bending over backwards (BOB) for going the extra mile to get the number I needed.

Day 350
Nancy Barnett

Because Nancy Barnett is a woman of few words, I will make my expression of gratitude short and to the point.

Nancy, I appreciate your effort with regard to getting the store stocked with all of the new CDs. Thank you for having them ready so that all you have to do today was add the cover. We will start again next week to restock since the ones you put out today sold out.

Grateful for your support and dedication to making it happen!

Day 351
Anthony Rendon

Unfortunately, we don't hear enough about the good that our young people do and what they contribute. Anthony Rendon, a violinist, accompanied the Embassy Church Praise Team on Sunday and he praised the Lord with the stringed instrument to perfection.

I love the violin and Anthony is an excellent young violinist. Noel Pointer, StÈphane Grappelli or Jean-Luc Ponty were my favoritesóI have a new favorite violinist: Anthony Rendon!

I understand that he joined the praise team on a very short notice; however, based on his excellent performance, I thought he had been practicing with them for some time. I am grateful that our youth use their talent to serve the Lord and do so cheerfully.

Day 352
Michelle Purtle, PA-C

Finally getting to meet Michelle Purtle, PA-C, Kingwood Skin and Laser center made for an enjoyable afternoon.

Before meeting Michelle in person, her stock with me was pretty high based on what I knew about her from our mutual friend. Her stock went higher after meeting her because she was even more professional, competent and caring than I imagined.

Mutual admiration and respect between Michelle and our mutual friend makes for an excellent work environment. No wonder my friend loves her job! I am grateful to know there are people like Michelle in the workforceóin the worldówho have so much compassion and respect for people. Meeting her certainly made my day.

Day 353
Sheila Blue

Winning a door prize is always a good thing–especially when the door prize is a collection of homemade goodies from Sheila Blue of Meal Masters.

I opened the container and the aroma made me want to eat one of each treat on the tray; however, I exercised some self-control. I shared with those at my table and the few good men who were in attendance at the WOAMTEC, The Woodlands luncheon. I admit that I did eat some of the fudge when I got home. OH MY!! The fudge was delicious - creamy, smooth, light and yummy.

I am grateful for whoever pulled my card out of the bowl and to Sheila for that labor of love. There is nothing like being able to enjoying homemade fudge. I have only eaten one more piece–honestly. THANK YOU Sheila!

Day 354
Designer Shoe Warehouse (DSW)

Oh happy day! I received my birthday coupon from DSW and I will use it to purchase a new pair of shoes I do not necessarily need.

DSW is one store that I have to "pop in" when I am in the area just to see what they have. I am grateful for a gift card and the DSW coupon which I will spend wisely.

Small things like a birthday coupon is something I am grateful for–nothing is too small for me to express gratitude for.

Day 355
Luis

So very often some service personnel are overlooked when we acknowledge others for what they do. I am grateful for Luis, the gentleman who collects our trash.

There have been times when we make a mad dash out of the house, back out of the garage and forget to put the 55 gallon trash can outside of the fence. That means Luis has to open the gate, come into the yard to get the trash can.

I am grateful that Luis goes the extra mile to make sure our trash is emptied. We ensure he knows he is appreciated but I want him to know how grateful I am that he performs him job in an exceptional manner. He does not have to do what he does but I am grateful he does.

Day 356
Yvonne Ybarra

As a member of Services Cooperative Association Advisory Board, I have gained unbelievable business acumen. Administratively, I have observed the efficiency of a well-run center by Yvonne Ybarra, the Center Manager.

Yvonne ensures the participants monthly board reports are delivered to each board member. She follows up and answers any questions we might have.

I am grateful she is committed to following up and making the meetings run smoothly as well as seeing to it that each board member has what they need. In my case, that would be an extra copy of the board report when I am not able to access it on my laptop. It is a pleasure working with Yvonne because she is thorough and has an easy going temperament.

Day 357
Ken, Mardel's Christian Bookstore

My Pastor wanted candles for service on the Sunday before Christmas – no problem–well, the problem was it was late Saturday afternoon! I called Mardel's Christian Bookstore in somewhat of a panic. Ken answered the phone and his calming voice settled me down enough to ask if they by chance had Devotional Candles with Drip Protectors. Ken asked if he could put me on hold and went to check to make sure they had the candles. I prayed! He returned with a "yes we have them" and I asked him to hold them for me. I flew to Mardel's, asked for Ken and sure enough, he had them waiting for me at the checkout.

Today, I express gratitude to Ken for going the extra mile and delivering exceptional customer service. Merry Christmas Ken at Mardel's on FM 1960.

Day 358
Saundra Mendoza and Embassy Church Teens

The teens at Embassy Church are the most cooperative, talented and respectful teens I have been associated with in a long time.

Our teens serve as greeters, in the nursery, the bookstore, the cafÈ, as well as serve as parking lot attendants. They are eager to serve. I asked Saundra Mendoza, one of our teens, to dust the pulpit and without reservation, talking back, or giving me "attitude," she grabbed a cloth and the spray and went to work.

I am grateful that our teens will serve anywhere and will do anything to uplift the kingdom. I am happy that our teens are the best I have had the pleasure of serving with in years and for that I am grateful.

Day 359
Rebecca Williams RN

When I reflect on the people who were instrumental in my professional development, I smile as I remember Rebecca Williams. Becky was a very classy lady who was all about business but enjoyed a good laugh.

She taught me to analyze documents/files, pay attention to details and to be able to support my decisions. With details in hand, I learned to "shoot from the hip" and hit my target. I must admit that it took some time for me to feel completely comfortable doing that. However, as I learned to pay close attention to details and with Becky's encouragement, I was able to "shoot" with a great degree of accuracy.

I learned to be firm but fair as I observed how she led her staff and how she followed her superiors. Becky walked the talk, gave excellence guidance, was professional in every sense of the word and was always ready to lend an ear. I am grateful that she shared freely with others and that our paths crossed.

Day 360

Sheryl Symonette

When someone is described as humble, we sometimes think the person is weak but I learned a long time ago that humility is power under control. Sheryl Symonette is graced with humility.

Sheryl has a soft, beautiful and friendly smile and being in her presence is such a pleasure. I am grateful that we are members of the same networking organization because that allows me to see her and chat with her often.

She has a calm and peaceful demeanor which further enhances her humble spirit. She is a true blessing to know and be around.

Day 361

Corey Sams

Gratitude, love and kindness fill me day. I am grateful for my salvation and for the love and kindness of my family.

My nephew, Corey Sams, called to wish me a Merry Christmas and that he was coming to visit. He drove a fairly long distance to visit and I was excited to see him and that he is doing well.

We had a fun time reminiscing about the things we did when he was a child and checking out a few pictures. I have his number so I will stay in touch. I will let him know how grateful I am that he chose to visit and introduce me to his girlfriend.

I had a wonderful day with my family.

Day 362

Cindy

I met Cindy at the HEB as we stood in line. We had never laid eyes on each other before.

She asked if I wanted to get in front of her since I only had one item – I declined the offer. We chatted as her husband removed the items from their basket. Cindy was there to pick up the ingredients for a key lime pie. I told her I love key lime pie and she responded by sharing the recipe with me. I took a picture of the recipe with my phone. We both chuckled and said "how did we survive before cell phones!"

As she prepared to leave the store, she turned and gave me the BIGGEST hug and said it was great meeting you. She walked away and the cashier commented "your friend is leaving you" and I responded that we had just met! The cashier said "you all were talking like you knew each other!" Then she said "kindred spirits I guess."

Cindy was a warm and friendly person and me, well; I guess I am also. Grateful that she felt it was ok to give me a hug!

Day 363
Sheila Rusk

Some people do not and will not ask for help because they feel they "can do it" without getting the guidance, advice and wisdom of others.

As I prepare to head into 2014 with a BANG that I sought help and received more than I could imagine from Sheila Rusk. Sheila is knowledgeable, approachable, direct and has a great sense of humor. She tells you like it is–and I love that because there is no hidden meaning in what she says.

I am grateful to be connected to people who don't waste my time by beating around the bush. I am ready for 2014. Thanks Sheila for your insight.

Day 364
Michael Harris

Solid wood furniture is beautiful and warm. My preference is hardwood: cherry, mahogany and oak. Michael Harris, a family friend taught me to properly care for our wood furniture.

The first thing he demanded was that I stopped dusting with a popular furniture spray. I got that message loud and clear. He also taught me how to cover scratches on the wood with a pecan – a really neat trick. Michael shared his resources for finding hardware for some of my furniture.

My favorite piece of furniture is an antique tiger oak china cabinet. When I followed his instructions on how to clean and polish the cabinet, it was simply beautiful. I am grateful that Michael was willing to share his knowledge about finding hardware and caring for wood furniture.

Love the beautiful look of wood after it has been properly cleaned and polished; grateful for our friend Michael for educating me.

Day 365
My Shreader

Grateful for my gift of a new fancy paper shredder– it has been ordered and will be delivered in 3-5 business days.

I thought about Harry Potter when I was told about this gift. This shredder is like the Firebolt racing broom Harry received as a Christmas present. I can't wait for it to arrive because I got some shredding to do! No more trips or pay money to Office Depot or Office Max to shred.

Love receiving this "prefect" gift. I am so appreciative and grateful that I was not given an ugly sweater!

CPSIA information can be obtained at www.ICGtesting.com
Printed in the USA
BVOW11s1156270116

434431BV00007B/86/P